Trekking in the Patagonian Andes

Clem Lindenmayer

Trekking in the Patagonian Andes
1st edition

Published by
Lonely Planet Publications
Head Office: PO Box 617, Hawthorn, Vic 3122, Australia
Branches: PO Box 2001A, Berkeley, CA 94702, USA and London, UK

Printed by
Global Com Pte Ltd, Singapore

Photographs by
Clem Lindenmayer
Front cover: Cerro Torre, Los Glaciares
Back cover: Laguna de las Tres Marías, Tierra del Fuego

Published
April 1992

Although the authors and publisher have tried to make the information as accurate as possible, they accept no responsibility for any loss, injury or inconvenience sustained by any person using this book.

National Library of Australia Cataloguing in Publication Data

Lindenmayer, Clem
   Trekking in the Patagonian Andes.

   Includes index.
   ISBN 0 86442 144 3.

   1. Patagonia (Argentina and Chile) – Description
and travel – Guide-books. 2. Andes Region –
Description and travel – 1991 – Guide-books.
I. Title.

918.2704

text & maps © Clem Lindenmayer 1992
photos © photographers as indicated 1992

Clem Lindenmayer

Clem has long held a fascination for the wild temperate lands of the southern hemisphere and has made extensive trips to the mountains of Tasmania and New Zealand. While returning to Australia after several years in Europe, however, he found Patagonia's wild beauty the most inspiring of all. Apart from alpine sports, his passions include languages and travel. Clem is currently studying Chinese and linguistics in Melbourne.

Acknowledgments

My wife, Romi Arm, first encouraged me to write this book and later helped me in drawing the preliminary maps. During my travels I relied heavily on the consistent goodwill of the Chilean CONAF and Argentinian SNPN. The staff of these organisations provided me with indispensable information regarding infrastructure and hiking possibilities within their national parks. My particular thanks go to *guardaparques* Carlos Mariosa (SNPN, Tromen, Lanín), Clement Jauffret (CONAF, Laguna de la Laja), José Urrutia (CONAF, Tamango), Felix Ledesma (CONAF, Conguillío), Luis Sautivañez (CONAF, Anticura), Claudio Godoy (CONAF, Coyhaique) and Adrian Falcone (SNPN, Chaltén). I would also like to thank the Club Andino Bariloche (CAB) of Argentina and the Federación de Andinismo de Chile for their special help in preparing club lists and other information.

In addition the help of the following people was much appreciated:

Carlos Alvarado García (Chaitén, Chile), Niki Schäfer (Cochrane, Chile), Claudio Hopperdietzel (Puyaguapi, Chile), Alberto Fontao (Buenos Aires, Argentina), José & Miguel Herrera Müller (Puerto Saavedra, Chile), Peter Hartmann (Coyhaique, Chile), Art Bloom (Juneau, Alaska), Bernard Faure (Banff, Canada), José Cordovas (Malalcahuello, Chile), Juan Pablo Izquierdo (Santiago, Chile), Karl Renoth, (Ushuaia, Argentina), Charlotte Mitchell (Hong Kong), Orv Voxland (Washington DC, USA), Carlos Alarcón (Santiago, Chile), Romi Arm (Zurich, Switzerland), Matthias Mayer (Engelsbrand, Germany), Olga Hohf (Lago Todos los Santos, Chile) Edwin 'Gogo' Marchén (Santiago, Chile), Enrique 'Quique' Chediak (Quito, Ecuador), Helene Römer (San Carlos de Bariloche, Argentina), Andi Hutter (Lucerne, Switzerland), Rita Gutierrez García (Chaitén, Chile), Pablo Petit-Brevilh (Santiago, Chile).

From the Publisher

This 1st edition was edited at the Lonely Planet office in Melbourne by Jeff Williams. Margaret Jung drew the maps and Vicki Beale corrected them. Vicki did the cover design and colour wraps while Ann Jeffree performed the layout and drew the illustrations. Michelle de Kretser proofed the final product.

Disclaimer

Although the author and publisher have done their utmost to ensure the accuracy and currency of all information in this guide, they cannot accept responsibility for any loss, injury or inconvenience sustained by people using this book. For example, they cannot guarantee that the tracks and routes described have not been overgrown or otherwise become impassable in the interval between research and publication.

All hiking times *exclude* rest stops, and unless otherwise stated, assume that the path is not obstructed by snow. The fact that a trip or area is described in this guidebook does not necessarily mean that it is a safe one for you and your hiking party. Although many of the areas covered are visited by mountaineering parties and rock-climbers, the actual itineraries included have been deliberately chosen to avoid the necessity of engaging in these activities. You are finally responsible for judging your own capabilities in light of the conditions that you may encounter. Buena suerte!

Warning & Request

Things change - prices go up, schedules change, good places go bad and bad places go bankrupt - nothing stays the same. So if you find things better or worse, recently opened or long since closed, please write and tell us and help make the next edition better!

Your letters will be used to help update future editions and, where possible, important changes will also be included as a Stop Press section in reprints.

All information is greatly appreciated and the best letters will receive a free copy of our next edition, or any other Lonely Planet book of your choice.

Contents

MAP LEGEND

International Boundaries *

Internal Boundaries

National Park Boundaries

Major Roads

Railways

Walking Trail

Indistinct Walking Trail

Ferry Routes

Cable Car, Ski Lift

Rivers, Creeks

Lakes

Spring

Waterfall

Glacier

Contour, Contour Interval

Volcanic Crater

Settlements

Church, Monastery

Ruins

Camping Area

Hut

Mountain, Peak

Mountain Pass

Bridge

Escarpment or Cliff

* These are approximate locations only, and are not necessarily officially recognised.

Introduction

Unique in otherwise hot and humid South America, Patagonia is a distinct geographical area that lies completely within the cool temperate zone at the southernmost tip of the continent. The Patagonian Andes are shared between Chile and Argentina, and have an average height and climate similar to that found in New Zealand's Southern Alps or the Coast Mountains of British Columbia.

Like many other countries in the New World, both Chile and Argentina have an excellent system of national parks. Along the 2000-km length of the mountain chain some 20 parks protect areas of superb alpine and coastal wilderness. Cool temperate rainforests, volcanic cones, alpine lakes and snow-capped glaciated peaks invite the more self-reliant trekker who is seeking something different or free from the hassles associated with travel in countries further north. Despite its exciting potential, Patagonia has remained surprisingly unknown outside South America, and seems to attract as many extreme alpine climbers as it does trekkers.

This first detailed guidebook to the area contains some 28 fully documented walks and also lists a number of other trekking alternatives. With one or two exceptions, the treks lead through national parks or reserves. A majority of the treks are in Chile, on the western side of the Andes. This is a reflection of the better walking opportunities and greater accessibility of those areas. A representative selection of environments and scenery typical for the far southern Andes is featured. The walking standard ranges from easy two-day treks to more strenuous trips of up to 10 days.

The book is not intended as a general travel guide, and only information considered to be relevant to trekkers is provided. The region covered is vast, and a few well-known areas could not be included. A considerable number of alternative treks are also suggested. Many other fine walks await your own independent exploration.

9

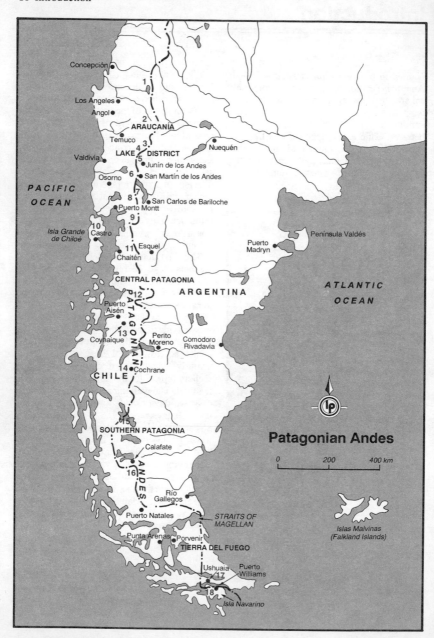

Patagonian Andes

Patagonian Andes

	Trekking Areas	Walking Routes
1	Parque Nacional Laguna del Laja (Chile)	Around Volcán Antuco
2	Parque Nacional Conguillío (Chile)	Sierra Nevada
3	Parque Nacional Huerquehue (Chile)	Central Huerquehue
4	Parque Nacional Villarrica (Chile)	Around Volcán Villarrica Villarrica Traverse (2 maps)
5	Parque Nacional Lanín (Argentina)	Ascent of Volcán Lanín Queñi Circuit
6	Parque Nacional Puyehue (Chile)	Puyehue Traverse
7	Parque Nacional Nahuel Huapí (Argentina)	Nahuel Huapí Traverse Paso de las Nubes
8	Parque Nacional Vicente Pérez Rosales (Chile)	Termas de Calláo
9	Parque Nacional Alerce Andino (Chile)	Pangal-Chaica Track
10	Parque Nacional Chiloé (Chile)	Río Anay Walk
11	Volcán Chaitén (Chile)	Walk to the Caldera
12	Reserva Nacional Río Simpson (Chile)	Cerro Catedral
13	Reserva Nacional Cerro Castillo (Chile)	In and Around Cerro Castillo
14	Reserva Nacional Tamango (Chile)	Tamango Circuits
15	Parque Nacional Los Glaciares (Argentina)	Cerro Torre Cerro Fitz Roy Lago Toro Glaciar Viedma
16	Parque Nacional Torres del Paine	Torres del Paine Lookout Torres del Paine Circuit Lago Pingo Pingo-Tyndall Circuit
17	Parque Nacional Tierra del Fuego	Lago Kami Circuit
		Tierra del Fuego Mini-circuit
18	Isla Navarino	Dientes Circuit

Facts about the Region

HISTORY
Indigenous Peoples of Patagonia

Before the arrival of the Spanish conquistadors, Patagonia was inhabited by a variety of indigenous peoples whose ancestors crossed from Siberia into North America perhaps as long as 30,000 years ago. How and when they reached the extreme south of the continent is uncertain.

Archaeologists have found evidence that American Indians have lived in the southern Lake District of Chile for at least 13,000 years, and it is now believed that humans first appeared in Tierra del Fuego about 7,600 years ago, thereby completing humanity's most far-reaching migration.

Among the original inhabitants, by far the most numerous were the tribes of northern Patagonia, usually referred to collectively as the Araucarians, or Mapuche. Upon the arrival of the first Spanish explorers, the Mapuche were occupying lands mostly to the west of the Cordillera. They were apparently attracted by wild herds of introduced cattle and, by the 16th century, they had already begun to migrate eastwards from their Andean heartland to the east Patagonian steppes.

Although they more or less spoke one common language, the Mapuche people were divided into numerous autonomous warrior tribes. These varied according to their local environments and Mapuche tribes had a diverse range of customs and lifestyles. The Pehuenches were a Mapuche tribe which inhabited the Andean region of northern Patagonia, and in late summer and autumn harvested the fruit of the araucaria pine, their staple diet.

The Mapuche of the north Patagonian steppes were a tall race of nomads. In the forested areas of the Araucanía and Lake District and the coastal zone including Chiloé, the Huilliche, Cunco and Puelche were the principle Mapuche tribes. They had a rather more settled lifestyle, practising a slash-and-burn form of agriculture.

To the south of the Mapuche territory, the Tehuelche people occupied the vast plains of central and southern Patagonia right down to the Straits of Magellan. At times, they ventured into the Cordillera from the east along the open river valleys. The Tehuelche were an exceptionally tall race of essentially nomadic hunters. They followed the large herds of guanaco across the Patagonian steppes, much as certain North American Indian tribes once followed the bison.

The flat northern part of the great island of Tierra del Fuego, where it begins on the southern shore of the Straits of Magellan, was inhabited by tribes of the Ona people. As well as spears, bows and arrows both the Tehuelches and the Onas used the *boleadoras*, an ingenious device of heavy rounded stones attached to a strong cord which is used to trip up and bring down their prey of mainly guanaco and ñandú. A small and largely unknown people called the

Major Indian Groups in South America before the Spanish conquest

12

Haush lived on the eastern tip of Tierra del Fuego.

The long west Patagonian coast stretching down as far south as the islands of Cape Horn was the territory of two sea-dwelling races, the Alacalufe and the Yaghan. Living on a rich diet of seafood, they occupied one of the most inhospitable areas on earth. These hardy marine nomads traversed the storm-battered waters of the archipelago in intricately constructed, lightweight bark canoes, which could be easily carried across the narrow isthmuses which separate the channels and fjords.

Exploration & Colonisation

After sailing steadily southwards for some months in search of a sea passage to the

Araucanian Indians

Pacific, the Dutch mariner Willem Schouten in February 1516 sighted the last land of the South American coast. Foggy conditions caused Schouten to erroneously chart the exposed rocky island he saw as a part of the continental mainland, and he gave them the name Cape Hoorn after his hometown in Flanders. Just three years later, in 1519, another tiny fleet arrived at the far southern Atlantic shores of South America. The fleet was captained by the navigator Ferdinand Magellan, who, like Schouten, was also seeking a safer, enemy-free trading route to India. Although Portuguese-born, Magellan was in the service of the Spanish king.

Magellan called this new land 'Patagonia'. Since *pata* is colloquial Spanish for 'foot', historians have generally assumed the name to be a reference to the supposedly big-footed native inhabitants, who were almost certainly Tehuelche Indians. Another theory links Magellan's coining of the word Patagonia with the fictitious land of Gran Patagón taken from a Renaissance story, *Primaleon of Greece*. This romance of chivalry had been published in Spain several years before Magellan set sail. In 1520, as he sailed through the straits that now bear his name, the discoverer called the great island immediately to the south *tierra del fuego,* or 'land of fire', after the multitude of glowing campfires he observed there during the dark and overcast nights.

The first European expeditions into Patagonia, scarcely a decade later, were inspired by the search for the legendary Ciudad de los Césares. A sort of southern El Dorado, this was supposedly a fantastically rich city situated somewhere in the Andes of Patagonia. Jesuit missionaries, seeking to convert the 'savages' to the Christian faith, also ventured deep into Indian lands and many were killed during hostile encounters with the natives.

To the west of the Cordillera, the Spanish conquistador and founder of Chile, Pedro de Valdivia, began the conquest of the forested zone south of Santiago. By 1567, in spite of extremely fierce resistance from the Mapuches, many settlements had been established along coast as far south as the great island of Chiloé. However, by the end of the 16th century the Indians' hostility reached a climax, and the Spanish invaders were unable to resist the sustained Mapuche offensives. Their cities were sacked and burnt, the survivors withdrew north. Chiloé, where interracial mixing had created a loyal Creole population, was cut off from the rest of the Spanish Empire to the north. As a result of this enforced isolation, a distinctive Chilote culture developed and this was to be an important influence on settlement in the rest of Patagonia.

With such unyielding native populations and seemingly little else to offer, Patagonia was largely neglected for the next two centuries. Neither the Spaniards nor any other European colonial power made serious attempts to settle or develop the region economically. Only after Chile and Argentina won independence in the early 1800s did the two nations move to expand and consolidate their territories.

In 1833 the *Beagle* sailed down the coast of Argentina. On board was the young naturalist Charles Darwin, who made frequent excursions into the Patagonian interior. It was largely observations of the local biology and geology during this journey that led Darwin to develop his theory of natural selection. As a cruel irony, the Darwinian notion of 'survival of the fittest' was soon to be used as a justification for the extermination of the 'inferior' indigenous races.

An interesting and curious episode in the history of Patagonia was the so-called Reina de la Araucanía, a 'kingdom' founded in 1859 by an opportunistic Frenchman, Orélie-Antoine de Tounens. Gaining the trust of the local Mapuche tribes, whose own *cacique* (chief) had prophesied the coming of a White saviour just before his death, Orélie-Antoine was made the Indians' monarch. The new king immediately declared the independence of the Araucanía, the Mapuche nation of northern Patagonia, and in another bold decree he annexed all remaining lands south of 42° right down to Cape Horn.

Ferdinand Magellan

Not surprisingly, the governments in Santiago and Buenos Aires initially ignored this new self-proclaimed monarchy. However, after he attempted to mobilise his Mapuche warriors the following year, Orélie-Antoine was captured, incarcerated and eventually deported. Orélie-Antoine made several attempts to return to his Patagonian kingdom but these were thwarted.

The farcical and essentially non-existent Reina nevertheless still captures the imagination of Argentinians and Chileans of both Hispanic and Indian descent. When the modern-day prince, Phillippe Boiry de Araucanía y Patagonia (who ascended to the throne by a dubious series of 'hand overs' that have taken place since the first king died without an heir in 1878) toured his kingdom in 1989 his visit aroused considerable curiosity and press coverage in Chile and Argentina. Prince Phillippe visited Mapuche and Tehuelche communities on either side of the Cordillera and his trip served to raise the issue of the indigenous peoples' rights and welfare.

Rather than save the Indian peoples of the south, however, Orélie-Antoine's original Reina was more a tragi-comic interlude before their almost total destruction. As in most parts of the New World, European colonisation proved catastrophic to the indigenous races. In the military campaigns of the late 1870s and early 1880s that were called by later historians the 'Conquista del Desierto', Mapuche and Tehuelche tribes of the southern plains of Argentina were systematically wiped out or driven onto reserves. Similarly, the 'reconquest' of the Chilean south progressively brought Indian lands under government control, leaving the way open for a steady influx of European settlers. The Mapuche, the only indigenous people in the Americas to successfully resist the domination of the Spanish Empire, were finally subdued. The Ona of Tierra del Fuego, who once numbered some 12,000, were completely wiped out by the invading settlers and gold prospectors. Disease and maligned negligence have left fewer than 30 surviving pure-blood members of the Yaghan and Alacalufe races.

Towards the end of the 19th century, the Indian tribes of Argentina had ceased to be a menace to colonists. In 1865, immigrants from Wales arrived at Puerto Madryn, on the dry Atlantic coast of Argentina, and not long afterwards Welsh settlements were gradually established throughout northern Patagonia. Moving up the Río Chubut, Welsh-Patagonians later founded the towns of Trevelin and Esquel in the Andean foothills. One of these newcomers, a young woman settler, wrote a literary classic of the Welsh language, *Dirngo'r Andes* ('Climbing the Andes'). Other immigrants – English, Basques and Germans – followed the coast south, moving into the drier interior along the more hospitable river valleys.

The sparse southern plains were turned over to profitable sheep and cattle grazing. The *gaucho* culture, a powerful influence in Argentinian folklore, spread from the Buenos Aires *pampa* into Patagonia. Unfortunately, vast tracts of the open steppes soon fell under the control of large Buenos Aires landowners. Other small-time sheep ranchers were forced to move westwards into the foothills of the Cordillera, often taking up tracts of new land without ever establishing

a legitimate title. This made the new settlers vulnerable during disputes with the large landholders, whose legal resources were hard to match.

To a lesser extent, this process was repeated on the Chilean side of the Andes, where the only available land was frequently in mountainous country or at the end of isolated fjords. Many of these smaller *estancias* were to survive little more than a generation, as low returns and isolation forced their abandonment.

In colonial times the Chilean-Argentine boundary had simply been the 'sierra nevada' of the Andes. Since the mountains between Santiago and Mendoza are such an obvious barrier, this seemed sufficient. As it became clear that a more precise understanding of the national border was necessary, a treaty in 1881 established the frontier line as 'the highest peaks which divide the waters'. However, in certain parts of Patagonia, the glaciers of the Pleistocene age had left their terminal moraines well to the east of the mountains. This diverted formerly eastwards-flowing rivers back towards the Pacific Ocean through latitudinal fractures in the southern Cordillera and as a result the highest peaks do not always form the watershed. In some places the Atlantic/Pacific divide lies only a few km from the Pacific while in other areas it is far to the east of the main line of peaks.

Under British arbitration, Chile and Argentina each established an official boundary commission. These Comisiones de los Límites sent numerous expeditions to their presumed Andean frontier lands in order to assess or assert their nations' territorial claims. During the last two decades of the 19th century all the important areas of the Patagonian Cordillera were reconnoitred. In Chile, explorers such as Hans Steffen and the geographer Luis Riso Patrón surveyed the rugged coastal areas of western Patagonia. In the service of the Argentine Boundary Commission, the naturalists Clemente Onelli and Perito Moreno (later rewarded with large tracts of land) made extensive journeys into the Cordillera from the east.

The absurdity of seeking a purely 'geographical solution' to the frontier dispute became evident when at the instigation of its own boundary commission the government of Argentina ordered that a section of an ancient moraine wall be cut away in order to change the course of a river. This audacious piece of landscape surgery shifted the watershed westwards, allowing Argentina to successfully claim the eastern part of the lake now called Lago Buenos Aires by Argentinians.

In 1902, Chile and Argentina accepted the decision of King Edward VII of England, whose borderline ran across the summits of some of southern Patagonia's most prominent peaks – San Lorenzo, Fitz Roy, Murallón and near to Cerro Stokes. Edward's border also created a number of other 'international lakes', dividing Lago Palena/Vintner and Lago Cochrane/Pueyrredón between the two countries. Unfortunately, the two enormous iccaps of southern Patagonia, the Hielo Norte and Hielo Sur, were still unknown, and this provided further grounds for dispute. Even today, some areas of the frontier are vehemently claimed by both Argentina and Chile.

In the second half of the 19th century, the California goldrush and the expanding settlement of the North American west coast led to a boom in maritime traffic around Cape Horn. This dangerous route via the southern tip of South America was still the only sea passage from the Atlantic to the Pacific, and of the numerous vessels that 'rounded the Horn' one in 50 was lost in the almost perpetually stormy waters. The port of Punta Arenas, founded on the Straits of Magellan to service passing ships, became a symbol of Patagonian prosperity. Early this century work began on an ambitious project to cut a canal through the Península de Taitao at the Laguna San Rafael. The aim of the canal was to create an almost unbroken shipping lane through the naturally sheltered canals of the Chilean Archipelago, but funds and fantasy were soon exhausted. With the opening of the Panama Canal in 1915, the Taitao project was abandoned forever. From then, until the discovery of oil in the inter-war period Punta Arenas slipped into decline.

International interest in the region was growing, and from the turn of the century Patagonia was visited by quite a number of scientific expeditions. In 1908-09 a party led by the Swedish botanist Carl Skottsberg travelled south from Bariloche along the eastern foothills of the Andes to reach Tierra del Fuego. In the first decades of the century the North American palaeontologist Simpson also made numerous important expeditions into central Patagonia. The polar explorer Otto Nordenskjöld explored the mountains around the two continental icesheets, the Hielo Norte and Hielo Sur.

Parallel to developments in the other parts of the New World, the need to protect the beautiful yet fragile mountains from excessive exploitation began to be understood. When in the early 1920s Perito Moreno was granted a sizable tract of land around the great lake Nahuel Huapí, he donated this back to the nation as its first national park. Soon afterwards, the first Chilean national park was created on the west side of the Andes. Directly adjacent to Nahuel Huapí, Parque Nacional Vicente Pérez Rosales was named in honour of a pioneer.

In both countries *clubs de montaña* were set up in some of the larger provincial cities along the Cordillera. Founded chiefly by immigrants from the European Alps in 1931, the Club Andino Bariloche became the largest mountaineering club in Latin America. Its members played an important part in opening up new climbing and hiking routes throughout the Patagonian Andes and constructed refugios in the surrounding mountains.

Between the wars the remarkable Italian Andinist and priest Father Alberto Maria de Agostini explored much of the southern Cordillera. Agostini made first ascents of various important summits and published an excellent mountaineering atlas of the Patagonian Andes that even today is still unsurpassed. Agostini's work was warmly appreciated by the goverments of both countries, and Chile recently named a national park in the Darwin

A	B	C
	D	
E	F	G

A Frutilla de magallanes
B Wildflowers
C Wildflowers
D Lenga branch in autumn colours
E Spiky cushion plant in flower
F Cushion plant
G Wild orchids

Top: Arrayán trees, Parque Nacional Nahuel Huapí
Middle: Beech rainforest, Queñi Circuit, Parque Nacional Lanín
Bottom: Lenga forest with autumn colours, Parque Nacional Los Glaciares

Range of western Tierra del Fuego in his honour.

During the 1940s and 1950s all of the highest unclimbed peaks of Patagonia such as Tronador, Cerro Fitz Roy, Monte San Lorenzo, San Valentín and the Paine Grande were conquered by mountaineers. In the 1960s the British explorer Eric Shipton ventured into the ranges of western Tierra del Fuego and the continental icecaps. Since the war, skiing and other mountain sports have become popular activities amongst better-off Argentinians and Chileans, and many new national parks have been established.

Recent Politics
In the 1970s, military governments seized power in both Chile and Argentina. Under these brutal dictatorships tens of thousands of suspected left-wing sympathisers were murdered, tortured or sent into exile. Despite their raw political similarities, the two regimes came close to war in 1979 over the sovereignty of a few small islands south of the Beagle Channel. The conflict was later settled by Pope John Paul II, who decided largely in favour of Chile.

In Argentina, the Falklands war fiasco and economic chaos had brought a cessation to military rule by 1983. Despite some initial successes however, the civilian government which followed (led by the Radical Party president Raúl Alfonsín) was unable to stabilise the Argentine economy. After a landslide victory in the 1988 elections, the Peronist candidate Carlos Menem assumed the presidency of Argentina under conditions of alarming hyperinflation and resulting social upheaval. Menem has imposed rigorous fiscal measures and embarked on a large scale privatisation program aimed at reviving the national economy. Menem's pardoning of former military junta members for their role in the notorious 1970s anti-terrorist 'dirty war' has angered and disgusted many Argentinians. This policy has failed to gain the loyalty of a small reactionary section of the military, who have periodically revolted against the government. More recently, the president has been linked to

allegations involving the complicity of his own family and close friends in a massive cocaine trafficking operation.

The 16-year long dictatorship in Chile began to end when the people rejected President Pinochet as the junta's candidate in the November 1988 plebiscite on whether to extend military rule until 1997. This led to presidential elections in December 1989, in which the candidate of the united Chilean opposition, Patricio Aylwin, soundly defeated the government-backed candidate. In contrast to Argentina however, the frugal Pinochet regime left Chile with the most dynamic economy in Latin America, a marginally falling foreign debt and a high growth rate. Since taking office in 1990, the Aylwin government has satisfactorily balanced more humane and just social policies with cautious economic management.

GEOGRAPHY
The Andes constitute a relatively young mountain chain which has been created over the last 70 million years as the oceanic Nazca Plate was slowly pushed under the continental South American Plate. In Patagonia, the initial uplifting of the range was accompanied by intense volcanic activity. Clearly, these great volcanic eruptions must have been extremely sudden, very widespread and quite catastrophic for the existing vegetation. Forests of proto-araucaria and other coniferous trees were smothered below thick layers of volcanic ash. This is how the fascinating 'petrified forests' found in the Chubut and Santa Cruz provinces of Argentina were formed. As the Cordillera gradually rose, the passage of moisture from the Pacific was blocked, drying out the land on the Andes' eastern side. Approximately two million years ago the Andes finally reached the elevation that they have today. The mountain-building is still occurring, and as a consequence the Andes experience a high level of seismic activity.

Over the last two million years the Cordillera has undergone several periods of intense glaciation during which much of its present topography was formed. At the height of these ice ages the entire Cordillera and a considerable part of the Patagonian lowlands were covered by an icesheet many hundreds of metres in depth. The glaciers released enormous quantities of moraine debris which was washed out from the mountains and deposited over the steppes of southern Argentina.

Approximately 14,000 years ago the last (Pleistocene) ice age began to end, and the glaciers that had intermittently covered most of the Andes retreated back into the Cordillera. This natural global warming allowed the plants and animals to recolonise areas previously under ice, and probably facilitated the arrival of the first humans not long afterwards.

Definitions of Patagonia

Depending on your definition, Patagonia comprises roughly one million sq km. The Patagonian region is just under one third of the land area of both Chile and Argentina but less than 5% of either nation's population actually lives there. Yet Chilean Patagonia is geographically very different from Argentine Patagonia. While the coastline of southern Chile is a wild and wet strip of densely forested mountainous country, most of Argentine Patagonia is a broad semi-arid plateau out of which rise eroded tablelands (called *mesetas*). It is only where these 'two Patagonias' meet, namely at the Patagonian Andes, that the area's continuity actually becomes apparent.

Politically speaking Patagonia is not much more than a somewhat vague geographical area that merely forms the southern part of Chile and Argentina. Like the rest of the land in both countries, Patagonia is divided into administrative units or 'states'. In Chile these are the numbered *regiones* and in Argentina *provincias*.

In Argentina, Patagonia officially includes all the land south from the Río Colorado (at 36°S). This vast area takes in the Argentinian Lake District in the provinces of Neuquén and Río Negro, as well as Chubut, Santa Cruz and the territories of Tierra del Fuego and the Malvinas (Falkland) Islands. People

who live in the so-called *provincias patagonicas* are entitled to certain tax and travel concessions from the Argentine government, which wants to promote development in the area. For years governments in Buenos Aires have talked about 'argentinising Patagonia' in order to integrate it more fully into the national economy. During the 1980s the decision was made to gradually transfer the capital to Viedma, a small city situated just inside Patagonian territory on the south bank of the Río Negro.

To the west of the Cordillera the situation is less definite. In Chile, only the strip of land extending south from Puerto Montt (which Chilean geographers call the *Sur Grande*) is normally considered a true part of Patagonia, a definition that excludes the Chilean side of the Araucanía and Lake District and usually also the island of Chiloé. Even this would come as a surprise to some Chileans, many of whom prefer to use the term Patagonia exclusively for the southern steppes of the Argentine also known colloquially as *la pampa*. However, the Araucanía and Lake District on either side of the Andes show a very high degree of geographical homogeneity, and 'Patagonia' is used loosely in this book to include all the Chilean territory south of the Río Bío Bío (at roughly 37°S), in addition to the 'true' Patagonia of the Argentine steppes.

THE PATAGONIAN ANDES

Unlike the rest of South America, which has a sticky tropical to subtropical climate, Patagonia's position at the most southernmost tip of the continent produces a cool and temperate climate. Chile and Argentina share (but quarrel over) the Patagonian Andes, whose ranges lie mainly on the Chilean side. Very roughly speaking, the main peaks of the Patagonian Andes have an average height of around 2000 metres. The climate is not unlike that found in the mountains of western Canada or New Zealand's Southern Alps.

Throughout their roughly 2000 km length the southern Andes do not always form an unbroken chain. Rather, the mountains appear as a series of separate parallel ranges with their own geological characteristics running more or less in a north-to-south line. The extensive high plateaus that typify the Andes further to the north are completely absent. In Patagonia, the Andes' overall width is reduced to an average of less than 100 km. Repeatedly interrupted by formerly eastwards-flowing rivers that have been forced back through the mountains to Pacific, in Patagonia the Cordillera ceases to be a continental divide or true geographical watershed.

The Patagonian Andes can be divided into three longitudinally arranged zones. Each of these zones is roughly 600 km in length and has a relatively distinct geographical character. The mountains of Tierra del Fuego and its countless islands form an additional zone below the South American mainland.

Northern Patagonia
(The Araucanía & Lake District)
After reaching their greatest height of almost 7000 metres at the latitude of 30°S around Mendoza and Santiago, the character of the Andes changes in a gradual yet dramatic manner. Moving towards the south, the mountain passes and peaks become steadily lower and the Cordillera itself narrows. As rainfall increases the dry sparsely vegetated north slowly changes into a fertile and perpetually green landscape of rich farming country and moist forests. Major rivers such as the Río Imperial and the Río Bío Bío descend from the main divide of the Cordillera through a wide and fertile valley, (which Chilean geographers call *la valle longitudinal*), before breaking out through the lower Coastal Range (the Cordillera de la Costa) to meet the Pacific Ocean.

On the western side of the mountains the landscape is increasingly dominated by intense volcanic activity, and volcanoes are almost always the highest summits. Towering over the lower basalt ranges, their cones are scattered randomly along the line of the main divide between 36°S and 43°S, with one volcano roughly every 30 km. The two highest peaks of this area, the extinct volcanoes Lanín (3776 metres) and Tronador

(3460 metres), lie directly on the Argentine-Chilean frontier and form part of the Pacific/Atlantic watershed.

The centre of volcanic activity lies at the Andes' western edge, however, and for this reason most of the dormant and active volcanoes are west of the Cordillera in Chile. The perfect cone of Volcán Osorno (2652 metres) is known as the 'Fuji of the Andes' and is a great favourite among Chilean climbers and skiers. Small and major eruptions are quite common, and the inhabitants of towns and settlements close to volcanoes are continually on the alert.

Sudden eruptions have caused destruction and loss of life in the past, though never on the same scale as recent Colombian and Peruvian disasters. On the higher volcanoes there is the danger that an eruption may cause the rapid melting of snow and glacial ice to create a deadly avalanche of volcanic mud (known in English by the Indonesian word 'lahar'). Some years ago Volcán Lonquimay had a minor yet highly spectacular eruption which continued for some four months, attracting bus loads of tourists. Volcán Villarrica churns out smoke and gases constantly, and has erupted several times in the last generation or so. Literally hundreds of *termas*, or thermal springs, dot the countryside, most still completely undeveloped.

Araucaria trees

This volcanic belt corresponds reasonably closely to the area of Greater Araucanía, the trans-Andean territory originally inhabited by many different tribes of the Araucarians, or Mapuche people. Today perhaps 250,000 full and mixed blood Mapuche still live here, mainly on the Chilean side of the Cordillera. The southern part of the Araucanía takes in the beautiful Región de los Lagos, or Lake District. With more than 20 great lakes gouged into the precordilleran landscape during the last ice age, and many hundreds of smaller lakes set higher up among snow-capped peaks, the Lake District is often promoted as the 'Switzerland of South America' – a title that conveniently disregards the total absence of volcanoes on the landscape of the Alps!

Fertile volcanic soil and the area's mild and moist climate have made the Lake District a prime agricultural region. Lush native rainforest still covers the higher ranges and large parts of the coast, but in the Chilean longitudinal valley, situated between the Pacific and the Cordillera, most of the original forested land has been cleared for farming and grazing. The mean level of the tree line is between 1700 and 2000 metres above sea level, with alpine grasslands covering the mountainsides to the permanent snow line some 300 to 400 metres higher up.

On the Chilean side of the Lake District, the major lakes are situated mostly in the Andean foothills. Here, even the larger lakes are warm enough for swimming in summer (especially when compared with the chilled waters of the Pacific beaches). Chileans sometimes attribute the relatively warm water of their lakes to subterranean volcanic activity, but lower elevation (generally under 350 metres) is a more likely cause than any thermal heating effect. The clarity of the water in the Chilean lakes can be surprising, often allowing visibility to depths of 15 metres or more. This seems to be due to the naturally low levels of nutrients in the water which hinders the growth of algae.

In the adjacent Argentinian Lake District, the major lakes are deeper and more elevated (usually at least 750 metres) and, therefore, quite a few degrees colder. The Argentine lakes also tend to take a more classically glacial form, with fjord-like arms stretching westwards deep into the Cordillera. Lago Nahuel Huapí is the best example of this.

In both countries the Araucanía and Lake District are closer to the major centres than the rest of the Patagonian Andes. In Argentina, the major provincial cities of Junín de los Andes, San Martín de los Andes and San Carlos de Bariloche are connected by excellent roads that skirt the eastern shores of the large lakes, while in Chile the Panamerican Highway leads north-south through the regional capitals of Temuco, Osorno and Puerto Montt. The area's splendid scenery and wildlife and its relatively easy access from the bigger cities has lead to the development of a sizable tourist industry. Investment in winter sports has been particularly high. Brown and rainbow trout have been introduced for the benefit of anglers.

Virtually the entire Argentine Lake District lies within two vast national parks, Parque Nacional Lanín and Parque Nacional Nahuel Huapí. These parks straddle the eastern side of the Cordillera and are multi-use areas, with controlled harvesting of timber in certain designated sectors. There are eight or so Andean national parks in the Chilean Lake District and the Araucanía. These parks are much smaller than those in Argentina, but have complete protection. The largest are Vicente Pérez Rosales and Puyehue, two adjoining parks which front Argentina's Parque Nacional Nahuel Huapí in the southern Lake District. Nearby is another smaller park, Alerce Andino, situated on the coast east of Puerto Montt. Chile's other important Lake District parks are much further to the north. The national parks of Huerquehue and Villarrica are near the tourist town of Pucón, and Conguillío/Llaima are east of Temuco. The most northerly area covered by this book, Parque Nacional Laguna del Laja is high up in the mountains just north of the Río Bío Bío. The Chilean Lake District also has large expanses of semi-wilderness outside of national parks.

The natural beauty of the Lake District

and the Araucanía is easily underestimated. Visiting trekkers often assume northern Patagonia to be less interesting than the more rugged south, simply because in both Chile and Argentina the area is more integrated into the national infrastructure. While it is true that development has left the Lake District and Araucanía a lot less wild and challenging than the central and southern regions, this northern third of Patagonia has more national parks, a greater diversity of plant and animal species and a much warmer climate in which to enjoy it all than the southern zones. The more settled and easily accessible character of the Araucanía and Lake District offers walkers a gentler introduction to the southern Andes.

Central Patagonia

South of the Chilean city of Puerto Montt at roughly 42°S the long western coastal plain begins to break up. The more or less continuous series of broad longitudinal valleys that further north are so much a characteristic of the Andes' western side now disappear completely. After dropping briefly below sea level at the narrow straits of the Canal Chacao, the Coast Range continues for some 180 km as the backbone of the great island of Chiloé, before suddenly fracturing into a wild maze of narrow channels and islands below 44°S. Known as the Archipiélago de los Chonos after their original inhabitants, these rainy and windswept islands are formed by the crests of the submerged Coast Range. The islands of the Chonos considerably shelter the shipping lanes to as far south as 47°S, where the twisted-fist shape of the Península de Taitao juts out into the Pacific and blocks any further passage. Here, at the Laguna San Rafael, the Ventisquero San Rafael descends from the northern Patagonian icecap. The Ventisquero San Rafael is the world's 'most equatorial' (ie situated closest to the equator) glacier that reaches the sea.

Compared with areas of a similar latitude in the northern hemisphere, mean annual average temperatures on the coast are not only relatively warm, but also surprisingly constant. July (mid winter) has an average temperature of around 3°C as against the January (mid summer) average of some 11°C. These climatic conditions have produced impenetrable temperate rainforests, where in places the continually cool temperatures even prevent fallen trees from rotting for hundreds of years. The coastal soils are leached and poor, and agricultural development is mostly limited to drier areas to the east that are sheltered by the coastal ranges.

From about 41°S the main range of the Cordillera is increasingly dominated by hard granitic rock types. There are still isolated centres of intense volcanic activity down through the Patagonian Andes (almost entirely on the Chilean side) as far south as about 46°S, where in August 1991 Volcán Hudson erupted violently, causing extensive damage.

Until recently many Chilean localities along Patagonia's central-western coast were accessible only by boat or via long and dusty overland routes from Argentina. This changed during the 1980s with the construction of the Carretera Austral, when military workers bulldozed and blasted their way south from Puerto Montt through the spectacular mountains that front the Chilean fjords. Originally conceived both as a means of promoting development in Chile's remote and sparsely-settled XI Región and breaking the local dependence on Argentina, this modest gravel road was christened *huella a la oportunidad*, or 'trail to opportunity'.

As the only north-south route on the western side of the border, the Carretera connects the few settlements of this region of Chile. The Argentine counterpart to the Carretera Austral is the Ruta 40, which leads south from Bariloche along the eastern edge of the Patagonian steppes through the small towns of El Bolsón, Esquel, Alto Río Senguerr and Río Mayo.

In Argentina, the central Patagonian Andes more or less correspond to the eastern strip of Chubut Province. In Chile this zone takes in the northernmost two thirds of the XI Región. On the Chilean side there are three main national parks. These are Parques Nacionales Chiloé, Queulat, Isla Magdalena, plus many other large national reserves such as Cerro Castillo, Río Simpson and Jeinimeni. On the Argentine side there is only one national park, Los Alerces, in the north of Chubut.

Of the four zones discussed here, the Andes of central Patagonia are the most thinly settled. The total population on both sides of the border is probably not more than about 250,000. Particularly in Argentina, transport and access are still the most difficult factors. Due to its wet weather, poor infrastructure and remoteness, central Patagonia is rather more demanding of trekkers. Yet the greater difficulties involved in visiting the Andes of Central Patagonia reflect the region's much wilder nature, and the extra hardship is worth enduring.

Southern Patagonia

Below 46°S volcanoes appear only sporadically and the Andes' average height once again increases. The climate becomes steadily more extreme and more heavily influenced by the closer proximity of the sea. Antarctic ocean currents with relatively low salt concentrations and an average temperature of 4°C drift along the coast. Fierce and almost perpetual storms batter and drench the ranges in south-western Patagonia. Miserable weather is (even more) common here, and in the few isolated coastal settlements like Puerto Eden (at 49° on Chile's Isla Wellington) three, or even two, straight days without rain are quite rare. Annual rainfall in certain areas exceeds eight metres, the highest levels of precipitation experienced anywhere outside the earth's tropical zone.

The Andes of southern Patagonia are dominated covered by the most extensive area of glaciers outside the world's polar regions. Situated at an average elevation of around 1500 metres between 46°S and 51°S, two massive longitudinal sheets of glacial ice, many hundreds of metres thick, smother all but the higher mountains. Mountains within these frozen plateaus appear as rock islands which mountaineers call *nunataks*, their summits projecting out spectacularly from their white surroundings. Many of the

higher peaks are covered by thick deposits of so-called *hongos de hielo*, or 'ice mushrooms'. This phenomenon, almost unique to the far southern Andes, occurs when moisture carried by the severe and incessant Pacific winds freezes directly onto exposed surfaces. Hongos reportedly have a brittle consistency similar to polystyrene and peaks where rock is covered by this type of ice can be extremely difficult and dangerous to climb. The icecaps are fed by extremely heavy snowfalls and kept from melting by almost continual cloud cover. Unlike other great expanses of glacial ice, the Hielo Norte and the Hielo Sur move out in all directions from the centre and have few crevasses.

The northern icecap is the Hielo Patagonico Norte, some 100 km long and comprising almost 4500 sq km. The Hielo Norte is the smaller of the two and lies completely on Chilean territory. The highest peak in Patagonia, the 4058-metre Monte San Valentín, towers from its north-eastern flank. The largest icecap is the more southerly, the Hielo Patagonico (or Continental) Sur. The Hielo Sur comprises roughly 14,000 sq km and stretches some 320 km from north to south. Although most of its mass is in Chile, parts of the southern icecap's eastern fringe edge over the frontier.

Most of the highest peaks in southern Patagonia are associated with the great icebound ranges around the two main icecaps. It is here that Patagonia's classical peaks of over 3000 metres are found, and names like Cerro Torre, Cerro Fitz Roy and Cerro Paine are known to climbers all over the world. An exception to this is the great lone massif of Monte San Lorenzo (called Cerro Cochrane in Chile), whose 3706-metre granite summit forms the Chile-Argentina border.

On the Andes western side, glaciers from the inland icecaps slide down to calve in the deep fjords that extend far inland from the Pacific Ocean. To the east, huge glaciers of Alaskan proportions spill off east into enormous lakes fringing the Argentinian pampa. Unlike those of the Argentine Lake District far to the north, these lakes are low-lying, with an average altitude of just 200 metres above sea level. The most northerly of these is Lago General Carrera/Lago Buenos Aires, the second largest natural lake in South America. At around 47°S, Lago General Carrera and the adjacent Península de Taitao both form a botanical and climatic division between the more temperate flora zone of central Patagonia and the frigid areas of the far south.

South of the Hielo Sur, the Patagonian Andes rapidly lose height. The higher peaks average little more than 1500 metres and are entirely within Chilean territory, stranded on offshore islands and peninsulas almost cut off from the mainland by canals and deep sounds channelled out by colossal glaciers during recent ice ages. Large icecaps cover some of the higher and more exposed ranges, but never reach anything like the proportions of the Hielo Norte and the Hielo Sur. It is at Puerto Natales, on Seno Última Esperanza, that for the first time the dry zone of Patagonian steppes extends eastwards right to the water line on the Pacific coast. Below Península Brunswick, the most southerly point on the South American mainland, the Cordilleran islands connect with the intensely glaciated ranges of Tierra del Fuego. Here, on the Fuegian Peninsula, the Cordillera Darwin has a number of 2000-metre peaks that soar above the surrounding wild seas.

Chile's Carretera Austral, the southern road leading down the Pacific coast of central-western Patagonia, ends at Tortel, a small coastal village near the mouth of the Río Baker and just south of the Hielo Norte. Another inland section is currently in construction and will go to Villa O'Higgins, a tiny settlement on the remote Lago O'Higgins near the Argentine border. Southwards from here the many glaciers that descend from the southern continental icecap to meet the Pacific Ocean make any southern extension via Chilean territory unfeasible for the moment. Nevertheless, ambitious (but probably unfeasible) plans have been drawn up that would push the Carretera south around the Hielo Sur as far as the Beagle Channel, with a series of car ferries to breach the numerous fjords. South of the Hielo Sur good roads lead southwards to Punta Arenas on the Straits of Magellan. Punta Arenas is the largest Chilean city south of Puerto Montt.

In Argentina the Ruta 40 follows a zigzag route along the eastern edge of the Andean foothills from the town of Perito Moreno in northern Santa Cruz through Calafate to Río Turbio near Puerto Natales in far southern Chile. This remote road has many dusty turn-offs that lead west to small settlements or sheep ranches close to the Cordillera. The Ruta 40 connects with surfaced roads that go to Río Gallegos, the most southerly city on the Argentine mainland.

In Chile the zone of the southern Patagonian Andes takes in the southern third of the XI Región (chiefly the O'Higgins Province) and the mainland area of the XII Región (Magallanes). On the Argentine side, this zone corresponds fairly closely to the western part of Santa Cruz Province.

There are five main national parks in southern Patagonia. Two of the national parks, Laguna San Rafael and Bernando O'Higgins, encompass the northern and southern icecaps and are in Chile. The Ventisquero San Rafael is most often visited by tourists on three-day boat trips from Puerto Aisén. Both of these vast parks are total wilderness areas, with extreme conditions, very difficult access and no visitor infrastructure whatsoever. Immediately south of the Hielo Sur is the outstanding Torres del Paine area, probably Chile's most famous national park. The two Argentinian national parks in the southern Patagonian Andes are Perito Moreno and Los Glaciares. It is in the enormous Parque Nacional Los Glaciares that most visitors actually get to view the great glaciers that spill down east from the Hielo Sur. Parque Nacional Perito Moreno is a remote but remarkable area south of Monte San Lorenzo/Cochrane.

Tierra del Fuego

As they near the tip of the South American continent, the Andes swing around into an east-west line. For the first time in its entire length the Cordillera dips completely below sea level into the Straits of Magellan, only to surface again a little further south to meet the great island of Tierra del Fuego.

On Tierra del Fuego the mighty Cordillera Darwin, situated on a great peninsula stretching 250 km west-to-east, forms the main range of the Andes. These rugged and ice-choked mountains rise up directly from the frigid seas to well over 2000 metres, sending numerous glaciers back down into deep fjords. This entire peninsula is part of the remote Parque Nacional De Agostini, an area seldom visited by anyone but the occasional mountaineering expedition or fishing boat. Not surprisingly, the Darwin Range is seldom visible due to its notoriously poor weather. To the west and south a multitude of larger and smaller islands surround the Isla Grande, forming an intensely glaciated and storm-battered archipelago.

The Darwin Range peters out at its eastern end about 20 km west of the frontier. The ranges that continue eastwards into the Argentine part of Tierra del Fuego are much lower and never exceed 1500 metres. Although still exposed to winds from the south, the mountains on the Argentine side are somewhat sheltered from the moister westerlies. This produces a slightly more moderate climate with lower precipitation levels, but decidedly subantarctic climatic conditions still prevail. Very small glaciers hang from the higher peaks and the permanent snow line lies at around 800 metres.

Cape Horn lies less than 100 km from Tierra de Fuego, and is usually regarded as the most southerly extension of the South American continent. However, although the Cordillera continues as a deep submarine ridge that reaches south as far as the Antarctic Peninsula, the rugged and windswept Staten Island ('Isla de los Estados' in Spanish), due east of Tierra del Fuego, is the Andes' true point of southern termination.

Geographically, Tierra del Fuego belongs to the Patagonian mainland, and the northern part of the island is essentially a continuation of Patagonia's arid steppes. The elongated form of Lago Kami, a deep glacial lake over 100 km in length, almost cuts Tierra del Fuego in two and more or less marks the halfway point between the dry flat north and the Fuegian Andes on the island's shattered southern coast.

When its numerous larger and smaller islands are included, over two thirds of Tierra del Fuego is Chilean territory. Despite this, the Argentine sector has a considerably higher population and is more homogeneously settled. Under the Argentine national government's development policies Ushuaia on the Beagle Channel has now displaced Río Gallegos as the largest Argentine city south of Comodoro Rivadavia. Apart from a few isolated estancias along the coast and south of Lago Blanco, the southern part of Chilean Tierra del Fuego is hardly populated and virtually inaccessible. As a kind of southern extension to its Carretera Austral, the Chilean government has approved plans for the construction of a road south across the Río Azorpardo to the Fuegian south coast.

CLIMATE

The vast unbroken stretch of ocean to the west and south of the South American continent leaves the Patagonian Andes very exposed to the saturated winds that circle the Antarctic landmass. The north-south line of the range forms a formidable barrier to these violent westerlies (known to English speakers as the Roaring Forties and the Furious Fifties), which dump often staggering quantities of rain or snow on the ranges of the Patagonian Cordillera.

Although, by Andean standards, the average height of the Patagonian mountains is relatively low, they capture virtually all the air-born moisture, leaving the vast Patagonian plains on the leeward side in a severe rainshadow. Nowhere else on earth do precipitation levels drop off so dramatically over such a short distance. In places the vegetation changes from dense, perpetually wet rainforest to dryland tussock grasses and low shrubs in as little as 10 km. Having left their moisture behind in the Andes, the now dry and cold westerly winds sweep down across eastern Patagonia to the Atlantic, drying out the already arid steppes even more.

The strong marine influence makes for highly unpredictable weather in the Patagonian Andes. Particularly in spring or early summer, fine weather may deteriorate almost without warning, as violent westerly storms sweep in from the Pacific Ocean. During such disturbances snowfalls occur on all but the lowest ranges, even in mid summer.

As a rule, climatic conditions become steadily harsher the further south you go. This is reflected in the upper limit of alpine vegetation and the level of the summer snow line. Although there are major variations depending on many local factors such as exposure and precipitation, both the tree line and summer snow line drop dramatically with increasing distance south. For example, in the Araucanía of Argentina's northern Neuquén Province, the stunted high alpine vegetation reaches about 2000 metres in places, but around Cape Horn only species of lichen have adapted to grow above 400 metres.

The highest average levels of permanent snow are also on the Argentine side of the northern Araucanía at roughly 2400 metres, while in the subantarctic islands of far southern Chile snow fields come down to as low as 450 metres.

The severe winds for which Patagonia has become notorious arise from strong low pressure systems over the Argentine steppes. These low pressure systems build up in summer as a result of the sun's warming effect and constantly draw in masses of moist air from the Pacific. As a general rule, winds become progressively more severe with increasing distance south, where very strong winds are a major nuisance and a real danger to walkers and mountaineers in all high or exposed areas. Strong westerly winds are usually at their worst from November to January, but typically continue through to the end of April. Winter is surprisingly wind-free, with long periods of virtual stillness.

Local weather is generally rather more stable in northern Patagonia, with less wind and longer, warmer summers. From the Lake District down to Aisén, signs of approaching bad weather often include strong, moist and suspiciously warm winds blowing in from the north. In northern areas isolated thunder storms regularly build up in the mountains during hot summer weather. Storms of this type usually bring heavy rain but pass quickly. Areas of the Cordillera with an easterly aspect (generally on the Argentine side) also tend to have somewhat less severe weather, though frosts are more frequent due to higher valley elevations and a much more typically continental climate.

South of about 47°S the climate comes more heavily under the influence of the subantarctic zone. Here extremely strong and incessant winds tend to blow westerly, but can vary from north-westerly to southerly. West to south-westerly winds generally indicate an approaching cold front and imminent storms. If a new westerly storm is approaching, winds may again begin to turn south-westerly and very cold after only a few days of fine weather. On the other hand a southerly airstream usually brings fine and stable conditions, although accompanied by very cold weather conditions.

Certain cloud formations such as long wispy streams of high cirrus cloud known as 'mares' tails', and heavy lens-shaped or lenticular clouds called 'hogs' backs' that hover above higher peaks, are another possible (but by no means definite) indication of a breakdown in the weather.

In the southern hemisphere, star formations appear upside down to people from Europe and North America, and the sun shines in the *northern* half of the sky. This generally gives north-facing mountain sides milder weather. On the other hand, slopes with a southerly aspect are shady and cold, allowing snow and ice to accumulate more readily. For this reason glaciers tend to form on the south sides of ranges, and here and there glacial action has sheered out rounded cirques that also usually open out southwards.

Seasons

Patagonia lies completely within the world's southern temperate zone, and the year is divided into four very distinct seasons, as in North America or Europe. The seasons of the southern hemisphere are offset to those in the north by six months, which means that during the southern summer the northern hemisphere is experiencing its winter and vice versa.

Due to the peculiarities of the earth's rotation cycle, the seasons in the two halves of the globe do not have an identical pattern of daylight distribution. For example, Punta Arenas, situated between 53°S and 54°S, enjoys more summer daylight but less winter daylight than the English city of Manchester, which is located at precisely the same latitude (or distance from the equator) in the northern hemisphere. Patagonia might therefore be expected to experience hotter summers and colder winters than comparable areas of Europe or North America. The enormous expanse of ocean (covering about 80% of the southern hemisphere's surface) serves, however, to even out seasonal temperature differences and to moderate the climate of the whole region. In high summer (late December) the maximum period of daylight ranges from around 15 hours in the far north at Laguna del Laja to 19 hours in Tierra del Fuego.

FLORA

The vegetation of Patagonia shows strong links with the plant life found in other parts of the southern hemisphere. The similarities are an indication of a common geographical past, when during Carboniferous times the earth's southern landmasses were joined together in a single supercontinent called Gondwanaland. When Gondwanaland began to break up 100 million years ago plants that had grown all over the supercontinent were left stranded on each of the newly formed continental islands. The vegetation continued to evolve in isolation, gradually developing into new species as South America slowly drifted away. Visitors from Australia's Tasmania and New Zealanders in particular will notice a close resemblance to their own native flora.

Very broadly speaking, the vegetation of the southern Cordillera can be divided into three main zones which extend southwards through the Patagonian Andes in more or less longitudinal bands. Vegetation zones largely reflect the climatic change moving eastwards from the mild wet lowland conditions to a colder and slightly drier montane environment before dropping down to the semi-arid steppes on the lee side of the ranges. Due to steadily harsher climatic conditions, the temperate rainforest and deciduous forest zones become gradually lower with increasing distance south.

The zone of the evergreen temperate rainforest (*selva fría*) is made up of mixed evergreen tree species and occupies all areas west of the Cordillera. This is the most luxuriant and diverse of the three zones, and includes virtually all the important species. In the Araucanía and Lake District, temperate rainforest is species-rich and grows from sea level up to about 1400 metres. In the far south, however, the rainforests are composed of only a few species (dominated by the *guindo* or coigüe de magallanes) and are only found close to sea level in sheltered locations. Temperate rainforest is generally very dense and this can make off-track hiking a very difficult proposition.

The zone of deciduous forest (*bosque deciduoso*) is subalpine and extends from as low as 600 metres up to tree line in the Lake District, (where the local term *bosque valdiviano* is frequently used). The factors favouring the distribution of deciduous forest are mainly better drainage and more severe winters rather than just lower rainfall.

There is usually no definite transition point and the rainforest zone tends to merge gradually into deciduous forest. Although very attractive, these forests have a much poorer range of species, with deciduous southern beech species (chiefly lenga) being dominant. Especially in southern Patagonia where there is little undergrowth, mosses and herbs make an attractive 'park lawn' type landscape.

The steppes fringe the eastern side of the Cordillera and generally are sparsely vegetated. Classed as *monte* by Argentine geographers, but known more colloquially simply as *pampa*, this type of terrain consists of tussock grasses and rounded pale-green thorny plants that from a distance look a bit like sheep. Sporadic clusters of low trees (especially ñirre) and calafate scrub grow in sheltered places and along the river courses.

Trees

Southern Beech The Andean-Patagonian vegetation is strongly characterised by the southern beech (with literally the same common name in Spanish of *haya del sur*). Southern beech are of the genus *Nothofagus*, whose member species are also found in other parts of the South Pacific such as New Zealand, Australia and Papua New Guinea. The 10 species of beech that grow in South America are all endemic to the Southern Andes, and do not grow north of the subtropical zone above 30°S. Their distribution is determined by factors of climate and elevation, but although many other tree species

may also be present, beech forms the basis of the forest in virtually all areas.

The three evergreen coigüe (usually called coihue in Argentina) species are mostly found at lower elevations, or where marine influence produces milder climatic conditions. Coigüe de magallanes (*Nothofagus betuloides*) is the most widespread, and can be identified by its stratified form and tiny deep-green leaves. Coigüe de magallanes is sometimes also known by its common Mapuche name, guindo. Coigüe de chiloé (*N. nitida*) has scaly, almost triangular-shaped leaves of a lighter colour. Vigorous and highly adaptable, the common coigüe (*N. dombeyi*) has larger and more serrated leaves and grows to well over 50 metres, often attaining a truly massive girth.

Deciduous species of beech are found with increasing altitude or distance south. Of these, lenga (*N. pumilio*) is easily the most common, and grows in a variety of forms. In early summer the leaves of the lenga are of a soft colour, and have neat, rounded double indentations. A beautiful tree, lenga grows in the mountains of the Araucanía and Lake

Various beech leaves & relative sizes

Raulí

Roble

Ñirre

Lenga

Coigüe de chiloé

Common coigüe

Coigüe de magallanes or guindo

District up to the tree line, where it forms low impenetrable thickets. In the far south lenga may be found at sea level. Under extreme conditions lenga can appear in a miniature form reminiscent of a Japanese bonsai tree.

Ñirre (*N. antarctica*) is a small tree that frequently occupies difficult sites such as poorly drained moors or windswept steppes, and has distinctive crinkled leaves of an irregular shape.

Two other lovely species of deciduous beech are found in the forests of the Araucanía and northern Lake District. These are raulí and roble. Raulí (*N. alpina*) has leathery leaves of up to 15 cm long, and gives a much-prized red-grained timber. The roble (*N. obliqua*) has a straight untapered trunk reaching up to 35 metres. As its Spanish name indicates, the tree has distinctive 'oak-like' leaves with deep serrations. In April and May, mountainsides all over Patagonia turn golden-red with the autumn colours of the southern beech species, giving the landscape a peculiarly 'northern hemisphere' feel.

Araucaria (or Pehuén) The araucaria 'pine' (*Araucaria araucana*) typifies the Araucanía and northern Lake District, and its name is inextricably linked with the Araucarian (or Pehuenche) Indians, local Mapuche Indian tribes whose staple diet was the araucaria nut. The graceful umbrella-like conifer has sharp-pointed leaves shaped like scales which are attached directly to the branchlets. Mature trees produce a kind of cone at the tips of their branches, rather the size and shape of a pineapple, which ripens towards the end of summer.

The araucaria is also known as the monkey-puzzle tree, because the first Europeans to inspect it were reportedly 'puzzled' at the question of how monkeys could possibly climb the spiny branches in order to reach the fruit. There are no monkeys in this part of South America of course, but the araucaria does provide food for much of the forest life. A member of the parrot family, the loro cachaña (*Microsittace ferruginea*), lives almost exclusively on the nuts, as do some 50 species of insect.

Essentially a montane species, araucarias thrive in the Andean foothills between 1000 and 2000 metres, and are often found right at the tree line. Individual specimens have been measured at 50 metres in height and 2000 years of age. The high commercial value of the timber has led to over exploitation of the tree in years past, but national parks and forest reserves now ensure the protection of the araucaria. The Chilean national park authority CONAF has adopted the araucaria as its official symbol.

Alerce (or Lahuén) Reminiscent of the North American sequoia, the alerce (*Fitzroya cupressoides*) is an extremely slow-growing conifer that reaches enormous proportions and great age. These majestic trees have green scaly segmented branchlet-leaves and a reddish spongy bark. Once widespread even on the coastal plains of the Lake District, alerce forests are now mainly limited to national parks and reserves. Although it is prohibited to cut down the trees, alerce wood can still be sold legally and it is in demand for use as highly durable roof shingles.

Mañíos Three species of mañío grow in the forests of the Lake District and Chiloé. Members of the genus *Podocarpus*, mañíos grow to be very large and attractive trees. They are recognisable by their distinctive waxy elongated leaves, and produce edible red fruit. The trunks of older trees are reddish-brown in colour and often deeply twisted, yet mañío produces timber of a high value.

Arrayán The arrayán (*Myrceugenella apiculata*) is a rainforest tree usually found growing in moist areas with a more moderate coastal climate. Covered with smooth pinkish-red bark that peels off leaving strips of white, the arrayán typically develops multiple trunks, forming beautiful dimpled twisted branches. The tree has abundant white flowers which grow into edible purple berries.

Laurels Two almost identical species of the genus *Laurelia* grow throughout much of the southern rainforests. Known as tepa (*L. philippiana*) and laurel or trihue (*L. sempervirens*), these tall, straight trees have thick sappy leaves with deep serrations. When crushed, the leaves of the tepa (and less so the trihue) give off a pleasant and intense aroma.

Cipreses (Cypresses) Two native members of the conifer family *Cupressaceae* are commonly called ciprés.

The ciprés de la cordillera (*Austrocedrus chilensis*) grows in dry highland areas of the northern Araucanía. The medium-sized tree has dark-green branchlet-leaves ordered like scales in flattened twigs. In October, when the trees are flowering, great clouds of pollen blow around the forests. The ciprés de la cordillera has been overexploited, and its habitat has been much reduced. At Parque Nacional Laguna del Laja intact forests of this tree still exist.

In stark contrast to the former species, the ciprés de las guaitecas (*Pilgerodendron uviferum*) thrives in waterlogged ground in the intensely wet coast of western Patagonia from around Valdivia to Tierra del Fuego. The tree looks similar to the alerce and is also very much prized for its fine timber, but the species is much smaller than the alerce and does not have the same reddish bark.

Avellano The avellano (*Gevuina avellana*) is a medium-sized tree found in a number of the varying habitats of northern Patagonia.

The tree's shiny leaves have a superficial resemblance to coigüe de chiloé and it can often be identified by its more or less smooth bark with white spots. Individual trees flower heavily between January and March while the reddish breast-shaped fruits from the previous year still hang on the same stem.

Tineo The tineo (*Weinmannia tricho-sperma*) is another Gondwanaland genus scattered across the South Pacific and is found in northern and central Patagonia. A very large tree, the tineo sometimes grows to a height of 50 metres and has small attractive branchlets with opposing leaves vaguely like a fern. The tineo blooms in December when white flowers appear, growing into red capsules in summer to give the whole tree a reddish colour.

Canelo A beautiful rainforest tree, the canelo (*Drimys winteri*) is sacred to the Mapuche and is found all over the Patagonian Andes. The canelo has thick light-green elongated leaves that grow out radially around the branchlets and reaches 30 metres and a diameter of one metre. Between September and November the tips of the branchlets are covered with fragrant white flowers which develop into inedible red berries in March and April.

Bushes & Wildflowers

Calafate The calafate (*Berberis buxifolia*) is a thorny bush found all over Patagonia. Growing from one to three metres high, the calafate has attractive bright yellow flowers in spring, and yields tasty round purple berries. Many other similar species of the widespread *Berberis* genus grow throughout the southern Andes, and these also produce edible (though usually less palatable) berries.

Chilco The chilco (*Fuchsia magellanica*) grows in cool humid areas, near waterfalls or by rivers. The flowers have a very distinctive fuchsia form, with bright red sepals and petals of a bluish-purple colour. Many cultivated varieties of the chilco are grown in gardens all over the world.

Nalca (or Pangal) The nalca (*Gunnera scabrosa*) is a vigorous annual that grows up to three metres in very moist areas. The nalca's remarkable giant 'elephant ear' leaves and its succulent thorny stems has seen this plant likened to giant rhubarb.

Notro The notro (*Embothrium coccineum*) is a distant relative of the spectacular South African and Australian proteas and normally grows as a large bush with leathery oval-shaped leaves. Notro blooms early (around October) producing attractive red elongated flowers that develop into seed pods.

Quila & Colihue These species of the native bamboo genus *Chusquea* grow in all areas covered by temperate rainforest, except for the far south. Extremely vigorous and hardy, quila (*Ch. quila*) has thin yellow canes that tend to spread out horizontally to colonise clear areas. Quila regrowth is normally the first stage of regeneration after a forest fire, forming quite impenetrable thickets.

Colihue (*Ch. couleu*) is found further south than quila and has thicker canes. It generally grows in a more erect form, reaching up to eight metres. Colihue canes are used commercially for furniture making.

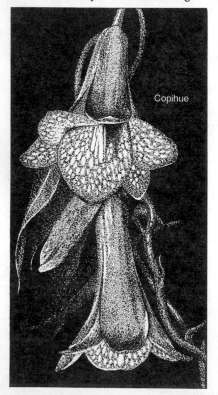

Copihue

Copihue The national flower of Chile, the copihue (*Lapageria rosea*) is a climbing plant often found growing on tree trunks in the rainforests of the Araucanía and Lake District. In late summer the copihue vine produces delicate pink flowers with a yellow stamen.

FAUNA

South America was once an isolated continent with a largely marsupial fauna, in some ways comparable to present-day Australia. However, with the creation of a natural land bridge at the Isthmus of Panama some three million years ago, large scale migration of more sophisticated North American placental mammals occurred. As a result South American wildlife is generally more closely related to the fauna of regions further north. Many newly introduced animal species, such as pigs, horses, rabbits, beavers, exotic deer and even reindeer run wild and have altered local ecosystems.

Herbivores

Guanaco The guanaco (*Lama guanicoe*) is a cameloid relative of the vicuña (and its domesticated breeds of alpaca and llama). Guanacos are found mainly on the Patagonian steppes, but also inhabit mountain areas, where their tracks sometimes seem like well-graded hiking trails. The animals are sleek but powerful, with a brownish-white body and long necks. Their herds have been drastically reduced but guanaco still survive because of the unrelenting persecution of their chief predator, the puma, by humans.

Huemul The huemul (*Hippocamelus bisulcus*) was once abundant throughout the entire southern Andes. Ravaged by civilisation and forest fires, the numbers of this graceful native deer species are now alarmingly low, and the huemul is seriously threatened with extinction. The huemul is brown with a black snout, and has a shoulder height of about one metre and an approximate length of 1½ metres.

Male huemul throw their two-branched antlers each year after mating. Agile with extremely acute hearing, herds of up to sixty individuals normally inhabit the alpine areas above the tree line, descending into the protection of the forested zone in winter. Now strictly protected, huemul are the subject of an extensive program (in Spanish, *Proyecto Huemul*) which aims to stabilise and restore their populations to sustainable levels.

Pudú The pudú (*Pudu pudu*) is the smallest of the world's deer species. Standing only 40 to 50 cm from the ground, the pudú only weighs about nine kg at maturity. The male has pointed, branched horns. Found principally in the dense forests of the Araucanía and Lake District, this shy and timid creature is now seriously endangered and rarely sighted.

Predators
Puma The puma (*Felis concolor*) is a large predator very closely related to the cougar of North America, and is present everywhere on the Patagonian mainland where there is sufficient natural protection from its sole enemy, the human race. Both male and female pumas have a coat of a uniform sandy-brown colour, except for the dirty-white muzzle, and reach over two metres from head to tail.

Although officially protected by law, the puma is still persecuted by farmers, whose livestock it sometimes preys upon. Pumas kill their prey, typically guanaco or huemul, by grasping the animal from behind and breaking its neck instantly with a powerful backward stroke of one front paw.

The puma is considered virtually harmless to humans. Although you may occasionally hear stories of puma attacks on people, the truth is these are very rare indeed. When such attacks occur they are invariably as an act of self defence by a cornered animal, or are the result of a puma mistaking a person for its natural prey. In fact, pumas seem to have a fear or respect for humans that is unknown among other large feline predators. Trekkers will be lucky to glimpse this principally nocturnal beast, although puma paw prints, about the size of a man's fist, are quite often seen in soft earth or snow.

Zorro Culpeo The second largest predator in Patagonia, the zorro culpeo (*Dusicyon culpaeus*) is a native fox. Due to its prized reddish-brown fur coat, the animal has been hunted and trapped extensively. The zorro culpeo (also called zorro colorado) is nocturnal and lives primarily in lightly forested country.

Zorro Gris The zorro gris (*Dusicyon gymnocercus*) is a smaller fox that lives in open country of northern Patagonia, eating a wide diet of rodents, insects and berries. The zorro gris itself has few natural enemies, apparently due to the animal's highly unpalatable flesh. Even when dead, condors and flies are reluctant to touch the carcass, which simply dries out and rots without ever becoming worm-infested.

Zorro culpeo

Rodents & Small Mammals

Coipo An aquatic rodent, the coipo (*Myocastor coypus*) is sometimes also called the falsa nutria, or 'false otter'. The animal looks more like an oversized hamster however, with sharp and prominent front teeth. Feeding on herbs, roots and fish, the coipo lives in freshwater streams, where it builds burrows under the banks. Coipos are nocturnal, and most commonly seen at dusk. Exploited almost to extinction for its valuable pelt in the earlier part of this century, the animal is now protected by law.

Llaca (or Monito del Monte) The only surviving member of the marsupial order left in the southern Andes, the llaca (*Dromiciops australis*) is a possum-like creature that inhabits the rainforests of the Lake District. The animal is often called *monito* ('little monkey') because its hands and feet have adapted to resemble those of monkeys, with four fingers and an opposing thumb to facilitate climbing. The llaca lives entirely in the trees, feeding on fruits and insects. Highly adapted to the area's temperate environment, the animal goes into a seasonal torpor during the winter months.

Monito del monte

Chingue (or Zorrino) Closely related to the North American skunks, the chingue (*Conepatus humboldtii*) has a black coat with a single white stripe down its back between a bushy tail and a round-pointed snout. Like its cousins, it protects itself by secreting a powerfully unpleasant odour. The animal preferably lives in open areas, feeding mainly on worms and insects. The chingue is also fond of birds' eggs and small rodents.

Birds

Cóndor The cóndor (*Sarcorhamphus gryphus*) is found throughout the Andes, building its nests on exposed and inaccessible rock ledges that afford easy take off and protection. This rather hideous member of the vulture family is nevertheless superbly adapted for flight. It has a wingspan of over 2½ metres, which apart from the wandering albatross, is the greatest of any flying bird. Often seen soaring around remote mountain peaks, condors are all black except for white feathers on the bird's collar and the tips of its wings. Condors are voracious eaters – a single bird weighing perhaps eight kg can reputedly eat an entire guanaco carcass in a week – and live on carrion or small live rodents.

Ñandú (or Rhea) A flightless member of the ostrich family, the ñandú (*Pterocnemia pennata*) roams the dry steppes of eastern Patagonia, occasionally venturing into the Andean foothills. Smaller than their African cousins, adult birds stand around 1½ metres high. The ñandú can run very quickly, avoiding its enemies by constantly changing direction as it flees. After the eggs have been laid, the male incubates and hatches the chicks.

Aguilucho The aguilucho de cola rojiza (*Buteo ventralis*) and the common aguilucho (*B. polyosoma*) are native eagles that live in the forests throughout the southern Andes. These large birds prey on insects, small mammals and other birds.

Bandurria Related to the ibis, the bandurria (*Theristicus caudatus*) is found throughout Patagonia in coastal and wetland areas where it feeds on frogs and other small aquatic creatures. This large bird has a curved beak and a reddish yellow neck. Bandurrias have a distinctive short dull-toned call.

Cisne de Cuello Negro The cisne de cuello negro (*Cygnus melancoryphus*) is a large white swan with the characteristic elongated neck, which is black except for a strident red tip just behind the bird's bill. This adaptable swan inhabits both salt and freshwater areas and has extremely oily feathers enabling it to remain in the water for several weeks at a time. The goslings can occasionally be seen riding tucked between the wings and body on the backs of adult birds.

Carpintero Negro The carpintero negro (*Campephilus magellanicus*) can be found throughout the entire forested belt of the southern Andes. This energetic woodpecker can frequently be heard picking away at tree trunks and branches. Males have a striking red head.

Patos (Ducks) There are a dozen or more species of duck in Patagonia. Of particular interest are the quetru vapor (*Tachyeres pteneres*, also called quetru no volador, or flightless steamer duck). The quetru vapor mostly inhabits the southern islands or other coastal areas where there are fewer predators. This large ground-dwelling bird is of a blackish-grey colour and has small under-developed wings that serve as 'paddles' to move quickly across water.

The pato anteojillo (*Anas specularis*) is also found in southern areas. This colourful bird lives along larger rivers where it builds its nest on small islands. Another duck frequently sighted in southern waters is the pato juarjual (*Lophonetta specularioides*).

Gansos (Geese) The caiquén (*Chloephaga picta*) is a native goose common to the riverflats of southern Patagonia. Male caiquenes have white and grey feathers while the female of the species is coffee-black in colour. Another common member of this genus is the canquén (*C. poliocephala*, also called cauquén). The canquén is of a light brown colour and also prefers open moist areas. The bird has a short beak with a sharp point ideal for cutting through grass.

Picaflor (Hummingbird) The smallest of some five species of hummingbirds native to the southern Andes region, the tiny picaflor (*Sephanoides galeritus*) inhabits the moist rainforests of the Araucanía and northern Lake District. This colourful bird feeds largely on nectar, supplementing its diet with insects.

Cisne de cuello negro

PEOPLE
The Argentinians

The Argentinians are a cultured and sophisticated people of almost entirely European origin. Since the last century, successive waves of immigrants have given Argentine society a cosmopolitan flavour unique among Latin American nations. Of these migrants, Italians were easily the most numerous, and their influence is all-pervasive. There are also strong and recognisable elements of British, German and Yugoslav influence. With their relatively high standard of living and strong links with the Old World, the Argentine people have traditionally considered themselves rather less 'South American' than their neighbours. The Argentinians are very outgoing and passionate, with a strong artistic flair. They tend to say what they think with little hesitation, and have a strong sense of identity and national pride that is sometimes mistaken by visitors as arrogance.

Lake District farmer

The Chileans

Bordered by the Atacama Desert in the north and the mighty Cordillera to the east, Chile is geographically cut off from the rest of South America, and Chileans sometimes refer to their isolated country as *el último rincón del mundo*, or 'the last corner of the world'. The result of this isolation was that Chile's European and indigenous peoples mixed gradually to create an overwhelmingly *mestizo* population.

The massive European immigration that shaped Argentina's growth did not occur on anything like the same scale in Chile, and the population has been modified relatively little by new arrivals. Politics notwithstanding, the Chileno is typically a cool-headed and modest person, not given to overly exuberant behaviour. This slightly reserved nature is sometimes considered a sign of their introversion, yet the people of Chile are friendly and hospitable and they possess a sharp and ironic sense of humour.

The Patagonians

Patagonia is the meeting place of Chile and Argentina. The lower average height of the Cordillera in Patagonia has traditionally encouraged movement between the two countries, even in precolonial times.

For more than a century, Chileans have migrated east to seek work on Argentine estancias or as labourers in the towns. A great number of the migrants were Chilotes, the mixed-race inhabitants of the island of Chiloé, who also established settlements along the west Patagonian coast. Until quite recently many of these settlements were accessible only by boat, or via Argentinian territory.

Even today almost half the inhabitants of certain southern provinces of Argentina are actually Chilean nationals or their children. Especially noticeable to the visitor is the high proportion of people in Patagonia with distinctly Indian features. Continual contact has left a greater homogeneity and sense of common destiny among Patagonians than elsewhere within the two countries.

LANGUAGE

Both Argentinians and Chileans speak Spanish, or *castellano*, a term generally preferred in the Americas to *español*. In the cities quite a number of people know some English, but in the countryside this is rare. In certain parts of the south, small but influential communities of German, English, Yugoslav and even Welsh settlers continue to speak their languages. In some areas indigenous tongues still survive, the most notable being the Mapuche dialects of the Lake District. Most Mapuche Indians are now able to speak Spanish as well as or better than their traditional languages.

On the whole, the Spanish language is not a difficult one, and you should try to gain some knowledge of simple conversational Spanish before you travel. Being able to communicate even at a very basic level with locals will be helpful and satisfying. Due to the common Latin roots in many English and Spanish words, it can be surprisingly easy to understand written Spanish. Spelling follows simple phonetic rules, and pronunciation is quickly grasped. Despite the common Hispanic colonial past of Chile and Argentina, there are major differences between the forms of Spanish spoken in each country.

Argentinian Spanish

Argentinian Spanish has some interesting features. Pronunciation and accent have been heavily influenced by Italian immigration, which has given this dialect a pleasant, melodic sound. Vowels are often lengthened and pronunciation is more decisive. Many Italian words have also been absorbed into the national vocabulary. Another strong characteristic of Argentinian Spanish is the continued universal usage of the archaic word *vos*, meaning 'you'. Vos (pronounced 'boss') completely replaces *tú* as the familiar singular form, and in the present tense requires special verb conjugations such as *vos pagás, vos tenés, vos sos* ('you pay', 'you have', 'you are'). In Argentina the Castillian sounds represented by the letters 'll' and 'y' are either pronounced like a French 'j', as in

Jean-Jacques, or more strongly like an English 'j', as in Jessie Jackson.

Chilean Spanish

Chilean Spanish is invariably spoken rapidly, and often has a high-pitched, lilting intonation that makes this dialect immediately recognisable. Having been described as the 'Australians of the Spanish speaking world', many Chileans speak without appearing to move their mouths very much, and often mumble their words. The habit of some Spanish speakers to drop the letter 's' is almost universal in Chile, making it hard to tell whether feminine nouns are in the singular or plural form.

Chileans have developed a great amount of local idiom and slang. Particularly in the south of the country, some Chileans are inclined to pronounce the consonants 'll' and 'y' in a similar way to the Argentinians, though with less force. Don't be too surprised or worried if you have (great) difficulty understanding the Chileans at first.

Patagonian Spanish

In Chile and Argentina the different national forms of Spanish extend more or less right down into Patagonia. Nevertheless, there are certain words and phrases that make the speech of native Patagonians easily recognisable to their northern compatriots. For example the construction *puro...no más*, instead of simply *puro*, produces phrases like *puro tábanos no más* ('nothing but houseflies'). Another common tendency is to add *de* to expressions like *a caballo* and *a pié*, giving *de a caballo* and *de a pié* ('by horse', 'on foot').

Naturally, there are also many words of indigenous origin that describe things peculiar to Patagonia, such as *mogote*, referring to the native cushion plants and *puelche*, a warm wind that blows across the steppes from the north. Another example is the Tehuelche word *toldo*, meaning tent, which in modern-day Patagonian Spanish has been extended to produce *toldería*, meaning a camp.

Books

A phrase book and a small pocket dictionary are more or less essential. Avoid material that is based on European Spanish however, because there is just too much variation (such as the difference between a Spaniard's and an Argentinian's use of the verb *coger*). Surprisingly, neither Chile nor Argentina seems to have a 'national dictionary' (such as the Webster, Macquarie and Oxford dictionaries used in English-speaking countries) to document the locally spoken Spanish. Two popular Spanish/English dictionaries that specifically cover Latin America are *The New World* and *University of Chicago* dictionaries, which are published in cheap paperback forms. Lonely Planet has produced a handy pocket-sized *Latin American Spanish Phrasebook*.

The following are some useful sentences for typical situations in which trekkers may find themselves.

Hike Preparation

Where can we buy supplies?
Dónde podemos comprar víveres?
Can we leave some things here a while?
Puedo dejar algunas cosas acá por un rato?
Where can we hire a mountain guide?
Dónde podemos alquilar un guía de montaña?
I'd like to talk to someone who knows this area.
Quisiera hablar con álguien que conozca este sector.
How much do you charge?
Cuánto cobra Usted?
We are thinking of taking this route.
Pensamos tomar esta ruta.
Is the trek very difficult?
Es muy difícil la caminata?
Is the track (well) marked?
Está (bien) marcado el sendero?
Which is the shortest/easiest route?
Cuál es la ruta más corta/más fácil?
Is there much snow on the pass?
Hay mucha nieve en el paso?

We will return in one week.
Volverémos (or *vamos a volver*) *en una semana.*

Transport

When does the next bus leave for...?
Cuándo sale el próximo bus a...?
I'd like to charter a boat/taxi.
Quisiera contratar un bote/taxi.
How much do you want for taking us to...?
Cuánto quiere por llevarnos a...?
Come to pick us up in five days.
Venga a buscarnos en cinco días.
Is there space for three people?
Hay lugar para trés personas?
Can you take me to...?
Puede llevarme a...?
I want to get off at the turnoff.
Quiero bajar en la bifurcación.
I'm going to hitchhike.
Voy a viajar a dedo.
We'll leave tomorrow.
Vamos a partir mañana.

Weather

What will the weather be like?
Qué tiempo va a hacer?
It's going to rain.
Va a llover.
It's windy/sunny.
Hace viento/sol.
It's raining/snowing.
Está lloviendo/nevando.
It has clouded over.
Se ha nublado.
Tomorrow it will be cold.
Mañana hará frío.
The rain held us up.
Nos atrasó la lluvia.
At what time does it get dark?
A qué hora caye la noche?

On the Trek

How many km to ...?
Quántas kilometros son hasta .....?
How many hours' walking?
Cuántas horas son caminando?

Is there a bridge across this river?
Hay un puente que cruce este río?
Which is the best place to wade the river?
Cuál es el mejor lugar para vadear el río?
How do you reach the summit?
Cómo se llega a la cumbre?
Does this track go to ...?
Va este sendero a .....?
Where are you coming from?
De dónde vienen ahora?
Where are you going to?
A dónde va usted?
May I cross your property?
Puedo cruzar su propiedad?
Can you show me on the map where we are?
Puede señalarme en el mapa dónde estamos?
What is this place called?
Cómo se llama este lugar?
We're doing a hike from ... to ...
Estamos haciendo una caminata desde ... a ...
Would you like to accompany me as far as ...?
Quieres acompañarme hasta ...?

Camping
Where is the best place to camp?
Dónde está el mejor lugar para acampar?
Can we put up the tent here?
Podemos armar la carpa acá?
Is it permitted to make fire?
Es permitido a hacer fuego?
There is no firewood.
No hay leña.
I have a gas/petrol stove.
Tengo una cocinilla/anafe a gas/bencina.
I'm going to stay here two days.
Voy a quedarme dos días aquí.

Difficulties
Help!
¡Soccoro!
Careful!
¡Cuidado!
We've lost the way.
Hemos perdido el camino.
I'm looking for ...
Estoy buscando ...

Can you help me?
Puede ayudarme?
I'm thirsty/hungry.
Tengo sed/hambre.
Could you give us some water?
Nos puede dar agua?
Do you have food to sell?
Tiene comida para vender?
Can you repair this for me?
Puede arreglarme ésto?
Where is the nearest doctor?
Dónde está el próximo médico?
Is the water OK to drink?
Se puede beber el agua?
I don't understand.
No entiendo.
Please don't speak so quickly.
Por favor, no hable tan rápido (or *Más despacio, por favor).*

General Conversation
Good morning!
¡Buenos días!
Good afternoon!
¡Buenas tardes!
Hello!
¡Hola!
My name is ...
Me llamo...
What's the time?
Qué hora es? (or *Cuántas horas son?)*
Where are you from?
De dónde es Usted?
Do you live here?
Vives acá?
Wait for me here.
Espéreme aquí.
It's a very beautiful spot.
Es un lugar muy lindo.
I'm sightseeing.
Estoy paseando.
We're getting to know the area.
Estamos conociendo.
See you later!
¡Hasta luego!
Goodbye!
¡Adios! or *¡Chau!*
Farewell!
¡Que le vaya bien!

Nationalities
Alternate -a forms are for women.

American	*Estadounidense, Norte Americano/a*
Argentinian	*Argentino/a*
Australian	*Australiano/a*
Belgian	*Belgo/a*
British	*Britano/a*
Canadian	*Canadiense*
Chilean	*Chileno/a*
Dutch	*Holandés(a)*
English	*Inglés(a)*
French	*Francés(a)*
German	*Alemán(a)*
Irish	*Irlandés(a)*
Israeli	*Israelita*
New Zealander	*Nueva Zelandés(a)*
Scot	*Escocés(a)*
Swede	*Sueco/a*
Swiss	*Suizo/a*
Welsh	*Galés(a)*

Ways of Transit

circuit	*circuito*
highway	*carretera*
path, trail	*sendero, picada, senda*
shortcut	*atajo*
road, vehicle track	*camino*
route (unmarked)	*huella, ruta*
sidewalk, footpath	*vereda*

Artificial Features

border post, customs house	*aduana*
bridge; footbridge	*puente; pasarela*
campground; caravan park	*camping; autocamping*
ditch	*zanja*
farm	*finca* (Arg) *chacra* (Ch) *fundo*
fence	*cerco, valla, alambrado*
firebreak	*cortefuego*
hut, mountain refuge	*refugio*
homestead	*caserío*
house, building	*casa*

jetty, landing pier	*muelle*
lighthouse	*faro*
park entrance	*portería*
ranch	*estancia*
ranger station	*guardería*
skilift; skitow	*aerosilla; andarrivel*
skifield	*cancha de esquí*
stockyard, corral	*galpón*
town; village	*pueblo; aldea*

Trail Terms

accommodation, lodgings	*alojamiento*
to arrive	*llegar*
bivouac	*vivac*
to camp	*acampar*
campfire; fireplace	*fogata; fogón*
campground	*campamento*
camp site	*sitio (de acampar)*
to carry	*llevar*
climb; to climb	*escalada; escalar*
firewood	*leña*
to fish	*pescar*
to follow	*seguir*
ford, wade	*vado*
hike	*caminata, andanza*
mountaineering	*andinismo, alpinismo*
horse ride; by horse	*cabalgata; a caballo*
rubbish	*basura*
signpost	*cartel indicador*
traverse	*traversía*
to walk; go on foot	*caminar; ir a pie*

Clothing & Equipment

altimeter	*altímetro*
anorak, rainjacket	*campera, chaqueta impermeable*
backpack, rucksack	*mochila*
batteries	*pilas, batterías*
billy, cooking pot	*olla*
boots	*botas*
camp stove	*cocinilla, anafe, infiernillo*
candles	*velas*
canteen, water bottle	*cantimplora*
cap, 'beanie'	*gorra*
carabiner	*mosquetón*
compass	*brújula*
crampons	*grampones, trepadores*
gaiters	*polainas*

gas cartridge	*cartucha*	cowboy	(Arg) *gaucho*
gloves	*guantes*		(Ch) *huaso*
ice axe	*piolet*		
	(Arg) *piqueta*	**Wildlife**	
pocketknife	*cortaplumas*	beaver	*castor*
provisions,	*víveres,*	cow; cattle	*vaca; ganado bovino*
food supplies	*abastecimientos*	deer	*ciervo*
runners, tennis shoes	*zapatillas*	dog	*perro*
rope	*cuerda*	duck	*pato*
sleeping bag	*saco de dormir*	eagle	*águila*
sleeping mat,	*colchoneta aislante*	fish	*pez*
('*Karrimat*')		flea	*pulga*
sunglasses	*gafas de sol*	fly	*mosca*
tent	*carpa*	fox	*zorro*
torch, flashlight	*linterna*	frog	*sapo, rana*
walking stick	*bastón*	cat	*gato*
white gasoline,		hare, rabbit	*liebre, conejo*
('*Shellite*')	(Arg) *nafta blanca*	hawk	*halcón*
	(Ch) *bencina blanca*	horse	*caballo*
		horsefly	*tábano*
		sheep	*oveja*
Climate & Weather		swan	*cisne*
clear, fine	*despejado*	seagull	*gaviota*
cloud	*nube*	tree	*árbol*
fog, mist	*neblina, niebla*	trout	*trucha*
frost	*helada*	vulture	*buitre*
high/low tide	*altamar/bajamar*	wild pig	*jabalí*
ice	*hielo*	woodpecker	*carpintero*
overcast, cloudy	*nublado*		
rain; to rain	*lluvia; llover*		
snow; to snow	*nieve; nevar*		
spring melt, thaw	*deshielo*		
storm	*tormenta, tempestad*		
summer	*verano*		
good/bad weather	*buen/mal tiempo*		
whiteout, clag	*borrina, encainada*		
wind	*viento*		
winter	*invierno*		

People

border police	(Arg) *gendarmería*
	(Ch) *carabineros*
backpacker	*mochilero/a*
foreigner	*extranjero/a,*
	gringo/gringita
Indian mountain	*Indio guía de*
guide	*montaña, baqueano*
mountaineer	*andinista*
park ranger	*guardaparque*
rancher	*estancionero*
traveller	*viajero*

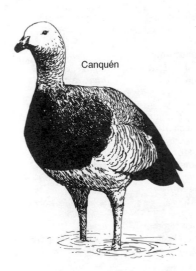

Canquén

Directions

ahead/behind	*mas adelante/atrás*
adjacent	*al frente, contiguo*
ascent/descent	*subida/bajada*
before/after	*antes (de)/ después (de)*
below/above	*debajo de/encima de*
beside	*al lado de*
between	*entre*
early/late	*temprano/tarde*
east/west	*este/oeste*
flat/steep	*llano/empinado*
here/there	*aquí, acá/allá*
height/depth	*altura/profundidad*
high/low	*alto/bajo*
(to the) left/right	*(a la) derecha/ izquierda*
near/distant	*cerca/lejos*
north/south	*norte/sur*
on the other side of	*al otro lado de*
southern	*austral, meridional*
towards/away from	*hacia/desde*
up/down	*arriba/abajo*

Map Reading

altitude difference	*desnivel*
contour lines	*curvas de nivel*
frontier mark, border stone	*hito*
map	*mapa, carta*
spot height	*cota*
tree line (timberline)	*nivel del bosque*

Landforms

Andean meadow	*alpage, coironal*
avalanche	*alud, avalancha*
bay; cove	*bahía; caleta*
beach	*playa*
bog, swamp	*pantano, mallín*
branch of a lake/river	*brazo*
brook	*riachuelo*
cairn	*mojón, pirca*
cave	*cueva, caverna*
chasm	*abismo*
cliff	*acantilado, barranco, farellón*
coast, shoreline	*costa*
(snow) cornice	*cornisa (de nieve)*
crag	*peña, peñón*

crater (of a volcano)	*caldera*
creek, small river	*estero, arroyo*
crevasse	*grieta*
drainage basin	*hoya, cuenca*
face of a mountain	*muralla, vertiente*
fjord, sound	*fiordo, seno*
forest	*bosque*
frontier, border	*frontera, límite*
gap, narrow pass	*portillo, pasada*
glacier	*ventisquero, glaciar*
gorge, canyon	*cajón, barranca*
hill	*morro, colina, loma*
hillside, mountainside	*faldeo, ladera*
iceberg	*témpano*
island	*isla*
lake	*lago, laguna*
landslide	*derrumbe*
location, spot	*lugar, paraje*
lookout	*mirador*
moor	*turbal, mallín*
moraine	*morrena*
mountain chain	*cordillera, cordón*
mountain	*cerro, montaña, monte*
national park	*parque nacional*
outlet stream	*desagüe*
névé, permanent snowfield	*nevero, campo de hielo*
pass	*paso, portezuelo, abra*
pinnacle	*pináculo, aguja, diente*
plain, flat terrain	*llanura, planicie*
plateau, tableland	*meseta*
range, massif	*sierra, mazico*
rapid	*catarata*
reserve	*reserva*
riverbank, shoreline	*ribera, orilla*
ridge, spur	*filo, espolón, cresta*
river	*río, quebrada*
river bed	*cauce, lecho*
scoria (volcanic rockform)	*escoria*
scrub; underbrush	*matorral, sotobosque*
slope, rise	*cuesta, pendiente*
source of a stream	*nacimiento*
spring	*fuente, manantial*
steppe, plain	*estepa, pampa*
stone, rock	*piedra*
strait	*estrecho*

stream junction	*horqueta, confluencia*	gol	*stake, stick, pole*
summit, peak	*cumbre, cima, pico*	huapí	*island*
thermal springs	*termas, aguas*	hue	*place, location*
	calientes	hueico	*tiny lake, puddle*
torrent,	*chorro*	lafquén	*sea, lake; plain*
gushing stream		leufú	*river*
valley	*valle*	lemu	*forest*
volcano	*volcán*	nahuel	*tiger*
waterfall	*salto (de agua),*	mahuida, mavida	*mountain*
	cascada	mallín	*moor*
		mapu	*land, earth*
Essential Mapuche & Tehuelche		pile, pilén	*frost, ice*
antü	*sun; day*	pillán	*volcano*
buta	*large, great*	puelche	*warm northerly wind*
cacique	*Tehuelche Indian*		*in Patagonia*
	chief	púlli	*mountainside*
cautín	*a native duck*	quilla	*moon*
co	*water*	repú	*path, track*
cura	*rock, stone*	tromén	*cloud*

Facts for the Trekker

VISAS

Entry requirements may change over a period of time and you should check on the current situation before departing.

Chile

Visas for Chile are not required by citizens of most countries. Australian, British, Canadian, US and most West European nationalities *do not* need visas. New Zealanders, South Africans and French *do* require visas. Upon arrival in Chile you receive an entry stamp which allows you to stay in Chile for 90 days. This can be renewed for a further 90 days. To stay in Chile longer than six months, it is usually easiest to travel to Argentina and then reenter Chile.

Argentina

Visas for Argentina are required by everyone *except* Canadians, Japanese, and citizens of most West European (including the Republic of Ireland) and some Latin American countries. Australians, New Zealanders, British and US citizens *do* need visas. Diplomatic relations with Britain have now been restored, and citizens of the UK should have little difficulty getting a visa.

For travel in Patagonia multiple entry visas are the most convenient as you will probably want to cross the border a number of times. Multiple entry visas cost around US$20, and are valid for 90 days from the first date of entry. US citizens are issued with free visas valid for four years, but must still exit after a stay of 90 days. Tourist visas can be renewed for an additional 90 days. To stay in Argentina longer than six months, travel to Chile (or any other neighbouring country) and get a new visa issued before reentering.

Visas are not issued at the border, but must be obtained from embassies or consulates. In the south of Chile there are Argentinian consulates in Puerto Montt and Punta Arenas.

MONEY

In Latin America, the US dollar is the universal shadow currency. The only really secure way of carrying your money is in the form of US$ travellers' cheques. Unfortunately, in remote areas of southern Chile and Argentina exchanging travellers' cheques for a reasonable rate is not always easy. Heavy commissions are often charged for this service. In both countries a parallel (or 'grey') market trading in US$ is widespread and more or less tolerated by the authorities. Parallel market rates are approximately 10% higher than the official exchange rate offered by banks.

At the time of writing the cost of living (and travelling) was somewhat lower in Argentina than in Chile. In southern Patagonia, prices are generally about 25% higher than they are further north. Most people travelling for longer periods in these countries budget for between US$200 and US$400 per month. For obvious reasons, the more time you spend in the wilds the cheaper your holiday will be. All prices throughout the book are given in US$.

Chile

The Chilean unit of currency is the peso (Ch$). Notes come in denominations of 500, 1000 and 5000 pesos. Coins are in one, five, 10 and 100 peso denominations. During the last decade or so Chile has had relatively moderate inflation, by Latin American standards, of roughly 25% per annum. At the time of writing the peso had a conversion rate of approximately US$1 = Ch$300. No doubt the economic policy of the new democratic government will largely determine the peso's future rate of exchange.

Argentina

The Argentinian unit of currency is the austral (A). At the time of writing Argentina was experiencing appalling hyperinflation of more than 6000% per annum. This has caused the austral to drop against strong foreign currencies at a bewildering rate. Consequently, notes of increasingly higher denominations must be regularly printed, and quoting any exchange rate is pointless. As long as this situation persists only small amounts of money should be exchanged at a time. Another currency reform will probably be undertaken within the next year. Travellers' cheques and banknotes in small US$ denominations will be handy.

WHEN TO GO
From May/June to October/November deep snow normally covers all of the higher ground. At this time ski-touring and winter treks are exciting possibilities, but these activities require special skills and equipment. The trekking season begins around November and continues until about mid-May. During the local holiday season of December and January, transport and accommodation is often heavily booked, which may interfere with your travel plans. On the other hand, tourist services and public transport to certain remoter areas (particularly in the south) starts to wind down after about the end of February. For a balance of convenience and weather, February and March are definitely the best two months for a trekking trip to the Patagonian Andes.

The Seasons
Spring (early September to late November) comes first to the Araucanía and Lake District due to this region's more northerly position. Lower level treks can be undertaken here as early as late October, when the first wildflowers are coming out. However, at this time snow-fed streams may still be impassable and weather tends to be very unpredictable.

Summer (from early December to late February) can actually bring quite hot weather in the mountains of northern Patagonia, with temperatures occasionally rising to above 30°C. Further south, summer days tend to be milder with a somewhat less settled weather pattern.

The early autumn period (March to mid-April) typically brings cooler, but slightly more stable weather. The red-gold colours of deciduous native tree species make this an especially pleasant time to trek. Towards the middle of May the period of daylight is becoming rather short and temperatures are falling steadily, yet conditions are often still suitable for trekking in the Araucanía and Lake District. Parties undertaking treks at this time should be equipped for possible heavy snowfalls.

WHAT TO BRING
It is difficult to buy most quality trekking equipment at a reasonable price in both Chile and Argentina. It is, therefore, advisable to bring whatever you will need with you. Of all trekking equipment, this applies most particularly to tents. Items that are locally available are indicated below. There are few specialist trekking shops, but fishing/hunting suppliers normally have a small range of general outdoor gear. Local mountain clubs sometimes have good new and used equipment for sale. For the Spanish names of items, see the previous Language section in the Facts about the Region chapter.

General Clothing
Warm Weather Wear Especially above the tree line in volcanic areas of the Araucanía and Lake District, summer conditions can get quite hot, and lighter clothing such as shorts and cotton or polyester shirts can be worn. Wear a hat with a broad visor to keep the sun off your face. Regardless of how conditions are when you set out, warm clothing should always be carried in case the weather suddenly deteriorates.

Cold Weather Wear It is essential that you carry least one very warm 'fibrepile' or woollen sweater. This will retain much of its insulating ability even if it gets wet. Trekkers who are very sensitive to cold might consider buying a lightweight down jacket (but keep it dry!). A pair of warm trousers should also be carried. Thermal underwear can be worn in the sleeping bag or in cold conditions. Silk garments are exceptionally warm for their weight and very pleasant to wear. A woollen cap or balaclava should be carried. Gloves or mittens are also highly recommended.

Rainwear

An essential piece of clothing that must be carried by all trekkers is a waterproof and windproof rainjacket. This should have a hood which properly covers your head. Experienced trekkers often prefer totally impervious rubberised rainwear to the newer 'breathable' garments, as the latter tend to leak after a few hours in extremely wet conditions. Waterproof ponchos, usually large enough to slip over the pack, are popular with local walkers. Ponchos don't offer the same protection from the elements as tailored rainwear, however, and tend to catch on branches as you pass. A pair of waterproof overpants is also highly recommended.

Footwear

Lighter style trekking boots with good ankle support are best. A pair of lightweight running shoes should also be carried as alternative footwear and for wading streams. In the boggy terrain of the west Patagonian Archipelago and Tierra del Fuego, local trekkers often prefer walking in rubber boots. It is advisable to impregnate boots with a waterproofing agent to protect the leather and keep your feet dry. Gaiters (*polainas*) should be worn – especially with shorts – to protect the lower legs.

Reasonably well made leather trekking boots can be bought locally in Buenos Aires or the Argentine Lake District, especially in San Carlos de Bariloche.

Tent

Good tents are almost impossible to buy in this part of the world, so you should *definitely bring one*. Even in the few places where there are good refugios, it is advisable to trek with a tent. Perhaps more than any other piece of equipment, a high quality tent is well worth paying extra for. Make sure it is absolutely waterproof. Modern 'free-standing' design tents are far better able to withstand the windy conditions you will

doubtless encounter. A tent is also an alternative form of accommodation. Carrying one makes travel more flexible, and even between treks camping out is often a pleasant and cheaper option.

Backpack

Another item that must not let you down. Be sure there is enough carrying capacity for the gear you take (or may accumulate) on the trip. Internal-frame rucksacks with 60 to 75 litres of volume are usually preferred. Removable daypacks that attach to the top of the pack are a convenient innovation, but side pockets are less recommended as they often get caught on bushes, bus racks etc.

'Convertible' packs that can be zipped up to look like hand luggage should be avoided since they compromise severely on trekking comfort. Packs are never completely waterproof. The contents can be kept dry either by packing everything in plastic bags or using a neatly fitting pack cover. Poor to fair quality imported Korean packs are available locally.

Sleeping Bag

Sleeping bags should have a rating of at least minus 10°C. For treks in the far south or anywhere early or late in the season, bags with a lower rating are preferable. Some trekkers keep weight down by wearing their warm clothing in bed. If you are sure you can keep it dry, a sleeping bag with a filling of super down is recommended.

Dacron filled bags are bulkier and heavier for their warmth, but will still insulate your body when they are wet. Dacron sleeping bags also dry very quickly and are much cheaper. Quite good down sleeping bags (as well as other down products) are made in Argentina, principally in Bariloche. Prices are reasonable, but not cheap.

Portable Cooker

In all areas fire is neither a reliable nor an environmentally sound means of cooking, and all parties should carry a camp stove. The most practical cookers are those that can burn a range of fuels like standard kerosene, petroleum or white gasoline ('Shellite').

Some stoves, such as the durable MSR, can burn several types of fuel.

Petrol (gasoline) is known as *bencina* in Chile and *nafta* in Argentina, and kerosene is called *parafina* or *kerosen*. Petrol is usually full of impurities, and should therefore be filtered before use. *Bencina blanca* or *nafta blanca* are the local terms for white gas. In Chile, white gas is sold in every second pharmacy or hardware store, but has become hard to find in Argentina where its sale may now be prohibited. For trekkers with 'Trangia'-style alcohol-burning stoves, methylated spirits is widely and cheaply available in local supermarkets and hardware stores.

'Camping Gaz' type stoves have become popular among local backpackers. Gas cookers are safe and virtually foolproof to use, and make a good alternative to the somewhat more hazardous liquid fuel stoves. However, gas stoves won't operate effectively in low temperatures, so the apparatus must always be kept warm. Remember that it is prohibited to take gas canisters on all aircraft. Canisters are now often available even in quite small towns, where they are usually sold in hardware stores. At around $1.50, 'Gaz' canisters cost roughly the same as a litre of white gas. Cheap Brazilian-made versions of the cookers are available locally – if you buy one, check it carefully first.

Cooking Ware

Depending on the size of the party, a number of cooking pots should be carried. Suitable aluminium utensils of quite good quality are manufactured in both Chile and Argentina. Fans of stainless steel should bring their own. A pot-grip is a very handy device.

Thermal Mattress

For sleeping comfort and insulation, some kind of lightweight mattress is essential. Closed foam cell mats weigh no more than a few hundred grams, but are bulky and awkward to pack. Reasonably priced Taiwanese-made versions are locally available. 'Thermarest' or integrated 'Stephenson's' type inflatable mattresses are heavier and

much more expensive, but offer greater sleeping comfort and take up less room in the pack. To avoid punctures clear the ground of any sharp matter (such as araucaria needles and calafate thorns) before setting up the tent.

Optional Extras

Some of the additional items that you may consider taking along include:

Ice Axe – may be necessary if you intend climbing the higher summits early in the season. For general summer and autumn trekking the considerable weight of an ice axe and crampons cannot be justified.

Length of Rope – sometimes useful for packhauling, crossing smaller streams or as a clothes line.

Machete – will come in handy where tracks are overgrown, and should be carried on all off-track expeditions. A leather glove will prevent blistering.

Pocketknife – a very practical instrument. 'Swiss army' type pocketknives are most recommended. Preferably bring one with cutting saw and Phillips head screwdriver functions.

Barometer/Altimeter – measures air pressure to show your approximate altitude and gives an indication of the approaching weather. Reasonably accurate barometers can be bought (but probably not in South America) for under $US50.

Watch/Alarm Clock – this instrument ensures an early start to make the most of your day. Should be completely shockproof and waterproof.

Camera – lightweight compact cameras are increasing sophisticated and therefore the recommended type. SLR owners might find a polarising filter often gives best results. All types of camera batteries can be bought locally. Film can be bought duty-free in Punta Arenas and Ushuaia, but is otherwise quite expensive throughout Chile and Argentina.

Walkman/Shortwave Radio – nice to tune in to on moonlit evenings.

Binoculars – a must for bird and animal watchers and also help you to scout out the route ahead. Excellent compact and lightweight models are now made, but are expensive.

Sunglasses – should be carried on all higher treks, particularly if early in the season when snowfields may have to be crossed. For maximum eye protection UV-Polaroid lenses are most recommended.

Battery Recharger – a portable traveller's recharger (*encargador de pilas*) for AA size batteries may prove a good investment, especially if you carry more than one electrical item. Locally made batteries are unreliable and relatively expensive, and using rechargables is more environmentally friendly. Chile and Argentina have compatible power plugs, and a battery recharger can be bought at local electrical stores in larger cities of either country for around $US25. High-tech solar-powered models have recently been released, but are unlikely to be available locally.

TOURIST OFFICES

There is quite a sizable internal tourist industry in both Chile and Argentina, and each country has well organised tourist offices (*oficinas de turismo*) which during the summer months (December to February) operate in even quite small towns. Staff are generally helpful and sometimes know some English. They have lists covering accommodation in all price ranges, and tourist maps and pamphlets are available free of charge. It is always worth visiting the local tourist office to check information in your travel guidebook.

National Park Administration

Both countries have a well-organised system of national parks and national reserves (*parques nacionales, reservas nacionales*). The parks are run by dedicated rangers (*guardaparques*) who work with very limited resources and generally do an excellent job. Even if you do not speak enough Spanish to converse with staff, it is generally well worth visiting the national parks offices or information centres before setting out. Ranger stations (*guarderías*) are frequently located at the start of the trek. Where relevant, the address of the nearest regional national parks office is given in the notes for each trek.

Chilean National Parks

In Chile the national parks are administered

by the Corporación Nacional Forestal, or CONAF. At most national parks there is at least one guardería. CONAF is also responsible for Chile's large tracts of national forest, and have many regional offices throughout the country. These include the following:

Santiago – Avenida Bulnes 285, 7th floor (☎ 60783)

Chilean Araucanía & Lake District
   Temuco – 2nd floor, Fco. Bilbao 931 – IX Región (☎ 23 8900)
   Angol – Calle Prat – IX Región (☎ 370)
   Pucón – Calle Fresia, Pucón – IX Región
   Puerto Montt – Ochagavia 464 – X Región (☎ 54358)
   Valdivia – Ismael Valdés 431 – X Región (☎ 12001)
   Osorno – Mackenna 674 – X Región (☎ 4393)

Chilean Central Patagonia
   Castro, Chiloé – 3rd floor, Calle O'Higgins – X Región (☎ 2289)
   Chaitén – Independencia 242 – X Región (☎ 2274)
   Coyhaique – Avenida Ogana 1060 – XI Región (☎ 21065)
   Puerto Aisén – Calle Ciro Arrendondo – XI Región (☎ 743)
   La Junta – Patricio Lynch 71 – XI Región

Chilean Southern Patagonia
   Chile Chico – Pedro Antonio González 31 – XI Región (☎ 325)
   Cochrane – Calle Teniente Merino – XI Región (☎ 164)
   Punta Arenas – Jose Menéndez 1147 – XII Región (☎ 22 7845)
   Puerto Natales – Ignacio Carrera Pinto 566 – XII Región (☎ 41 1438)

National Parks ticket

Argentine National Parks
In Argentina the responsible authority is the Servicio Nacional de Parques Nacionales. There are not as many SNPN offices throughout Argentina but those relevant are listed below:

Buenos Aires – Santa Fe 680

Argentine Araucanía & Lake District
San Martín de los Andes – Plaza de Armas – Neuquén
San Carlos de Bariloche – Calle San Martín 24 – Río Negro

Argentine Central & Southern Patagonia
Calafate – San Martín & 1 De Mayo – Santa Cruz

Tierra del Fuego
Ushuaia – Calle San Martín 56 – Tierra del Fuego

USEFUL ORGANISATIONS
Mountain Clubs
Usually calling themselves *club andino* or *club de montaña*, the larger provincial centres often have some kind of informal or organised mountain club. Not many of these have a permanent office address (and even fewer will answer your mail), so trying to locate them can be difficult, but the local tourist office may be able to help. Unfortunately, most clubs seem mainly interested in

CAB symbol

skiing and technical climbing rather than the simpler pleasures of trekking. The major exception to this is the (Argentinian) Club Andino Bariloche (CAB) which is very helpful and can give information on local treks and other advice. The CAB is listed below with the addresses of a few other useful mountain clubs:

Argentinian Mountain Clubs
Buenos Aires – Centro Andino Buenos Aires, (1033) Rivadavia 1255 (offices 2 & 3) (☎ 01-38 1566)

Argentine Araucanía & Lake District
San Carlos de Bariloche – Club Andino Bariloche, (8400) 20 de Febrero 30 – Río Negro (☎ 0944-22266/48)
Junín de los Andes – Club Andino Junín de los Andes, (8371) O'Higgins 369 – Neuquén
San Martín de los Andes – Club Andino San Martín de los Andes, (8370) Capitán Drury 872 – Neuquén

Argentine Central Patagonia
Esquel – Club Andino de Esquel, Darwin 639 – Chubut (☎ 0945-2318)

Tierra del Fuego
Ushuaia – Club Andino Ushuaia, (9410) Solís 50 – Tierra del Fuego (☎ 0901-92335)

Chilean Mountain Clubs
Santiago – Federación de Andinismo de Chile, Almirante Simpson 77 (☎ 222 0888)

Concepción – Club Andino de Chile – Concepción, O'Higgins 744, 3rd floor – VIII Región

Chilean Araucanía & Lake District
Malalcahuello – Club Andinismo y Ski 'Cóndores', Escuela E-260 – IX Región (see Jose Cordovas)
Valdivia – Club de Montaña de Valdivia, Avenida Argentina 3502 Pob 1, Corvi – X Región
Osorno – Club de Ski y Montañismo de Osorno, O'Higgins 887 – X Región

Chilean Central & Southern Patagonia
Chaitén – Club de Montaña 'Los Halcones', Ignacio Carrera P – X Región (see Carlos Alvarado García)
Coyhaique – Club de Ski y Andinismo 'Cóndores Australes', Magallanes 100 – XI Región (see Peter Hartmann)

BUSINESS HOURS
In general, bank hours are from 10 am to 4 pm, and offices are normally open from 9 am until 12 noon, then from 2 to 7 pm. In the bigger cities supermarkets and larger shops often stay open throughout the day. In more remote areas however, even in the cool climate region of the south, the siesta break can be as long as four hours, usually starting around noon.

POST & TELECOMMUNICATIONS
Post
Chile has quite an efficient mail service. Charges are moderate, and your mail is unlikely to get lost in the system. The post restante (*lista de correos*) service is well organised, but mail is only kept for 30 days. There is a small charge for each article of mail collected.

Although postal charges are lower, the Argentine mail service is rather less efficient and its post restante system can be very unreliable. Items of value are probably best dispatched from Chile. To the annoyance of philatelists, post offices in both countries frequently use franking machines instead of stamps.

Telephone
In both countries the principal telephone company is called ENTEL. All larger cities have a telephone centre from where internal and international long-distance calls can be made.

In Chile two 10-peso coins are used when making a local call from a public phone. The telephone system is fairly modern. Lines are generally good throughout Chile, and there is usually little difficulty in putting through your call. Charges for international calls are comparable to (or somewhat higher than) those in North America, Europe or Australia.

In Argentina public telephones use tokens (*fichas*) instead of coins. You can buy these at post offices and kiosks. Especially in Buenos Aires, the local telephone system is often hopelessly overloaded, making it almost impossible to get your call through.

International calls are a bit cheaper from Argentina, but reverse-the-charges calls (*cobro revertido*) can't be made to Australia or South Africa.

TIME
There is a one-hour time difference between Argentina and Chile. Argentinian time is three hours behind GMT while Chile is four hours behind GMT. Incidentally, you might be interested to learn that Santiago on the *west* coast of South America is actually one hour ahead of New York on the *east* coast of North America. The reason for this surprising fact is that the South America continent's relative position on the globe is a long way east of North America.

In both Chile and Argentina daylight saving operates from mid October to early March, making Summer Time one additional hour later in each country.

ELECTRICITY
Chile and Argentina use the same round twin-pronged power plug, and run 220-volt current. This means you can use devices that need mains electricity in either country. All but the smallest and most isolated townships have a reliable electricity supply.

BOOKS & MAPS
Considering the region's potential, surprisingly few books are published on the Southern Andes. The most interesting and useful titles are listed below.

Patagonian Exploration & History
An Englishman in Patagonia by John Pilkington (Century, 1991). A highly informative narrative by this well-known trekker-traveller who makes a point of getting off the beaten track.

In Patagonia by Bruce Chatwin (Jonathan Cape, 1977). A fascinating and thoroughly readable introduction to the people who inhabit the vast Patagonian steppes. Already a Patagonian classic.

From The Falklands To Patagonia by Michael Mainwaring (Allison & Bushby,

Top: Laguna de la Laja, Parque Nacional Laguna del Laja
Bottom: Volcán Antuco, Parque Nacional Laguna del Laja

   Top: Refugio Laguna Azul (with Volcán Lanín), Parque Nacional Villarrica
Middle: Volcán Lanín, Parque Nacional Villarrica
Bottom: Laguna Azul, Parque Nacional Villarrica

1983). The story of the Halliday family who resettled from the Malvinas to the Patagonian pampa earlier in the century. Especially interesting are chapters dealing with the Tehuelche Indian tribes and Patagonian fauna.

The Rucksack Man by Sebastian Snow (London, 1976). An account of the author's trek from one end of the South American continent to the other. His educated naivete is as amusing as it is infuriating.

The Totorore Voyage by Gerry Clark (Century, 1988). The story of a circumnavigation of Antarctica by yacht. The voyagers spent considerable time exploring the remote fjords and channels of the west Patagonian coast.

Voyage of the Beagle by Charles Darwin (London, 1839). Essential reading for all travellers to South America, this fascinating story tells of the journey during which Darwin began to develop the theory of natural selection. The author's insight is remarkable for his time.

The Springs of Enchantment by John Earle (Hodder & Stoughton, 1981). The story of two climbing expeditions to the mountains of Chilean Tierra del Fuego in 1963 and 1979. A number of first ascents of major peaks in the savage Darwin Range were achieved.

The Cockleshell Journey by John Ridgeway (Hodder & Stoughton, 1974). Another excellent account of an expedition by inflatable raft through the channels and fjords of southern Patagonia and Tierra del Fuego culminating in the first crossing of the small icecap Gran Campo Nevado.

Back to Cape Horn by Rosie Swale (Collins, 1986). The story of the author's journey through Chile on horseback. Rosie Swale spent over a year riding from Antofagasta to Cape Horn. Many treks can actually be undertaken on horseback and her book makes a sort of blueprint for novice riders as well as being a good read.

The Uttermost Part of the Earth by E Lucas Bridges. The story of the first pioneering family in southern Tierra del Fuego.

Land of the Tempest by Eric Shipton. An account of this famous explorer's expeditions in the southern Andes in the 1960s.

Tierra del Fuego by Natalie Prosser Goodall (first published 1970). A general but thorough history of the Isla Grande from pre-European times to the present. The book has a bilingual text in Spanish and English and is available from bookshops in Buenos Aires and southern Argentina.

Natural History Books

The Whispering Land by Gerald Durrell (Penguin, 1971). A narrative which introduces the fauna and marine life of east Patagonia as well as other areas of Argentina.

Flight of the Condor by Michael Andrews (Collins/BBC, 1982). Arguably the best layperson's introduction to wildlife of the Andean Cordillera. The first five chapters cover the continent's southernmost regions.

Trekking Guides

Backpacking in Chile & Argentina by Hilary Bradt & John Pilkington (Danvers, Massachusetts, 1989 – 2nd edition). The only other trekking guidebook available in English that includes treks in Patagonia.

Las Montañas de Bariloche by Toncek Arko & Irina Izaguirre (San Carlos de Bariloche, renewed periodically). A guidebook in Spanish on treks in the mountains of Parque Nacional Nahuel Huapí. At times the route descriptions are a bit vague.

A View of Torres del Paine by G Nancul & O Nenen, 1990. A new guidebook covering Chile's Parque Nacional Torres del Paine with emphasis on the wildlife. Text in English and Spanish.

Patagonia: Dreamland for Climbers and Trekkers by Gino Buscaini & Silvia Metzeltin (Bruckman, Munich, 1990). An excellent introduction to the southern Patagonian Andes with many colour photos and a number of maps. The book is primarily concerned with mountaineering and the history of Patagonian exploration. Editions in German and Italian only.

Travel Guides

Argentina – a travel survival kit by Wayne

Bernhardson & María Massolo (Lonely Planet, 1992). Another of Lonely Planet's titles which covers all of Argentina.

Chile & Easter Island by Alan Samagalski, (Lonely Planet, 1990). A practical travel guide for Chile.

Patagonia, Tierra del Fuego by Agustin Goenaga & Eusebio Novoa (SUA Edizoak, Spain). A not-so-complete Spanish-language guidebook to travel and trekking in southern Chile and Argentina. It includes some useful information on Torres del Paine and Los Glaciares national parks.

South America on a shoestring by Geoff Crowther et al (Lonely Planet, 1990), has recently been updated and gives a good overall coverage of the region. It contains a number of useful maps.

South American Handbook, Trade & Travel Publications (revised and published annually). The most comprehensive guidebook to all of South America – compact, lightweight, expensive.

Travel Companion: Argentina by Gerry Leitner (1991). A detailed, well-produced book that gives a good coverage of Argentina for travellers on various budgets.

Turistel, Editorial Lord Cochrane, Santiago (revised and published annually). A very good local publication available only in Spanish. Turistel caters chiefly for motor tourists, but also includes suggested excursions and is worth buying just for its excellent colour maps.

Other Books in Spanish

Andes Patagonicos by Alberto De Agostini (Buenos Aires, 1941, Italian edition, Milan, 1946). This classic work is a one-volume atlas to the central and southern Patagonian Andes. From his arrival in Tierra del Fuego in 1910 until he returned to his native Milan almost 50 years later, Father Alberto De Agostini energetically explored, climbed and photographed the mountains of southern Patagonia.

Somehow managing to combine his expeditionary activities with clerical responsibilities, Alberto De Agostini also wrote a number of other books relating his experiences in the southern Cordillera. His six odd books are long out of print but can often be found in the larger libraries of southern Chile and Argentina.

Chile, sus Parques Nacionales y otras areas naturales, (Incafo SA, Madrid, 1982). A now incomplete but very worthwhile catalogue of Chilean national parks and nature reserves. This large format book contains many excellent colour photographs.

Los Parques Nacionales de la Argentina y otras de sus areas naturales, (Incafo SA, Madrid, 1981). Another in Incafo's series on Latin American parks. Not as good as its Chilean counterpart but nevertheless worth having a look at. It is possibly still available from the odd bookshop, but otherwise you'll find it in most libraries.

Los Ríos Más Australes de la Tierra by Werner Schad (Marymar, Buenos Aires, 1983). The author has written other titles on canoeing and rafting the numerous wild rivers of Patagonia. In this book Schad has produced an informal guidebook to 23 river trips on both sides of the Cordillera. (The publisher, Editorial Marymar, has also published quite a number of other titles which concentrate on Patagonian exploration).

Maps

Where possible, try to obtain maps for all treks which in this guidebook are graded moderate or difficult. Even where navigation is straightforward, a map of the surrounding area will increase your appreciation and enjoyment of the landscape.

As in many Latin American countries mapping is carried out by the military, and Chile and Argentina both have a central mapping authority called the Instituto Geográphico Militar. You can only get IGM topographical maps in the national capitals, so if you are passing through Buenos Aires or Santiago be sure to buy all sheets there. It is possible to mail-order maps, but delivery time within the respective country is usually at least two weeks. The Chilean IGM produces a brochure-catalogue of available maps. The Argentinian IGM has a very bulky and out-of-date catalogue, and does not accept orders for less than US$45.

Cartographers in both countries have been busy during the last decade, but maps of large sectors of the southern Cordillera are still unavailable at a useful scale. Maps of a scale greater than 1:100,000 – the next size upwards is usually 1:250,000 – are generally unsuitable for accurate ground navigation. In areas where such maps are the only ones available exploratory trekking can be very challenging.

Maps start to disintegrate if they become damp or torn. It is a good idea to cover your essential sheets with transparent adhesive plastic foil (available locally) or a liquid map sealant.

Chile The Chilean IGM has two sales offices, both in Santiago. Their main office is at Dieciocho 369 in Santiago. (This is almost opposite the historical mansion and museum of the Braun-Menendez family, near metro station Toesca). They also have a less well stocked sales office at Alameda O'Higgins 240.

The Chilean IGM has divided the country into 12 sections (*secciones*), or mapping zones, given a letter from A to L. All Chilean treks in this book are within the (southern) mapping zones G to L. Individual sheets are numbered and have a name. At the Chilean IGM sales offices folders containing all sheets of a particular section will be given to you on request. Always quote the sheet's name, number and mapping zone letter when ordering (eg *Volcán Puyehue*, Sección H, No 27).

The standard series covering the south is scaled 1:50,000. Generally these are topographically quite accurate, though trekking routes are often not properly indicated. Prices have been raised considerably in the last few years, and each 1:50,000 sheet now sells for about US$7. Maps that are out of print (*hojas agotadas*) can be bought as single-sheet photocopies for the same price. You must order photocopies at least two days in advance. A cheap and very basic 'preliminary' series of 1:250,000 scale

sheets is also available. More detailed colour maps of the Chilean Lake District and Araucanía have been prepared at the same scale.

It is sometimes possible to borrow forestry maps from CONAF offices for photocopying. These are usually traced black and white sheets based on IGM maps. CONAF also produces sketch maps for some of the more popular Chilean national parks. Sketch maps show features not included on IGM maps (such as tracks and huts), but are usually unsuitable for serious navigation.

Argentina The Argentina IGM sales office is at Avenida Cabildo 381 in Buenos Aires. Take the subway (*subte*) to the termination of line B and trek three blocks north. All maps are identified by national grid reference numbers, but are catalogued under their provinces.

The sales office staff won't let you look at more than a few sheets at a time. If unsure about which sheets to buy, you should go to the IGM library next door. The IGM library can show you even out-of-print sheets. All maps may be borrowed free of charge for photocopying (maximum of five sheets at one time; staff will advise you where to go).

The standard scale for maps of southern Argentina is 1:100,000. Especially in Río Negro and Neuquén provinces, many sheets are hopelessly out of date and show topographical information poorly. Newer sheets are considerably better. Excellent new colour maps scaled at 1:250,000 are available for a few areas in the southern Argentine Cordillera. In areas very close to the border (eg Volcán Lanín), Chilean IGM maps overlapping into Argentine territory are sometimes more useful.

The SNPN produces topographical maps of Argentine national parks, but for southern areas all are currently out of print. Original SNPN maps can often be borrowed from regional offices for photocopying.

Compasses Especially on treks rated moderate and difficult, all parties should carry a compass to aid in navigation.

The entire area of Patagonia is within the South Magnetic Equator (SME) zone, and only compasses balanced for South American countries or southern Africa are suitable. Compasses set for magnetic conditions in Australasia, Europe or North America tend to give inaccurate readings. If buying a compass in South America, check whether the needle dips downwards at one end when held horizontally, as this indicates improper balancing.

Magnetic deviation in the Southern Andes is minimal, and very roughly ranges from close to 8°E in the northern Araucanía to about 14°E in the islands around Cape Horn.

Place Names Much of the Spanish nomenclature is monotonous. The southern Cordillera seems to have an endless number of lakes with names like 'Laguna Verde' or 'Lago Escondido', and rivers called 'Río Blanco' or 'Río Turbio'. While there are indeed a great many green-coloured lakes and white-water rivers, other equally descriptive but more interesting names might have been thought up instead. Many land features bear the names of battles or heroes from the wars of independence, such as Cordón Chacabuco, Lago O'Higgins and Cerro San Martín.

Naturally all places which were significant to native peoples already had names. These were often disregarded by the new settlers, or were swept away with the extermination of the Indians. In the Araucanía, however, the nomenclature often still shows indigenous origins, having been taken mostly from local Mapuche languages. Like other inhabitants of the New World, Chileans and Argentinians are slowly rediscovering their nations' indigenous past, and some native Indian place names are coming back into use. A complicating factor is the different dialects that were spoken by tribes on either side of the border. For example, a key Mapuche pass in the southern Lake District is called *vuriloche* in Chile and *bariloche* in Argentina, both meaning 'the people on the other side'.

In order to make the text less confusing and more interesting, land features which still don't have an official place name have sometimes been given (hopefully appropriate!) Spanish titles by the author. In such cases the particular lake, mountain pass or stream etc appears in this guidebook in inverted commas (eg 'Pasada Peñón') to emphasise that the name is not official. Where there are several place names, the more popular or simpler word has been taken. Some of the more common Mapuche words found in place names are listed in the Language section.

FILM & PHOTOGRAPHY
Few trekkers will want to do without a camera. If possible try to limit your overall photographic equipment to about one kg. SLR camera owners are advised to settle for a 28–110 mm zoom lens rather than taking three or more separate lenses. Compact cameras are reasonably priced and often weigh less than 200 grams. The latest versions have mini zoom lenses with variable angle (usually 35–70 mm) and are ideal for trekkers. If buying a compact camera, make sure its lens has provision for the attachment of a filter.

The fine gritty dust found particularly in volcanic highlands and on the dry windy steppes east of the Cordillera is a constant problem for photographers. A lens cap and a plain glass or UV filter are standard items for lens protection. Lens tissues and a 'puffer brush' should be used regularly to clean the camera. When changing film be especially careful to prevent dust entering the camera chamber.

A padded camera case with a shoulder strap will lengthen the life of your camera appreciably, and is a convenient way to carry it on short trips. When trekking in wet areas be sure to adequately protect your camera from water damage. This can be done by keeping it in a waterproof container, but watch out for condensation! A polarising filter is more or less essential for successful results where intense solar reflection is present – such as shots of scenes with glaciers, snowfields or lakes. All types of camera batteries can be bought locally.

Film can be bought tax-free in the far southern cities of Ushuaia and Punta Arenas (at the *zona franca*). Elsewhere in Argentina and Chile, film is quite expensive. There are no developing laboratories for Kodachrome anywhere in Latin America, and consequently this type of film is not sold locally. If you want to use Kodachrome you will have to bring enough film for the whole trip.

Serious photographers in Chile and Argentina generally use Fuji Professional film for the best quality. The brands Agfa and Pacific are also sold locally, but these are not as widely available as Kodak and Fuji (note its pronounced 'foo-xi' in Spanish).

HEALTH

Vaccinations are not required for entry to either Chile or Argentina. Standards of hygiene are generally high, and gastric complaints are less of a problem. However, in parts of Chile sewerage water is still commonly used to irrigate and fertilise crops, and fruits or vegetables that grow on or close to the ground (eg strawberries, lettuce and carrots) should not be eaten before they have been cooked or otherwise sterilised. Some travellers have themselves inoculated against typhoid as a precaution.

All travellers should take out basic health and travel insurance before they leave. Ensure that adequate cover is given for all the activities you intend doing on your trip. Standard travel insurance policies usually cover trekking, but often exclude the more dangerous mountain sports such as roped climbing or river rafting. It is wise to have a thorough dental checkup before you begin your journey.

For those who can afford it, good medical care is available in Chile and Argentina. For the treatment of minor complaints you can often simply consult a pharmacist. A wide range of medications can be bought without a prescription.

In Patagonia, only common sense health precautions need to be taken. There are no poisonous reptiles or insects, nor dangerous animals of prey in the entire area of the Patagonian Andes. However, in the vast South American tropical zone to the north conditions are very different, and travellers intending to go on to there should acquire a basic knowledge of tropical diseases and conditions.

Medical Kit Checklist

A small medical kit containing the basics for simple first aid should be carried by all trekking parties. The following items are recommended:

- Antibiotics – in both Chile and Argentina tablets can be bought 'over the counter' without a prescription
- Antihistamine (such as Benadryl) – useful as a decongestant for colds; for allergies; to ease itching caused by insect bites; or to help motion sickness
- Antiseptic powder or spray – to prevent infection of cuts and small wounds etc
- Bandages and band-aids – for minor injuries
- Burn cream
- Insect repellent – it might stop the *tábanos* for a while!
- Lomotil, Imodium or Kaolin preparation (Pepto-Bismol) – for the treatment of diarrhoea and intestinal troubles
- Painkillers and aspirin or panadol – for pain or fever
- Suncream and lip chap stick – the latter will save your lips from the dry and incessant winds encountered east of the Cordillera
- Tweezers and scissors
- Water sterilisation tablets

Liver Fluke Cysts

The only organism in Patagonia that is potentially very harmful is the liver fluke. The liver fluke (*Tenia equinococco*) is a worm-like parasite that usually lives in the digestive tract of sheep, but may also infect cattle or pigs. This parasite's eggs are often passed on to humans through contact with dogs that have fed on the entrails of infected animals. So-called hydatid cysts occur where the parasite establishes itself in organs of the body – especially the liver, kidneys or lungs – and develops gradually over a number of years. This condition (in Spanish, *hidatidosis*) is extremely serious, requiring surgery to remove the cysts.

To control liver fluke, an extensive government program is now underway to educate farmers not to allow their dogs into areas used for slaughtering animals. The parasite is found all over the world, and this simple precaution has largely eradicated it from countries such as Iceland and New Zealand.

It is advisable not to pet suspect dogs – such as those on more remote farms – or other canines that may be infected with liver fluke, and to boil all water when passing through grazing country. In wilder mountain areas, however, the risk of contracting liver fluke is virtually nil.

Hypothermia

Hypothermia, also known as exposure, is the ultimately fatal excessive cooling of the body temperature and is probably the most everpresent danger in all alpine areas. The Andes of Patagonia are renowned for the unpredictability of the weather, and hypothermia is a constant danger. Even in summer, severe storms can roll in suddenly from the Pacific, bringing heavy rain or snowfall. Trekkers should always be alert to signs of an impending breakdown of weather conditions. Familiarity with the typical symptoms of a developing hypothermic condition and methods of treating exposure is essential.

Key signs of hypothermia include slurred speech, dizziness, lethargy, difficulty with coordination, numbness of the the skin, lack of feeling in the extremities and irrational behaviour. Always carry enough warm clothing, including a completely windproof and waterproof garment that covers at least your upper body and your head. Avoid crossing (or camping in) high and exposed areas

in poor weather. Even in areas where there are refugios, carrying a tent will ensure you always have shelter in an emergency.

To treat hypothermia, first get the affected person out of the wind and rain. Have them remove all wet garments and put on dry clothing. Give the patient hot drinks (not alcohol) and simple sugary foods. If they still do not soon show signs of recovery, their condition is more serious. Put the patient into a well-insulated sleeping bag with another person to give additional body warmth. If possible place the patient in a warm bath.

Never treat a hypothermic person in the following ways. Do not rub the patient. Do not place the patient near a fire. Do not remove the patient's wet clothing unless they are under shelter from wind and rain. Do not give alcohol.

Heat Stroke & Sunburn

Patagonia is a decidedly cool-climate region, and consequently heat stroke is unlikely to be a real concern. Nevertheless very warm days do occur in summer in the northern Lake District and Araucanía. There, heat may become a problem, especially in exposed volcanic country above the tree line.

Heat stroke is usually the result of dehydration of the body and/or salt deficiency through sweating, diarrhoea or vomiting, and is characterised by fatigue, lethargy, headaches, giddiness and muscle cramps. During hot weather heat stroke can be easily avoided by drinking plenty of water and resting regularly.

Particularly in November/December, when the sun is high but there is still plenty of snow about, routes above tree line expose trekkers to relatively high levels of UV radiation. Since most trekkers dress lightly in such conditions, often wearing only a T-shirt and shorts, sunburn is often a problem. Remember the danger of sunburn is especially high when large snow drifts have to be crossed. Protect your skin by wearing a broad-rimmed hat and keeping your limbs and face either covered up or well smeared with a good UV suncream (available locally). A sturdy pair of polarising sunglasses is essential.

Altitude Sickness (AMS)

For trekkers, the generally lower elevation of the Andes in Patagonia virtually eliminates the danger of altitude sickness (which is called *soroche* or *puna* in South America). However, the threat of acute mountain sickness (AMS) is significantly greater to Patagonian climbers, as they are more likely to ascend to higher altitudes quickly and stay there for longer periods. In the treks described in this book, altitude sickness is extremely unlikely except perhaps for the ascent of Volcán Lanín (altitude 3776 metres). There seems to be wide disagreement regarding the lowest height at which true cases of AMS can occur, ranging from as low as 1800 metres to 3200 metres. However, 2500 metres above sea level is probably the lowest elevation, although serious cases of AMS are actually quite uncommon below 3000 metres.

AMS is basically caused by the body's failure to acclimatise to the lower atmospheric pressure of high altitudes. Because mountain air has a lower oxygen concentration, the alveoli in the lungs cannot pass on enough oxygen into the blood. The lungs begin to work harder and breathing is quickened. Fluid accumulates in between the cells in the body and eventually collects in the lungs and brain. As it builds up in the lungs, the fluid starts to cause breathlessness and a progressively worsening cough. If they do not descend, the patient is ultimately drowned by this fluid. This syndrome is called high altitude pulmonary edema (HAPE).

When the fluid build up occurs in the brain, the first symptoms are headache, loss of appetite and nausea. As the condition progresses the patient feels constantly tired and lethargic. If still allowed to progress, balance and coordination become distorted (ataxia), and eventually the patient lies down and slips into a coma. Unless they are immediately brought to lower ground, the patient will die. This dangerous syndrome is referred to as high altitude cerebral edema (HACE). HAPE and HACE can occur by themselves or in combination.

Similar symptoms to HACE can occur as a consequence of dehydration of the body, too much sun, or other unrelated illnesses. Sleeplessness and loss of appetite are a common reaction to rapid ascent, and do not necessarily indicate altitude sickness. If such symptoms seem to be getting worse, the only sensible thing to do is descend. Failure to do so could result in death.

Water

Water is often a problem in the far southern Andes, usually because there is just *too much of it*. For this reason it is usually unnecessary to carry more than a small canteen of water with you. Camp sites are invariably close to a good source of water.

The exception to this are the volcanic ranges of the Araucanía and Lake District and areas of dry land that fringe the Patagonian Andes. In volcanic areas heavy deposits of lava or pumice ash often make the ground so porous that surface water quickly seeps away into subterranean streams, making it difficult to find water. Walking over lava fields in sunny weather can be surprisingly hot work, and when trekking in such areas be sure to carry plenty of water to last the whole day.

Especially when trekking in popular areas, use common sense in your selection of a toilet spot. Defecate (ie crap) well away – say 20 metres – from streams and lakes on the downhill/downstream side of camp sites or houses. Cover up your doings properly, preferably by burying them in a roughly 20 cm deep hole. Thoughtful trekkers carry a small trowel for this purpose. These simple precautions may prevent walkers who later visit the spot from getting a nasty bout of diarrhoea.

Even in the towns and cities of Chile and Argentina, water is rarely a health problem. As anywhere, trekkers sensible enough to avoid drinking from suspicious water sources are quite unlikely to suffer stomach troubles. Provided there is no other source of water contamination (such as a farm or major camping area upstream), the water in remoter trekking areas is likely to be far purer than your tap water at home and should not need sterilisation. But if there is any doubt, boil it (see also notes on Liver Fluke Cysts in the Health section).

DANGERS & ANNOYANCES
Emergencies
Before setting out, read through the track notes carefully to decide whether you are sufficiently fit, well enough equipped and have the necessary experience to do the trek safely. Leave the details of the persons in your party, intended trekking routes and your expected date and time of return with the park authorities or police.

You should avoid trekking alone. Two is the minimum number for a safe walking party, and at least one additional person in the group will enable someone to stay with an injured trekker while another goes to seek help. When in remote areas, special care should be taken to avoid accidents. Caution is particularly called for when using potentially dangerous devices like gasoline stoves and sharp knives such as machetes. All walkers should have a basic knowledge of current first aid practices and carry adequate medical supplies for treating injuries.

In emergencies help may be three or four days' trek away. Border posts, ranger stations, police or military installations, and sometimes larger estancias have two-way radios. If absolutely necessary they will probably be able to organise the evacuation of an injured walker. Depending on how this is done, you may be asked to contribute all or a large part of the cost of the rescue.

River Crossings
Serious river crossings must be undertaken on some of the treks. These often require wading a fast-flowing glacial stream where fine sediment may so discolour the water that it is difficult to gauge the depth. Walking parties should be well practised in river crossing techniques. Where possible, wade at the bottom of a long pool to avoid being swept off your feet by the current. If necessary link arms with other party members and use a heavy tree branch to stabilise the group. Cross the stream with the branch in line with the flow of water. Ropes are sometimes useful for crossing narrow streams, but the rope itself may entangle and endanger a wading trekker.

It is important to consider that in mid to late spring (October/November) river levels may still be high. Remember that in warm sunny weather streams of glacial origin usually reach their highest level in the late afternoon, somewhat after the sun's intensity has begun to wane. In such conditions, a morning crossing will generally be the easiest. Heavy overnight rain can also make a stream impassable, and it is advisable to cross and make your camp on the other side wherever it is safe to do so.

Sharp Bamboo Stumps
Bamboo grows in the understorey of all but the most southerly temperate rainforests. Where tracks have been slashed through clusters of bamboo, short cut-off canes are left sticking out of the ground. These make sharp and potentially very dangerous obstacles. Particularly where the slippery bamboo rods have not been cleared off the track, there is the risk of slipping and falling onto the spikes. Walk very carefully anywhere the track leads through bamboo, especially on steep muddy descents.

Bloodsuckers
Chile is completely free of ticks and they are rare or absent in the Andes of southern Argentina as well. Ticks are best dislodged by dousing the bite with stove fuel. It is very important that the head of the insect is also carefully removed. Although leeches are very common in the extraordinarily wet rainforests of archipelagic Chile they are not dangerous and can easily be removed by applying salt, stove fuel, direct heat or even hot spices such as curry.

Among the relatively few blood sucking insects found throughout the southern Cordillera are various biting gnats, sometimes called *petros*. There are also mosquitoes, but surprisingly, these are generally much less bothersome than in other moist areas. Distinct from mosquitoes in tropical areas, those in Patagonia are not carriers of malaria nor any other known disease.

Tábanos, the collective name for a few different species of horsefly (but particularly the voracious black and red ones) appear for four to five weeks from Christmas until late February in the forests of the Araucanía and Lake District to as far south as Aisén. Insect repellents don't work for long against determined swarms of tábanos, and must be constantly reapplied. Dark clothing (especially blue) tends to attract these insects and should be avoided.

Tábanos are fond of sunny places close to lakes and streams, but will often pursue you tenaciously through rainforest and sometimes even above the snow line. The insect carries a tiny honey sack inside its abdomen which locals frequently remove and eat.

Security

Although you should never get too complacent about security, Chile and Argentina are unquestionably safer places for foreigners than certain countries immediately to their north. Outside of large cities serious incidents such as assaults are rare, and almost unheard of in the countryside.

The risk of robbery can be minimised by wearing an inconspicuous money belt under your clothes and by carrying your money in the form of travellers' cheques. In busy places such as bus and train stations, keep cameras and other valuable items out of sight and avoid putting your bag down. Don't pack valuables in the top of your rucksack and use small padlocks to deter petty theft.

THE TREKS

Most of the treks are intended for the more self-reliant walker. Nonetheless, even those rated difficult can be done by the inexperienced as long as there are some trekkers with experience in the party. The average length of the treks is three or four days, though taking optional sidetrips may considerably lengthen the trek. The track notes divide each trek into separate stages. These are intended as suggestions only, and in most cases there is nothing to stop parties from doing the trek differently.

Generally the treks follow foot tracks, but these are not always maintained or well transited. Although short sections of the first stages may involve walking along a road or 4WD track to where the path begins, none of the actual treks themselves involves following roads the whole way.

In most cases the routes have been cut specifically for trekkers or have gradually developed as foot traffic on popular routes has increased. With only a small number of exceptions, the routes outlined in this book go through national parks or reserves, and sometimes there are foot tracks providing access to small farm enclaves within the park boundary. Especially in the Lake District and Araucanía, such areas are more accurately described as isolated pockets of semi-wilderness rather than completely untouched wilderness.

Unlike treks you may have done in other trekking regions where the valleys and mountain ranges are much higher – such as in the Himalaya or Peru – trekking routes in the Patagonian Andes do not generally lead through mountain villages or remote alpine farms. Porters to carry gear and supplies are unnecessary and virtually unheard of in Patagonia. For extended excursions into the mountains (but outside national parks) horses and pack animals are sometimes used. Especially in the more popular trekking and climbing areas, mountain guides can be hired.

Obviously the selection of treks in this guidebook comes nowhere near to including all the possibilities in Patagonia, and trekking parties are limited only by their experience in backcountry travel. Walkers who are planning off-track exploration are advised that particularly in the Chilean Lake District dense vegetation often makes the going difficult, but above the tree line movement is generally both easier and more spectacular. Concise descriptions of other

58 Facts for the Trekker

TREK STANDARDS & TIMES

Country	Name of Trek	Days	Rating	Access	Special Features	Page
Chile	Around Volcán Antuco	3	Easy to Moderate	Bus	Volcano near large alpine lake	78
Chile	Sierra Nevada	2(4)	Easy to Difficult	Bus	Thermal springs, alpine scenery	82
Chile	Central Huerquehue	2(4)	Easy to Moderate	Tour Bus or Taxi	Lakeland plateau, thermal springs	88
Chile	Around Volcán Villarrica	4(5)	Moderate	Tour Bus or Taxi	Active volcano, forests of araucarias	93
Chile	Villarrica Traverse	4	Moderate	Bus	Volcanic alpine wilderness	97
Argentina	Ascent of Volcán Lanín	3	Moderate to Difficult	Bus	Spectacular ascent of volcano	105
Argentina	Queñi Circuit	3	Easy	Bus	Beautiful forests, thermal springs	110
Chile	Puyehue Traverse	4	Moderate	Bus	Volcanic plateau, geysers & fumeroles	114
Chile	Termas de Callão	3	Easy	Boat and Bus	Rainforest, thermal baths	121
Argentina	Nahuel Huapí Traverse	4(5)	Moderate	Bus	Mountain huts by alpine lakes	127
Argentina	Paso de las Nubes	3(6)	Moderate	Tour Bus and Boat	Superb alpine scenery in lush rainforest	133
Chile	Pangal-Chaica Track	4	Easy to Moderate	Bus	Glacial lakes, giant alerce trees	139
Chile	Río Anay Walk	3	Easy	Bus	Wild beaches and coastal rainforest	145
Chile	Walk to the Caldera	3	Moderate to Difficult	Car or Bus	Volcanic crater in rainforest	149
Chile	Río Simpson: Cerro Catedral in & Around Cerro Castillo	3	Moderate	Bus	Forested valleys, craggy summits	152
Chile	Tamango Circuits	4(7)	Moderate to Difficult	Bus	Rugged peaks, glaciers, lakes & moors	155
Argentina	Cerro Torre	3	Easy to Moderate	Bus	Subalpine lakes to sparse steppes	168
Argentina	Cerro Fitz Roy	2	Moderate	Bus	Stunning granite needle	172
Argentina	Lago Toro	4	Easy to Moderate	Bus	Granite peaks & glaciers	173
Argentina	Glaciar Viedma	2(3)	Moderate	Bus	Small lake at the terminus of huge glacier	177
Chile	Torres del Paine Circuit	2	Easy to Moderate	Bus	Major glacier descending into lake	179
Chile	Torres del Paine Lookout	7(9)	Moderate	Bus	Outstanding alpine scenery & wildlife	183
Chile	Lago Pingo	1	Moderate	Bus	Three distinct ice-capped pinnacles	189
Chile	Pingo-Tyndall Circuit	3(7)	Easy	Bus	Heavily glaciated landscape	190
Argentina	Lago Kami Circuit	5	Difficult	Bus	Wild, remote part of Torres del Paine	191
Argentina	Tierra del Fuego Mini-circuit	6	Difficult	Bus	Subantarctic moorland, lakes & forest	198
Chile	Dientes Circuit	3	Moderate	Bus	Gentle alpine valleys, moors & forests	203
		5	Moderate to Difficult	Boat or Plane	Wild and mountainous island scenery	205

recommended trekking areas are listed in regular Other Treks sections at the end of the track notes or chapters. These should help you go about planning your own treks.

Walking Times
The walking times given in the track notes are for average experienced trekkers carrying packs weighing between 15 and 25 kg. Given times don't allow for rests, lunch stops or sidetrips. A trek's overall length should always be calculated in terms of the required number of walking hours rather than its distance. However, to help you to better assess the walking standard, the length of each section is also given in kilometres (km).

Walking Standard
Walking standards given in this book rate the strenuousness and navigational difficulties of a trek. The trek's overall distance and the existence of mountain huts are other minor factors taken into consideration. The grading gives only a general indication of what to expect. Remember that the walking standard can vary considerably with the weather. Always read through the track notes before you begin the trek. The text will give you a much more detailed idea of the conditions to be encountered.

Walks in this book are graded as easy, moderate or difficult. Where conditions of difficulty vary, the intermediate gradings of easy to moderate, and moderate to difficult are also used. Although, on the whole, the more demanding treks pass through less disturbed wilderness areas, a trek's grading is in no way an indication of an area's natural attractiveness.

A description of these gradings follows:

- *Easy* treks follow generally well-marked tracks. These require little navigational skill and only an average standard of physical fitness. Track notes for treks given an easy grading are generally a bit more detailed.
- *Moderate* treks require somewhat more experience. These are best attempted after

a number of easy treks have been completed. More strenuous tracks, and well-marked but exposed routes may be encountered. At times you may have to do your own navigation.
- *Difficult* treks are exclusively for parties led by experienced walkers. They generally follow largely unmarked routes through rugged, exposed or remote country. A high level of navigational skill, self reliance and fitness is required.

Fishing
The southern lakes and rivers of Chile and Argentina are well stocked with introduced North American river trout, European brown trout and rainbow trout, as well as perch, salmon and Patagonian mackerel. Fishing is quite popular with locals, and the region is also attracting increasing numbers of fly anglers from all over the world. The season runs from about mid-November to mid-April, and in both countries you must have a fishing permit. Fishing permits are generally issued on a daily, weekly, monthly or seasonal basis and can be purchased at national parks offices. Anglers supplies are sold in all larger towns. In Chile, a periodically updated publication, *Guía de Pesca*, has plenty of useful information for anglers.

The Trans-Andean Frontier
The Southern Andes (though not always the continental divide itself) form most of the common border between Chile and Argentina. On the whole the two nations have cordial relations, but the frontier remains a sensitive area. As the topographical maps of either country often show, there is not always complete agreement about the exact location of the border. The two countries' most current conflict is over sovereignty of the Laguna del Desierto area between Lago O'Higgins and and the Fitz Roy sector of Parque Nacional Los Glaciares.

Border police patrol key sectors on either side of the frontier. In Argentina a special paramilitary force, the Gendarmería Nacional, is responsible for controlling the border.

In Chile this is done by sections of the regular police force, the Carabineros.

The Chilean authorities are chiefly concerned about preventing the spread of plant and animal diseases, particularly foot and mouth disease (*fiebre aftosa*). Apart from the patrol horses themselves, in Chile no livestock is permitted within five km of the border. It is prohibited to take most unprocessed foodstuffs and dairy products across the frontier from Argentina. These regulations are strictly enforced. Nevertheless smuggling of animals and various other goods still occurs, and in certain places close to the border there are well-trodden international paths that locals tellingly call *senderos de los contrabandistas*.

Theoretically, doing a trek that leads you across the frontier requires special permission from the authorities of each country, (that is, of course, unless you go via an official *aduana* or border post). All trans-Andean trails are marked by red tape, however, and arranging a permit – normally granted by the local constable of the country concerned – may turn out to be a time-consuming business. As there is some fine walking territory close to the frontier such restrictions are frustrating, but bear in mind that the border's very existence has probably kept many frontier areas wild and intact by hindering their development.

All of the important national parks in the Patagonian Andes lie directly alongside the border, and in more remote areas walking a short way over the frontier line is generally no problem at all. Obviously, you must return to the country from which you set out. In the (unlikely) event of meeting a border patrol, you will probably be expected to produce identification papers and your gear may even be searched.

ACCOMMODATION

Apart from during the seasonal vacation rush, finding clean and cheap accommodation is usually not too difficult even in out of the way places. In larger towns and tourist centres there is generally quite a range of accommodation. The local tourist office usually has the most up-to-date list of accommodation alternatives from the more humble *casas de familia* to the most expensive hotels.

Camping & Huts

Camping has become quite popular in Chile and Argentina and is quite safe. In Argentina especially, organised campgrounds with toilets and hot showers are usually very good value. During the busy summer holiday period, when cheap accommodation is scarce, 'wild' camping close to roads and towns is common among local backpackers, and is a well-accepted practice. While in an emergency you can camp just about anywhere, if possible ask for the owner's permission before camping on private land.

The track notes give recommended camp sites, but on the whole there are few restrictions on where you may camp within most national parks and reserves. In some very popular national parks camping is more tightly controlled and trekkers are often obliged to camp at designated sites. Where such controls exist it is usually necessary to get a permit from the park staff. Provided you don't light a fire and are otherwise respectful of the environment, however, these rules are usually not strictly enforced. Campfires should be kept small and never left unattended.

In certain areas, refugios exist for the benefit of trekkers. Some are just draughty wooden shacks with a dirt floor. Others, such as the refugios around Bariloche in the Argentine Lake District, are comparable with better mountain huts in New Zealand or Europe, with a fee payable to the resident warden. National park authorities and the military also erect huts for the use of their own personnel, and it's usually possible to arrange to stay in these. The Chilean CONAF has plans to build new refugios in some of the country's more popular parks in the coming years. Refugios can become overcrowded in wet weather or during the holiday season, and it is recommended that you carry a tent even in areas where there are good refugios.

Youth Hostels

The YHA network in Chile and Argentina is rather limited, but youth hostels (called *albergues juveniles* in Spanish) are probably the cheapest of all forms of accommodation. Many youth hostels only operate during holidays, and frequently use school buildings for dormitory accommodation. Charges are always minimal, and probably never more than US$1 per night. Unfortunately, it is sometimes hard to find out whether a town has a youth hostel until you actually get there. Ask at the local tourist office.

Casas de Familia & Hospedajes

These are usually the cheapest form of accommodation available to travellers. A *casa de familia* is a private home where the family lets out one or two spare rooms to travellers, often only during busier holiday periods. *Hospedajes* are similar, but tend to be more permanent. Both are generally very good value for money and have hot water. Prices per person range between about US$2 and US$4, often including a continental breakfast.

Residenciales & Pensiones

Although they are usually also family-run concerns, *residenciales* and *pensiones* are more up-market and (pensiones especially) generally offer better facilities and more privacy. Depending on price, rooms may even have their own bathroom. Prices per person range from around US$3 up to US$7, which usually includes breakfast.

Hotels

The term hotel is usually used for more up-market accommodation, but sometimes quite cheap places also call themselves hotels. 'Real' hotels offer rooms with at least a bathroom with hot water, and probably a private telephone. In larger towns there are many mid-range hotels, but international-style luxury accommodation is rarely found outside the main cities. Hotels charge upwards of about US$8 per person.

FOOD

Chile and Argentina have their own national cuisines. Argentine food is typified by meat dishes, especially roast lamb and beef. Argentina's famous gaucho-style roasts are called *asados*, where a whole sheep or calf is grilled on a vertical spit around a large open charcoal fire. Italian food is generally excellent in Argentina because of the profound cultural influence of Italian immigration. Pasta and real pizza – Chileans think pizza is a sort of lightly toasted cheesy bread sandwich – are served in restaurants throughout the country.

Fish and seafood is the great speciality of Chilean cuisine. Shellfish were first eaten by the Indians of the west Patagonian coast, and today oysters, mussels and clams form the base of various traditional soups and casseroles. *Curanto*, originally a dish from Chiloé, is a rich potpourri of various kinds of seafood, beef or chicken cooked with vegetables such as pumpkin and potato. On the coasts of Chiloé and Magallanes pink salmon are farmed both for export and domestic consumption, and salmon is served as a speciality in the south. In the Fuegian islands, king crabs known as *centollas* are harvested. A cheap and universal Chilean takeaway food is the *empanada*, a pastry filled with anything from sweetened maize *choclo* or vegetables to mince meat.

Chile is also world-renowned for its outstanding wines, particularly the smooth mellow reds. Argentine wines are not bad either, and are usually a bit cheaper than their trans-Andean counterparts.

Expresso coffee (*cafe de maquina*) is served in coffee shops in even quite out-of-the-way places in Argentina. In southern Chile real coffee is very hard to find except in the larger centres. Surprisingly, there are also quite a few vegetarians in Argentina and Chile, particularly among the alternative-lifestyle communities of the southern Lake District. Restaurants usually have at least one or two main-course dishes without meat.

Backpacking Food

Most practical are lightweight nutritional foods that can be quickly prepared. The longer the trek, the greater should be the proportion of dehydrated foods, but taking along some fresh fruit is always a good idea.

Although food (especially farm produce) can often be bought on the trekking route, it is very unwise and often even unfair to depend too much on locals for supplies. Make sure you you have enough to last for the whole trek.

Always carry one or two days' extra food for unplanned sidetrips, emergencies or miscalculation. With the exception of certain specialised freeze-dried products, supermarkets in Chile and Argentina stock a similar range of food items to those in Australasia, Europe and North America.

It is prohibited to take most unprocessed dairy and agricultural products across the border from Argentina into Chile. This is important to remember if you intend doing a trek immediately after crossing into Chile. Food is cheaper (and usually of better quality) in Argentina.

Naturally everyone has their own tastes and preferences in camp food. The following local specialities are particularly recommended and should be obtainable from most centres:

Cheese *(queso)* – excellent in Argentina. Try *pepato* and *roquefort*.
Wholemeal bread *(pan integral)* – available in larger supermarkets and occasional health food stores in most larger centres of both Chile and Argentina
Dried fruits *(frutas secas)*
Walnuts *(nueces)* – especially good in Chile
Callampas – dehydrated mushrooms available in small packets
Packet soups – try exotic flavours like *choclo*, *marisco* and *lenteja*
Dulce de leche or *manjar* – caramelised condensed milk eaten as a spread for bread and cakes
Dulce de batata, dulce de membrillo – a semi-solid dessert made from sweet potato or quince
Harina tostada – toasted wheat flour, mixed with milk to form a kind of instant porridge
Pasta and spaghetti *fideos* – a wide range is available in Argentina

Homemade chocolates – especially good in San Carlos de Bariloche, San Martín de los Andes and Calafate and other towns in southern Argentina
Mussels *(Cholgas)* – available in dried form at markets in Chile
Herbal teas – try *mate, boldo* and *manzano* flavours in particular
Wine and fruit juices – available in reasonably durable one-litre cardboard cartons

Wild Foods

Wild foods can usually only provide a small supplement to your diet, and should not be depended on for survival.

Berries Although there is the odd unpalatable variety, none of the 'edible-looking' fruits growing throughout Patagonia are poisonous. The most common treats are the abundant native berry species. February, March and April are the best 'berry months'.

Chauras

Chauras – These are red to white berries growing on heath-like bushes, usually at their best when found just above the tree line. There are a great many species growing throughout the southern Andes.

Calafates – The calafate is a seedy smaller version of the blueberry. At least five calafate species (genus *Berberis*) grow all over southern Patagonia. Sharp thorns protect the deep purple-coloured berries from excessive exploitation. A popular Patagonian folk song claims 'whoever eats the calafate comes back for more'.

Frutilla de magallanes – This is a bright red berry usually found growing in moist rich locations such as along streams. Burying itself in the ground, the frutilla has a flavour not unlike a raspberry.

Moras – Moras are introduced European blackberries, which are found growing beside country roads, particularly in the Araucanía and Lake District. The fruit ripens in mid to late March.

Murtas – Murtas are sweet red berries with a scaly skin. In Autumn murtas are plentiful in the Lake District and are often sold in local markets.

Other Wild Foods These include:

Piñones – These are the nut-like fruit of the araucaria pine found growing in the Araucanía and northern Lake District. Giant cluster-cones of piñones fall from the trees in late summer, scattering across the ground. The pinkish kernels look a bit like elongated cloves of garlic. After roasting or boiling they can be easily 'squeezed peeled' to reveal a starchy flesh that has a flavour something like chestnut, but with an interesting, slightly resinous aftertaste. Be sure not to collect germinating nuts, and always leave enough to allow proper regeneration.

Pan del indio – This is the local term for the round edible growths that form on the trunks and branches of southern beech (*Nothofagus*) species where parasites of the *Cyttaria* genus becomes established. The 'fruit' have the form of immature champignons, with a rubbery texture and a musty fungal taste. Although no great delicacy, pan del indio is an abundant source of carbohydrate and was a staple food for some indigenous tribes of the south.

Colihue and *quila* – Shoots of these native bamboo species can also be eaten. Chewing at the stems of new, succulent sprouts is considered a good thirst quencher. The juice of bamboo shoots may irritate the mouth and throat slightly, but this can be neutralised by cutting up and soaking the stems in vinegar or lemon juice.

Warning The eating of wild mushrooms is not recommended unless you are accompanied by someone with sufficient knowledge of edible native fungi.

FIRE & CONSERVATION

It would be difficult to overstate the devastation that forest fires have caused in the Patagonian Andes. Particularly in the colonisation of southern Chile, fire was frequently used as a means of clearing land for farming. Often strong winds would whip the flames out of control, resulting in enormous fires that soon became impossible to contain. It was not uncommon for such fires to remain burning throughout the whole summer, laying waste vast tracts of valuable forest as they spread.

During the worst periods of the 1930s and 1940s smoke and ash from huge forest fires in Chile's Aisén Región was deposited as far away as Argentina's Atlantic coast. It is estimated that in the southern Andes this century some two million hectares of virgin forest were destroyed in this way. Even today forests of dead trees are the enduring landmarks of many regions, often scarring entire mountain ranges.

Slow regeneration after forest fire makes soil erosion a severe problem in the Patagonia. The destruction of the forest along the middle course of the Río Aisén in Chile caused the river to silt up so badly that the city of Puerto Aisén became useless as a port. Fire is also partly responsible for the alarming decline in numbers of some animal species, most particularly the huemul and pudú.

If you must light a campfire, always exercise extreme caution, and *never* leave it unattended. Make sure the fire is properly extinguished before you leave. Never light a campfire in areas with peat soils. Peat largely consists of undecomposed organic matter that is often quite dry and porous, making it difficult to extinguish once ignited. Keep the rivers and lakes pure by not washing with soaps or detergents. Sand or a pot scourer will be just as good. And remember, if you carry it in, you carry it out!

NATIONAL CAPITALS
Buenos Aires

The Argentine capital, Buenos Aires, is one of the world's major cities and is home to some 12 million people. On the broad bay known as the Río de la Plata, or River Plate, the city has a moist subtropical climate that often produces unpleasant, sticky weather. Mass immigration has given Buenos Aires an ethnic diversity and cosmopolitan flavour found neither in any other regions of Argentina nor in other Latin American capitals.

As the undisputed cultural, political, and economic hub of the nation, Buenos Aires completely dominates the nation. Understandably, the city's rather self-indulgent atmosphere often annoys Argentinians from 'lesser' parts of the country (such as Patagonia), as does the sometimes arrogant manner of its inhabitants.

Buenos Aires' permanently overloaded telephone system and run-down underground suburban rail network are signs of Argentina's economic decline. With many parks, squares, cafes, pedestrian walkways and interesting architecture, central Buenos Aires is nevertheless quite an attractive place and there is a lot to see and do here.

One good reason for going to Buenos Aires is to buy topographical maps at the Instituto Geográfico Militar, as the IGM does not have sales offices anywhere outside the capital. The IGM is at Avenida Cabildo 381, which is best reached by taking the subway to the termination of B line then walking three blocks north.

The Argentine national parks authority, the SNPN, has its headquarters in Buenos Aires. The SNPN office is at Santa Fe 680 (around the corner from where the Florida mall ends). The most important mountain club in Buenos Aires is the Centro Andino Buenos Aires at Rivadavia 1255, (office Nos 2 & 3).

The Centro Patagonico is a commercial enterprise for the promotion of Patagonia. The Centro sells books, videos and artifacts from the south at its main shop on the Florida mall. A good tip for those with the time is a day trip to the nearby provincial capital of La Plata to see the natural history museum founded by Perito Moreno.

Santiago

Santiago is no longer the parliamentary capital since the restoration of the democracy, but as a city of six million it dominates Chile almost as much as its trans-Andean rival, Buenos Aires. Although Santiago itself is only about 600 metres above sea level, the city is still very much an 'Andean capital'.

Santiago looks out (through an increasingly thick layer of exhaust smog) onto the adjacent central Cordillera, whose towering snow-capped peaks reach over 6000 metres. The city has a pleasantly dry and warm climate, with maximum summer temperatures rarely going above 35°C. Summer nights in Santiago are relievingly cool, as chilled air from the Andes regularly descends on the city after sunset. The city has a modern Paris-style metro whose network is currently being expanded. Santiago has good art galleries, museums, restaurants, cafés and parks, and there is plenty to keep you occupied for quite a few days.

The headquarters of the forests and national parks authority, the Corporación Nacional Forestal (CONAF), is at Avenida Bulnes 285. The CONAF information office is on the 7th floor. Most Chilean mountain clubs are represented by the Federación de Andinismo de Chile at Almirante Simpson 77. There is some superb mountain country just outside Santiago, and the the federation has published a booklet (possibly again out of print) on trekking and climbing in the central Cordillera. The office has a small library and sells some imported mountaineering equipment. The Argentine Embassy is at Vicuña MacKenna 41.

REGIONAL CENTRES

Some of the regional centres may serve as a base for trips into the nearby Cordillera. In central Patagonia the largest settlements close to the Andes are almost always very small provincial towns with poor access.

Chilean Araucanía & Lake District

Los Angeles A regional capital just north of the Río Bío Bío at the far northern end of Chile's forested Araucanía, Los Angeles is the jumping off place for the Laguna del Laja and Tolhuaca national parks as well as many other potential trips into the nearby Cordillera. The city is on the Panamerican Highway and is easily reached from the north or south.

Temuco With a population of about 220,000, Temuco is the largest city within the region of greater Patagonia. The city is on the Panamerican Highway and has excellent transport connections to all locations in the Chilean Araucanía. Temuco is the starting point for trips to the national parks of Villarrica, Huerquehue, Conguillío/Los Paraguas, Nahuel Buta and Laguna del Malleco.

Temuco is not only the administrative centre of Chile's IX Región, but also the 'capital' of the Mapuche people. Over half of the population are Mapuche Indians, although most speak Spanish. Interesting features of Temuco are the fruit and vegetable market and the Mapuche handicrafts market. Excellent native wood products (such as salad bowls carved out of raulí), Mapuche silver jewellery, Araucarian belts and ponchos and other woollens can be bought at the markets.

Also worth a visit is the regional museum at Alemania 84, which specialises in Mapuche history. CONAF has its regional headquarters in Temuco at Fco. Bilbao 931 (on the 2nd floor).

Valdivia The only major coastal city between Concepción and Puerto Montt, Valdivia is a neat and attractive place. Valdivia is the starting or terminating point for treks between the Río Bueno and Corral on the coastal strip to the city's south (see the Other Treks section in the Lake District chapter). The local mountain club is the Club de Montāna de Valdivia at Avenida Argentina 3502 Pob 1, Corvi. The Chilean CONAF has its regional office at Ismael Valdés 431.

Osorno The city of Osorno is an attractive place, and is sizable with a population of around 110,000. It is ideally located as a base for trips into the mountains of the central Chilean Lake District. Osorno is on the Panamerican Highway and a major regional transport centre. The local CONAF office is at Mackenna 674 and the local mountain club is the Club de Ski y Montañismo de Osorno, at O'Higgins 887.

Puerto Montt This port city, also of some 110,000 inhabitants in the southern Lake District, lies on the sheltered northern shore of a wide bay called Seno Reloncaví. 'Frente al mar', Puerto Montt is the gateway to Chiloé island and the arrival and departure point for short and long-distance boat trips down the southern coast of canals and fjords. The city has many fine examples of southern Chilean wood and corrugated iron architecture. CONAF has its main regional office on Ochagavia 464. Surprisingly, there is no local mountaineering club. The Argentine Consulate is at Cauquenes 94 (on the 2nd floor) near the junction with Varas.

Castro With a population of about 20,000 Castro is the biggest town on Chiloé. Castro is an attractive place to stay and the best base for trips into Parque Nacional Chiloé. The town has fine examples of the typical wood and corrugated iron buildings (including its cathedral) and excellent seafood. The local CONAF office is on the 3rd floor of the municipal offices building in Calle O'Higgins near the Plaza de Armas.

Argentine Araucanía & Lake District

Junín de los Andes This is a small city of around 30,000 people situated on the dry steppes fronting the central Argentine Lake District, 41 km north by road from San Martín de los Andes. Junín is still largely a military base and not a very interesting place, but the city is the jumping-off point for trips to Volcán Lanín and Lago Huechulafquén, the largest lake in Parque Nacional Lanín. The Club Andino Junín de los Andes, or

CAJA, is at O'Higgins 369 and can give information on climbing Volcán Lanín.

San Martín de los Andes An attractive regional centre at the eastern end of Lago Lácar, San Martín de los Andes is the gateway to the mountains of Argentina's large Parque Nacional Lanín. San Martín is also a winter sports centre, with skiing at Cerro Chapelco. The SNPN has a national parks office on the Plaza de Armas and should be contacted for information on Parque Nacional Lanín. The local mountain club is the Club Andino San Martín de los Andes at Capitán Drury 872.

San Carlos de Bariloche The largest Argentinian city in the Patagonian Andes, San Carlos de Bariloche is easily the most touristy. The city is nevertheless a very attractive place although it can be expensive. Situated on the south-eastern shores of Lago Nahuel Huapí in the southern Lake District, Bariloche is the gateway to Argentina's superb Parque Nacional Nahuel Huapí.

The Museo de la Patagonia at the Civic Centre has interesting natural history displays. The regional SNPN has an office on the Plaza de Armas at Calle San Martín 24. The Club Andino Bariloche, or CAB, is at 20 de Febrero 30. The CAB has an excellent library and information service and is worth visiting.

Chilean Central Patagonia

Chaitén Although very small (population 3000) and fairly uninspiring, the port town of Chaitén has a number of ferry services to Chiloé island and is the most important town on the Carretera Austral north of Coyhaique. There is a small regional CONAF office on Calle Independencia (just off the Plaza de Armas). Chaitén also has a small mountain club, the Club de Montaña 'Los Halcones', at Ignacio Carrera P (see Carlos Alvarado García).

Puerto Aisén A small port at the end of a wide fjord, Puerto Aisén is the starting and finishing point for boats to and from Puerto Montt or Chiloé and for sea excursions to Ventisquero San Rafael. The town of around 15,000 has a rainy coastal climate but is surrounded by picturesque peaks. CONAF has a local office in Puerto Aisén at Calle Ciro Arrendondo.

Coyhaique The regional capital of Chile's remote IX Región, Coyhaique sits in a sheltered valley behind ranges to the west. Although a small city of 40,000 people, Coyhaique is nevertheless home to around half the region's population. The area still has a pioneering feel, and most of the people are not original Aiseños. Coyhaique is the only large base for trips into the national reserves such as Cerro Castillo and Río Simpson. Day walks directly from the city are easy and worthwhile. A small local museum, the Museo de Patagonia Central is situated on the pentagonal Plaza de Armas.

The regional CONAF office is situated at Avenida Ogana 1060 on the southern road out of town. Unfortunately, there is no Argentine consulate in Coyhaique, although in recent years the government in Buenos Aires has been making vague promises about opening one. There is an informal mountaineering club, Club de Ski y Andinismo, at Magallanes 100 (contact Peter Hartmann).

Cochrane Cochrane is 70 km south of Lago General Carrera and on the Carretera Austral. Although a very small and isolated town of around 1500 people, Cochrane is the only reasonably sized settlement in the far south of Chile's IX Región (Aisén). The town is very much sheltered by the Hielo Norte, the more northerly of the two Patagonian icecaps, which is situated roughly 60 km to the west. The entire icecap and much of the surrounding country is within the huge and savage Parque Nacional Laguna San Rafael.

Cochrane is only a few km south of Reserva Nacional Tamango, and is a logical starting point for long treks south to Lago Brown and Monte Cochrane (called San Lorenzo in Argentina). A new road is being pushed through to Chile Chico around the steep southern side of Lago Carrera. CONAF has a small office in Cochrane at Calle Teniente Merino (on the Plaza de Armas).

Argentine Central Patagonia

Esquel This town is at the edge of the dry Patagonian pampa just south of the Lake District in northern Chubut Province. The city has a population of 17,000 and makes a good base for trips into Parque Nacional Los Alerces. The surfaced Ruta 40 goes through Esquel. The local mountain club is the Club Andino de Esquel, at Darwin 639.

Comodoro Rivadavia This is an oil city of 120,000 on Argentina's Atlantic coast. Although nowhere near the Cordillera, travel connections may bring you here. A good surfaced road connects the city with the Lake District and LADE flights often land here. Comodoro Rivadavia is not a particularly interesting place, but the Museo Patagónico is worth visiting. The petrified forest (*bosque petrificado*) near Sarmiento, 160 km inland from the city, is fascinating.

Chilean Southern Patagonia

Puerto Natales This windy town of some 8000 people provides the usual access to Parque Nacional Torres del Paine. The city is also the southern port for the *Tierra del Fuego*. This large transport ferry makes the long three-day trip through the spectacular Chilean fjord-land between Puerto Natales and Puerto Montt five to eight times per month.

The CONAF office in Puerto Natales is on Ignacio Carrera Pinto (opposite the hospital), but if you want information about Torres del Paine the staff will probably tell you to ask out at the park itself. A visit to the Cueva de Milodon is recommended. Another way to fill in a day is to take the cold but rewarding boat trip over to Glaciar Balmaceda, which calves into the fjord at the northern end of Seno Última Esperanza.

Punta Arenas With a population of around 100,000, Punta Arenas is the only large city in southern Patagonia. Apart from some easy walking in the low ranges of the Península Brunswick the city is not a good base for trips into the Cordillera. Punta Arenas is the regional transport knot with flights and boats both from Chile's far north and to Isla Navarino and Tierra del Fuego.

Although extremely gust-prone the city is a reasonably interesting and attractive place with plenty to do. The Salesian Museum (Museo Salesiano) at the corner of Bhories and Sarmiento in Punta Arenas is one of the best in Patagonia and has good exhibits on local Indians (including the only surviving canoe built by the Alacalufe sea nomads) and wildlife.

A visit to the Instituto de la Patagonia, situated opposite the duty-free zone (*zona franca*), is well worthwhile. The institute has a zoo, an open-air museum and a good library specialising in Patagonian history, wildlife and geography. A worthwhile day trip is to a penguin colony near the city.

The Argentine Consulate is at Avenida 21 de Mayo 1878. CONAF has its main regional office in Punta Arenas at Jose Menéndez (downhill from the main square between Quilota and Montt).

Argentine Southern Patagonia

Perito Moreno This is a small regional town with a population of around 2000, which still makes it the largest settlement on or near the Ruta 40 between Esquel and Calafate. Perito Moreno is not to be confused with the Argentine national park of the same name, situated 250 km to the south-west. The town's remote location on the Patagonian steppes east of Lago Buenos Aires in the north of Santa Cruz Province is not especially convenient for trips into the Cordillera. However, visits to the Cuevas de los Manos and the Río Pinturas area 120 km south of the town are a must.

Calafate This town is on the south shore of Lago Argentino and is the gateway to Argentina's Parque Nacional Los Glaciares. Day visits to Glaciar Moreno, boat excursions on Lago Argentino and trips to the Fitz Roy area in the north of the park almost always begin and finish at Calafate. In the last decade or so the town has experienced phenomenal growth, fed completely by tourist interest in Los Glaciares. The SNPN has a large regional office in Calafate at the junction of San Martín and 1 de Mayo on the western side of town.

Río Gallegos Not far north of the Straits of Magellan is Río Gallegos, the capital of Santa Cruz Province. Río Gallegos is not a very interesting place but, like Comodoro Rivadavia, flights and bus journeys may lead you there. The city is a jumping-off point for trips to Tierra del Fuego, Calafate and Punta Arenas. The local museum is a worthwhile place to fill in time and has a good collection of fossils and Indian artefacts.

Argentine Tierra Del Fuego
Ushuaia A scenically located city, Ushuaia is built on the Beagle Channel in front of the Fuegian Andes. Ushuaia is the capital of Argentine Tierra del Fuego and has grown so rapidly in recent years that it is now the largest city south of Comodoro Rivadavia.

The city makes an excellent base for trips to the Tierra del Fuego or other nearby mountains. Boat trips on the Beagle Channel to see marine life and other tourist excursions can be made from Ushuaia. Although the city is a free zone, prices for most things are still quite high.

The Club Andino Ushuaia is at Solís 50, and the Argentine SNPN office is on Calle San Martín 56 (but the latter always seems to be closed). Caminante is also worth contacting for mountain guides.

Chilean Tierra Del Fuego
Porvenir This is a small town opposite Punta Arenas on the dry windy steppes of northern Tierra del Fuego. With just 4500 people, Porvenir is nevertheless the largest settlement on the Chilean side of the island. The town could serve as a base for trips to the nearby abandoned goldfields of the Cordón Baquedano and the Altos de Bosquerón or to the remote country around Lago Blanco. There is a regular ferry service between Punta Arenas and Porvenir.

Getting There & Away

South America is really only directly accessible by air, and getting to Chile or Argentina is relatively expensive, especially from Australia or New Zealand. Discount fares from 'bucket shops' are available in most countries. These are usually substantially cheaper than the normal airfare. Check on the maximum period you are allowed to stay. Some return airfares allow a maximum stay of only four months, so check before you book.

Until some years ago, many travellers from the northern hemisphere flew into cities in northern South America and from there travelled south (usually overland). However, in parts of the continent, and particularly in Peru and Colombia, the security situation has been tense – in places even downright dangerous – for some time. For this reason the overland alternative, while not altogether out of the question, has become less popular these days.

Please note that in most of the following examples the return fare quoted is a special excursion fare and, as such, is subject to certain conditions. Ask the relevant airline for further details.

TO/FROM PERU
To/From Chile
Peru has a southern border with Chile and this is the point of entry for many travellers. There are two ways of entering Chile from Peru. The only overland route possibility between Peru and Chile is from the southern Peruvian town of Tacna to the city of Arica in Chile in the far north. Tacna can be reached daily by either bus, train or taxi (*colectivo*).

AeroPeru has daily flights from Lima to Tacna for about US$80 one way. The other possibility is a flight from Lima to Santiago. AeroPeru flies from Lima to Santiago four days a week. The one-way/return airfare is around US$310/540. Together LAN-Chile or Ladeco have flights between Santiago and

other major cites in virtually every country in Latin America.

To/From Argentina
Peru and Argentina don't have a common border, so all route possibilities are by air. From Lima, Aerolíneas and AeroPeru fly regularly to Buenos Aires. The one-way/return airfare is around US$460/617.

TO/FROM BOLIVIA
To/From Chile
From Bolivia there are a number of route possibilities into Chile. Bolivia has a relatively long border with Chile, but most of the land traffic is between La Paz and Arica in Chile's far north. From La Paz there are train, *ferrobus* (a kind of bus mounted onto a rail carriage base) and regular bus services to Arica. The ferrobus and regular bus run frequently, but the train only runs twice a month and only as far as Calama. Lloyd Aéreo Boliviano (LAB) has two flights per week from La Paz to Santiago for US$175 one way. LAB also flys from La Paz to Arica three times weekly for about $85 one way.

LAN-Chile fares, LaPaz-Santiago are one-way/return US$215/345, but check with the airline about the conditions applying to the return fare.

To/From Argentina
The main land road link between Bolivia and Argentina goes via La Quiaca/Villazón on the northern border in Jujuy Province. From Villazón there are daily buses to the the the Argentine provincial capitals of Salta and Jujuy.

From La Paz the non-IATA carrier LAB have several daily flights to Buenos Aires. A one-way/return fare is around US$295/513.

TO/FROM BRAZIL
For many travellers, Rio or São Paulo is the arrival point in South America.

To/From Chile
There are many daily flights between Santiago and Rio de Janiero/São Paulo with airlines such as Varig, LAN-Chile and Ladeco. The one-way/return LAN-Chile fare for Santiago-Rio de Janiero is US$540/689.

To/From Argentina
Travellers coming from the north usually make the crossing from Brazil into Argentina at the spectacular Iguazú Falls. Regular buses leave from the Brazilian side of the falls at Foz do Iguaçu to Puerto Iguazú in Argentina.

From Río and São Paulo, Aerolíneas and Varig have daily flights to Buenos Aires. The airfare from Puerto Iguazú to Buenos Aires is US$160. There are also many daily buses to Buenos Aires and the more luxurious have sleeping compartments.

TO/FROM AUSTRALIA & NEW ZEALAND
Flights from Australasia to South America are expensive. For travellers going on to Europe or Asia, Round-the-World (RTW) tickets will probably work out to be much better value for money. If you are coming from Australia or New Zealand and intend travelling overland from the USA to Latin America, the cheapest option is to fly to San Francisco or Los Angeles and journey south through Mexico. Those intending to fly direct to South America from North America should refer to the separate section which follows.

A number of agents offer discounted airfares for flights out of Australia. Two of the main competitors are The Flight Shop and STA Travel. Customers of STA don't have to be students. There are also Flight Shops in the larger New Zealand cities. Look in the travel sections of newspapers for the most suitable and competitive airfares.

To/From Chile
From Sydney, Qantas and UTA fly to Tahiti. From Tahiti LAN-Chile has trans-Pacific flights via Easter Island to Santiago and then Buenos Aires. A regular return ticket includes all three stages of the journey sells for around A$2780, but airfare discounting will often bring this down to A$2400. This price generally includes transfers and tourist hotel in Tahiti, and a stopover on Easter Island may be made without additional cost.

Various RTW ticket combinations with one-year validity include this route as the first stage. Other more detailed itineraries, including stopovers on many different islands of the South Pacific, can be built into such tickets.

To/From Argentina
From Australia and New Zealand, the cheapest and most direct way to South America is with Aerolíneas from Sydney or Auckland to Buenos Aires (Aerolíneas likes to call these 'trans-polar flights', even though the plane only just skirts the Antarctic Circle). The fare is around A$2200 and there are two flights per week. It usually costs little or nothing more if you buy a connecting flight on to Santiago (or any other South American capital serviced by Aerolíneas Argentinas). This route is the first stage of various RTW ticket combinations from Australasia.

Aerolíneas flights from Sydney and Auckland usually land briefly in Río Gallegos for refuelling. Although itself an uninspiring place, this city's southern location may be a more convenient starting point for a Patagonian hiking trip. With prior reservation it is usually possible to disembark (or reboard the aircraft for your flight home) in Río Gallegos. In future some trans-polar flights may also make refuelling stops at the newly upgraded airport in Ushuaia on Tierra del Fuego.

TO/FROM BRITAIN & EUROPE
London and certain other capitals on the European continent are excellent places to buy cheap air tickets. In Britain, magazines like *Time Out, Business Traveller*, and *TNT* have very good information about cheap air tickets. STA Travel (which does not require its customers to be students) and Trailfinders are two recommended bucket shops. Journey

Latin America, based in London, is a well-known specialist on South American travel, sells discounted airfares and runs tours all over Latin America.

From London, the cheapest way into South America is flying to Bogotá in Colombia (around £450 return) and Caracas in Venezuela (about £600 return). However if you just want to get to the continent's far south and are not much interested in travelling overland, this alternative is probably not worth considering. The best direct airline connections from both Colombia and Venezuela are with Viasa, Avianca, British Airways or Air France to Buenos Aires.

Flights from continental Europe are a bit more expensive. It might possibly work out cheaper going to the USA or Canada and flying to South America from there. Amsterdam probably has the most competitive prices in Europe after London. France and Belgium are also good places to pick up cheap airfares – try WATS in Antwerp or Nouvelles Frontiéres at 74 Rue de la Féderacion, 75015, Paris. In Switzerland, Trottomundo or Globetrotters (both are based in Zurich) have the most competitive international air tickets.

To/From Chile

The Spanish airline Iberia has four weekly flights to Santiago, and Air France flies from Paris three times a week. Other important European carriers are Lufthansa, Alitalia, Sabena, SAS and Swissair. The LAN-Chile fare from Frankfurt to Santiago is DM3460 return.

To/From Argentina

Aerolíneas has direct flights to Buenos Aires from Amsterdam, Madrid, Rome, Paris and Frankfurt and Zurich. A great range of other carriers have flights from European cites to Argentina. For travellers wanting to fly direct from Bogotá or Caracas to Buenos Aires, the best airline connections are with British Airways, Air France, Viasa and Avianca.

TO/FROM NORTH AMERICA
To/From Chile

In Canada, non-students can also book tickets with the national student travel agency, Travel CUTS. Travel CUTS has offices in Toronto, Ottawa, Montreal, Halifax, Saskatoon, Edmonton, Vancouver and Victoria. In the United States the Student Travel Network (STN) and the American Student Council Travel (SCT) offer various route combinations to many places in Latin America. Both STN and SCT have discount prices and you are not required to be a student in order to buy a ticket from them. STN has offices in San Diego, Los Angeles, San Francisco, Dallas and Honolulu. SCT offices are in Boston, New York, Seattle and Los Angeles.

LAN-Chile flies to Santiago several times a week from Montreal, Los Angeles, Miami and New York. A one-way Miami-Santiago fare with LAN-Chile is US$800 and there is a three-month return excursion fare for US$1115.

To/From Argentina

The cheapest South America flights out of North America are with Canadian Airlines from Vancouver and Toronto to Lima. The economy return airfare to Lima starts at a little over C$700 return. The regular economy airfare to Buenos Aires or Santiago is around US$1100. Overland travel via Mexico and Central America may work out cheaper, but would take several weeks.

From the USA, Eastern Airlines has the widest range of flights into Argentina, with five direct weekly flights to Buenos Aires from New York and Miami plus one weekly flight out of Los Angeles. Eastern also flies twice a week from from Miami to Juyuy in northern Argentina. Aerolíneas Argentinas and Pan Am also have many direct flights from New York to Buenos Aires (off-peak with Aerolíneas – July to November – is US$900).

TO/FROM SOUTH AFRICA

The only direct flights between South Africa and South America are to Río de Janeiro.

SAA flies on Monday and Varig flies on Friday from Johannesburg via Cape Town. The standard return economy airfare is R6121 and the ticket is valid for one year (see the earlier section To/From Brazil in this chapter).

Getting Around

Chile and Argentina have modern, efficient and reasonably cheap systems of long-distance public transport. Access to the start of a trek is in most cases easy by local public transport.

AIR
Three airlines service the Argentinian region of Patagonia. They are the military-run Líneas Aéreas de Estado (LADE), Austral Líneas and Aerolíneas Argentinas. In southern Argentina, flying is usually cheaper than a combination of buses, but flights are heavily booked during busy holiday periods.

There is a special circle fare offered by Aerolíneas Argentinas in combination with LAN-Chile which is particularly suitable for people using this book. This 'Southern Lake Crossing' fare (Buenos Aires-San Carlos de Bariloche-Puerto Montt-Santiago-Buenos Aires) is US$318. A one-way Bariloche-Buenos Aires fare, for example, costs US$248.

In Chile, air transport is relatively expensive. The two main Chilean air carriers are LAN-Chile and Ladeco. There are also a number of small regional airways which service remote areas of the south. Both Chile and Argentina have organised special air passes offering flights all over the country within a set period (eg 21 days). The 'Visit Chile Pass' is US$250 and allows for such a trip as Santiago-Puerto Montt-Punta Arenas-Santiago.

BUS
In Chile (where there is no cheap air carrier such as in Argentina) bus travel is likely to be the main form of inter-city transport for budget travellers. Buses are usually the most reliable form of land transport and are both comfortable and fast. There are bus stations in all of the large provincial cities, and these serve as departure and arrival terminals for virtually all local and long-distance services.

On well-travelled routes there is a considerable difference in ticket prices between bus companies, so it usually pays to compare prices. On international routes, always remember that a bus service across the border will usually be much more expensive for the distance travelled than a combination of regular buses.

TRAIN
Unfortunately, the state-owned railways in both countries have been allowed to run down badly, and train services are slower and considerably less reliable than buses. Trains, however, are a much more pleasant way of travelling and often follow more scenic routes than the road.

In Chile, an electrified line goes from Santiago to Puerto Montt in the Lake District, but there are no railways further south. These trains are slower and less popular with the public than buses, and in busy holiday periods may be the only transport available.

Apart from an isolated 300-km stretch of rail from Río Turbio to Río Gallegos, the Argentine national network goes only as far south as Esquel. If travelling inland from Buenos Aires, the rail services from the capital to Córdoba and Mendoza are rapid, comfortable and well priced. Other trains, such as those to San Carlos de Bariloche or Neuquén, are very slow and only recommended for rail enthusiasts with plenty of time.

TAXI

Sometimes chartered taxis are the best way of getting to the start of the trek. Out of season it may be necessary to hire a taxi because tourist buses are no longer running. Depending on your travel budget, a long trip by taxi may only be economical for trekking parties of more than three or four. Bargain hard!

CAR

All non-resident drivers must have a valid International Driver's Licence issued by your own national/state automobile association. In Chile, motorists will require a Relaciones de Pasajeros document, and must present the original registration papers of their vehicle. To enter Argentina by car it is necessary to have the Carnet de Pasages en Douanes (Libreta de aduana) issued by a recognised automobile club. In Argentina, non-residents are not permitted to take a private vehicle out of the country. Apart from the main highways, roads in the south are usually unsurfaced.

BICYCLE

Particularly since the advent of the mountain bike, increasing numbers of travellers seem to be peddling their way around southern Chile and Argentina. Other kinds of bike are probably not robust enough for the mainly unsurfaced roads. Locally produced mountain bikes are reportedly of inferior quality and cope poorly on the area's testing roads.

When planning your route through Argentine Patagonia pay special attention to prevailing wind directions, which in summer tend to blow east to north-east. The frustration of peddling against eastern Patagonia's strong and incessant head winds causes some cyclists to give up. There are bicycle shops in all of the larger cities, but in out-of-the-way places spare parts can be hard to find.

HITCHING

The Spanish term for hitching is *viajar a dedo,* literally 'to travel by thumb'. Hitchhiking in Chile and Argentina is reasonably reliable along the main routes during the busy summer holiday period. Remember, that for many local backpackers hitchhiking is the only affordable way to see their country, so try not to compete with them for rides unless there is no other viable means of transport.

On lonelier stretches of road you may have to wait a long time – even days – for a ride. One of the slowest hitching routes in Patagonia is the 900-km stretch of the Ruta 40 between Esquel and Calafate. The Ruta 40 is a very long and dusty dirt highway which follows the Andean foothills in the Argentine provinces of Chubut and Santa Cruz. This area is thinly settled, and lengthy stretches along the Ruta 40 are best avoided as there is usually little traffic. The good coastal highway between Comodoro Rivadavia and Río Gallegos (Ruta 3) is much busier and carries most of the long-distance traffic bound for inland destinations.

Considering the low vehicle density, Chile's Carretera Austral has surprisingly good hitching. As the only possible north-south route, the Carretera channels all long-distance traffic onto one single road. The drivers in this remote region are also more inclined to stop. The Carretera Austral is popular with locals, and the hitchhiking routes (and the hitchers themselves) often reach saturation point.

The less densely populated south of both countries is relatively safe for travellers and assaults are rare. Even so, an unaccompanied female hitchhiker is more likely to get into dangerous situations than a lone male. Women who hitchhike are advised to travel with male company, or at least in pairs.

BOAT

In southern Chile, sea-based transport is very important, and for some isolated settlements boats are (still) the only means of access. Long-distance ferries ply the beautiful fjord-studded coast south from Puerto Montt, of which the *Tierra del Fuego* running between Puerto Montt and Puerto Natales is the best known. The larger lakes also have a number of ferry services.

In addition to maritime traffic, there are regular ferry services on many of the large lakes of southern Chile and Argentina that are an important means of transport for travellers. In some cases, such as on Lago Nahuel Huapí in the Argentine Lake District, these are mainly tourist boats. In areas such as Lago General Carrera in central Patagonia, ferry services are simply the most practical form of transport between two places.

In a few cases (the access to the Termas de Calláo for example) the best way to get to a walk is by chartered boat. Here you will have to negotiate payment and transport yourself.

CROSSING THE BORDER
The best way to see Patagonia's national parks is probably to start in the north and work your way southwards, crossing between Chile and Argentina a number of times. In the Araucanía and Lake District there are a good number of international routes with available public or tourist transport. In remote parts of southern and central Patagonia, however, most of the border crossings are in fairly remote and inaccessi-

ble areas. People with their own transport will have fewer worries on the remoter passes. Hitchhikers who are in a hurry are better off keeping to the more transited roads.

Below are the principal Chile-Argentina routes:

Pucón to Junín de los Andes
This is an attractive but largely unsurfaced road route across Paso Mamuil Malal (called Paso Tromén in Argentina) and is the point of access for treks in Parque Nacional Villarrica and for the ascent of Volcán Lanín. There are only eight bus services each week in either direction along this road, and there is not much other traffic. Buses generally run between Temuco and San Martín de los Andes via Pucón and Junín de los Andes.

Puerto Fuy to San Martín de los Andes
This is a very scenic boat and bus route of roughly 70 km. Puerto Fuy is situated on the remote north-western end of Lago Pirehueico and is accessible by daily bus from Panguipulli. From Puerto Fuy a ferry can be taken to the lake's south-eastern shore, from where passengers can meet a synchronised bus service to San Martín. The route gives direct access to the Quefíl Circuit trek just on the Argentine side of Paso Hua Hum.

Osorno to San Carlos de Bariloche
This is the most important international route in the Lake District and usually the quickest way across the border. A good surfaced road goes via Entrelagos across the Paso (or Portezuelo) Puyehue and around Lago Nahuel Huapí. In summer, there are quite a number of buses between Bariloche and Osorno, Puerto Montt, Valdivia and even Santiago. The route provides access to walks in both Puyehue and Nahuel Huapí national parks and it offers some very nice scenery.

Petrohué to San Carlos de Bariloche
This is essentially a route designed for tourists, and is slower and more expensive than the main Osorno-Bariloche road.

From Petrohué boats go across Chile's Lago Todos los Santos to Peulla, where a short section of international road leads to Laguna Frías in Argentina. From Puerto Frías another boat is taken to Puerto Alegre on Lago Nahuel Huapí, from where a third ferry can be boarded either to Llao-Llao or to Bariloche. This route offers superb Lake District scenery, and is highly recommended. The whole trip can take up to two days, and can be done as a complete package for around US$45 including meals and overnight accommodation.

Futaleufú to Esquel
This very scenic 75-km road route which starts from the remote village of Futaleufú links the Carretera Austral with the Argentine city of Esquel, which is the gateway to the large Parque Nacional Los Alerces. Colectivos run between Esquel and Futaleufú three times a week. There is moderate traffic along the road during the summer period, but the route is popular with local hitchhikers.

Coyhaique to Río Mayo & Comodoro Rivadavia
The unsurfaced road over the low Paso Coyhaique passes the small reserve of Dos Lagunas. Río Mayo is a remote settlement of roughly 400 people on Argentina's Ruta 40 road. Buses Giobbi runs some three international buses per week in either direction between Coyhaique and Comodoro Rivadavia on the Atlantic coast.

Chile Chico to Los Antiguos & Perito Moreno
This is a more popular route with travellers heading to the Argentinian town of Perito Moreno. The trip involves first taking the ferry across Lago General Carrera from Puerto Ingeniero Ibáñez on the lake's northern shore to the pleasant village of Chile Chico. From Chile Chico a short road route goes via the southern shore of Lago General Carrera (whose name changes to Lago Buenos Aires at the Argentine border) to Los Antiguos. The unbridged Río Jeinimeni must be forded (whether on foot or by 4WD

vehicle), and at times this crossing may be difficult or impossible due to flooding.

Cochrane to Bajo Caracoles
The is the most isolated of the international pass routes and leads through the Valle Chacabuco across Paso Roballos. There is no public transport and traffic is extremely thin, so the route is only suitable for those with their own transport or plenty of supplies, time and patience.

Puerto Natales to Calafate
This route is of key interest to trekkers because it connects these two 'gateway' towns to Torres del Paine and Los Glaciares national parks.

The scenic road across the Paso Baguales has recently been upgraded to allow the establishment of a regular minibus service. Buses Sur runs buses between Puerto Natales and Calafate three times per week from November to March. The fare is about US$40, which for a distance of less than 200 km is grossly overpriced. The route passes the 50-km turnoff road that leads into the Parque Nacional Torres del Paine about halfway. The road has little traffic during the tourist season from December to February, and virtually none outside that time, so hitchhiking carries the risk of a very long wait.

Puerto Natales to Río Turbio & Río Gallegos
This is an uninteresting route but may be your fastest way of getting to Río Gallegos. Workers' buses run roughly hourly across the border to the border town of Río Turbio. The fare is around US$12. About once a month the historic coal trains from Río Turbio to Río Gallegos couple on a passenger car for the benefit of railway enthusiasts.

Punta Arenas to Río Gallegos
Punta Arenas is connected to Río Gallegos by a 260-km surfaced road. The route follows the coast of the Straits of Magellan before heading inland at the border, and passes the road turnoffs to the Laguna Azul

and Pali Aike reserves. There are frequent buses between the two cities.

Puerto Williams to Ushuaia

This roughly 70-km route across the Beagle Channel is the most southerly border crossing possible. There is one weekly tourist boat between Puerto Williams on Navarino Island and Ushuaia on the mainland of Tierra del Fuego. The return fare is around US$15.

Puerto Williams can also be reached by plane or boat from Punta Arenas. Yachts sailing down to Cape Horn and Antarctica are often required to register with authorities at Puerto Williams on the way, and it is often possible to get a ride with one of these vessels.

The Araucanía

The Araucanía extends southwards from the Río Bío Bío to the snows of Volcán Villarrica. Like the Lake District, which shares many of its typical features, the Araucanía is extremely active volcanically, and offers a fascinating variety of natural phenomena such as many thermal springs, volcanoes and mountain lakes. The area is the heartland of the Araucarian (or Mapuche) Indians, who relied heavily on the edible nuts of the Araucaría 'pine' for food. These glorious trees still grow throughout the Araucaría, where they are protected by the region's many national parks and reserves.

Parque Nacional Laguna del Laja

Parque Nacional Laguna del Laja is situated just to the north of the Río Bío Bío, east of the Chilean provincial city of Los Angeles. The park represents the most northerly area covered in this book, and has a hot dry summer climate more like the mountain areas further north.

AROUND VOLCÁN ANTUCO

At the centre of the park is the near-perfect 2979-metre cone of Volcán Antuco, just one of the region's many dormant volcanoes. Modest skiing facilities have been developed on the mountain's unstable northern slopes. Immediately to the south-west is the Sierra Velluda. Towering above the surrounding countryside, this spectacular range rises to 3585 metres and is choked by numerous hanging glaciers and icefalls.

At the eastern foot of Volcán Antuco is Laguna de la Laja, a large highland lake

Araucaria (monkey-puzzle) trees

78

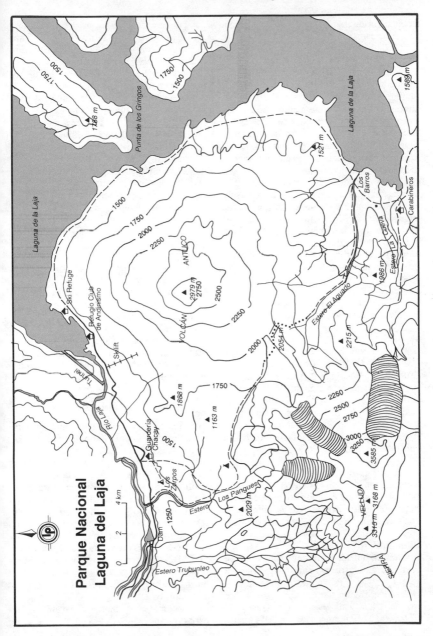

Parque Nacional Laguna del Laja

created during the volcano's 1873 eruption. Thick streams of molten lava blocked the Río Laja, impounding its waters and drowning the valleys upstream. Unfortunately, hydroelectric development has disturbed the laguna's natural shoreline, but the lake's setting amongst lofty peaks still presents a dramatic scene. Because Laguna de la Laja does not have a direct natural outlet, water seeps out through its porous volcanic subsoil. Flowing underground, the river emerges downstream in spectacular waterfalls known locally as *ojos*.

Due to its climate, height and recent volcanic activity, the park is relatively sparsely vegetated, but one feature of its flora is the ciprés de la cordillera (*Austrocedrus chilensis*). This small attractive conifer thrives in the drier alpine conditions, and can be seen on the surrounding mountainsides on the park approach road. In the spring and early summer, attractive hardy wildflowers grow sporadically in the loose volcanic earth. There are also small areas of evergreen coigüe and deciduous ñirre scrub.

Maps

The entire park is covered by one Chilean IGM 1:50,000 sheet, *Laguna de la Laja* (Section G, No 21). Although some higher areas are left uncontoured, this map indicates topographical detail very well. The walking track itself is not indicated and must not be confused with another high altitude traverse route through the Sierra Velluda which this sheet does show.

Days Required

The trek can be done in two very long days, but parties should plan to take at least three days. Volcán Antuco itself can be climbed in one day from the mountain's northern side.

Standard

The trek completely circumnavigates Volcán Antuco, and crosses bare and exposed country of lava flows and loose volcanic earth for virtually the entire distance. The first half of the walk goes from the Guardería Chacay at 1150 metres across a 2054-metre

pass, where deep snow may lie well into January. The route is fairly straightforward but largely unmarked. The long final section is along an easily navigable dirt road. Particularly lower down, fine weather can quickly make the going hot and unpleasant.

Volcán Antuco itself can be climbed from the mountain's northern side by experienced parties. Crampons and ice axe are generally necessary before about mid-January but this equipment is not available for hire at Chacay. The small CONAF museum near the guardería features the park's natural history and is well worth a visit.

The circuit can be walked in either direction, but the recommended way to walk is anticlockwise. The trek is graded easy to moderate. The total walking distance is 40 km.

Accommodation & Supplies

There are two ski lodges beside the road but these are closed in summer. Since there are no refugios for trekkers in the park, the trek cannot be done safely without a tent.

Supplies cannot be bought at Chacay. The nearest stores are in El Abanico and Antuco, but Los Angeles is by far the best option for stocking up.

Access

The trek begins at Chacay, the tiny park administration depot, 90 km by road east of Los Angeles. No public transport exists to the park itself, but there are seven buses daily from Los Angeles via Antuco to the nearby hydroelectric town of El Banico. Buses pass the turnoff to Chacay shortly before they get to El Abanico. From Los Angeles the trip takes about two hours. From the turnoff the remaining 11-km section of road to the Guardería Chacay leads up beside the rapids of the Río Laja and can be walked in three or four hours. There is usually little traffic but during the busy tourist season hitchhiking is a possibility.

A nominal entry charge is payable at the park portería.

Top: Puyehue Plateau, Parque Nacional Puyehue
Bottom: Volcán Casablanca, Parque Nacional Puyehue

Top: Victoria Island, Parque Nacional Nahuel Huapí
Bottom: Lago Triángulo, Parque Nacional Alerce Andino

**Stage 1: Guardería Chacay to
Estero Los Pangues Camp**
(4 km, 2½ to 3½ hours)
The one-hour return sidetrip from the
guardería to the Ojos del Laja is recommended. Follow the road uphill for five
minutes as far as the turnoff to the museum
on your right, and pick up a track opposite
this that leads down to the river. At various
points the subterranean flow of water from
Laguna de la Laja shoots out of the ground
in spectacular waterfalls.

After signing in, follow the path from just
above the guardería due south up the slope
past the clusters of mountain cypresses.
Head up a steep rocky ridge leading to a level
area overlooking the Río Laja after 45
minutes to one hour, where there is a
signposted junction.

The right branch goes to the Meseta de los
Zorpos (shown on IGM maps as Los
Pangues). To get there follow the track down
through light forest to a lovely grassy
meadow set amongst ciprés and coigüe trees.
There are good views across the valley
towards the adjacent rocky range. Just below
the spectacular torrent Estero Los Pangues
washes black volcanic scoria out from the
mountains. This easy return sidetrip takes
from 45 minutes to one hour.

Take the left branch (marked 'Sierra de
Velluda') up over sparsely vegetated ridge
mounds until you come to a lava flow. The
path skirts the edge of the lava, passing interesting tiny islands of quila scrub left
undisturbed in the mass of volcanic rock.
Watch for small cairns leading south-west to
meet the Estero Los Pangues, where another
track comes up the east bank of the stream.

Follow the path 50 metres through an old
cattle pen, and continue quickly upstream for
a further 20 to 30 minutes until you reach a
wide curve of the estero fringed by high
cliffs. Here hanging glaciers spill down from
the abrupt northern slopes of the Sierra
Velluda.

Camp Sites At Chacay there is good
camping by the Río Laja below the Ojos del
Laja, though the recommended camp site

close to the guardería is the Meseta de los
Zorpos. There are semi-sheltered sites near
the ruined corral, and camping further
upstream is more scenic but rather exposed.

**Stage 2: Estero Los Pangues Camp to
Los Barros**
(13 km, 6 to 9 hours)
Head south-west across the scoria towards
the obvious low point between the Sierra
Velluda to your right and the majestic form
of Volcán Antuco. Marked only by occasional cairns, the well-trodden track stays
within earshot of the Estero Los Pangues,
avoiding the vast expanse of broken volcanic
slag.

As you approach the pass, the tiny upper
valley widens. Make your way up left across
steepening loose slopes and continue east
into a bare gully that leads to the col, 2½ to
3½ hours from the Estero Los Pangues
Camp. The pass lies at 2054 metres, and
gives good views of the valley ahead. Due to
its south-eastern aspect the top is liable to be
snowed over and corniced well into January.

Do not descend immediately, but sidle left
200 metres before heading down easily
across snow or loose earth slopes to pick up
a faint trail at the stream-side. If coming from
the other direction, look out for a large cairn
opposite a cascading chasm a way before
you reach the head of the valley. This points
directly to the pass.

Proceed downstream through the sparsely
vegetated Valle El Aguado. The dusty path
follows the northern bank, crossing a
number of small seepage streams that
emerge from the southern slopes of Volcán
Antuco. After three to four hours you come
to a lone araucaria pine, from where it is a
short walk down to meet a small wooden
bridge on the Laguna de la Laja road. Known
as Los Barros, the flat shoreline to the south
is periodically inundated when the level of
the laguna rises.

Camp Sites There is no sheltered camping
along this section until you cross the pass. In
the upper Valle El Aguado occasional camp
sites can be found on the true right (ie south)

bank of the stream amongst ñirre thickets. There is also exposed camping in places around the muddy lake shore.

Stage 3: Los Barros to Guardería Chacay
(23 km, 8 to 12 hours)
This long section is probably best done in two days.

Fill your canteen before leaving the stream, and head off north along the road. Across the turquoise waters of Laguna de la Laja impressive bare eroding crags drop down to the shore. The road dips and rises constantly, passing a boat ramp and the curiously named narrow of Punta de los Gringos after 3½ to 5½ hours. Continue for a further three to 4½ hours through extensive lava fields past two skiing refugios (open only in winter) to the the lake outlet. Here an enormous band of lava dams the Río Laja. The road now descends in several switchbacks to reach the Guardería Chacay, 1½ to two hours on.

Camp Sites Except in the central section, where cliffs front the lake, there is poor to reasonable camping in many places around the shore.

Parque Nacional Conguillío

The national parks Conguillío and Los Paraguas are situated east of the Chilean provincial city of Temuco. Although officially still two separate parks, the area is more or less administered (and shown on maps) as one. The names of both these parks refer to the superb stands of araucaria pines that, together with mixed beech forest, dominate the subalpine slopes of the ranges. *Conguillío*, usually pronounced as 'con-gee-yo', is a Mapuche word meaning 'water with pine nuts'. *Paragua* is the Spanish word for 'umbrella', a reference to the araucaria tree's unusual form. In the past the local Pehuenche

peoples made special trips into these forested highlands to collect its rich supply of *piñónes*, or araucaria nuts, from which they prepared a kind of starchy meal. The area also has rich stands of araucanía rainforest with mixed beech species such as coigüe, raulí, roble and lenga.

The park has a relatively high elevation (lowest point 900 metres), which along with the inland location of the area produces a locally cool climate. Annual precipitation levels are about average for the northern Lake District, ranging from 2000 mm in the valleys to 2500 mm in the higher ranges. Normal mid-winter snow cover is around three metres in the valleys.

In the centre of the park is Volcán Llaima, a periodically active volcano that rises to 3125 metres. Even when seen from the Panamerican Highway some 80 km to the west, Llaima's distinctive form stands out prominently as a key landmark of the region. Recent eruptions have left an extensive volcanic wasteland surrounding the impressive double cone. In places, there are interesting islands of vegetation that were left untouched as the lava flowed around them.

Volcán Llaima's repeated intense volcanic activity has obstructed the nearby Río Traful-Traful to form three lakes around its north and western sides. The youngest of these lakes is Laguna Captrén, which was only created some 30 years ago by a lava flow. The largest lake, Laguna Conguillío, is set in a dramatic landscape bordered on its southern side by a barren expanse of broken volcanic rock. Lava flows descend from the slopes of Volcán Llaima almost to the shoreline. Behind Laguna Conguillío high ranges covered with rich temperate rainforest enclose the lake on three sides. The waters of Laguna Conguillío escape underground through the porous volcanic subsoil.

SIERRA NEVADA
Immediately to the north of Laguna Conguillío lies the Sierra Nevada, an interesting range of rugged glaciated peaks reaching to over 2500 metres. The range itself overlooks the volcanic lakeland

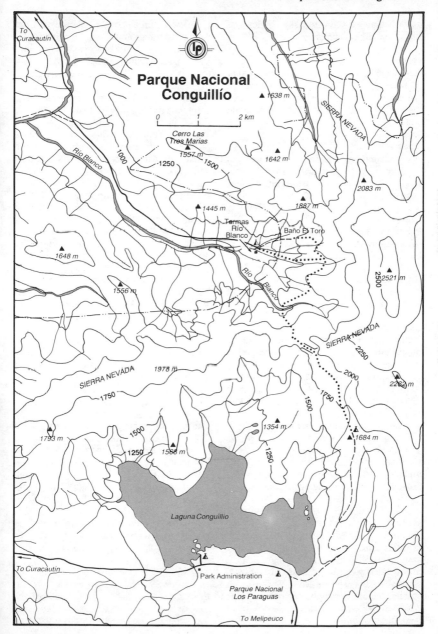

Parque Nacional
Conguillío

described above and offers superb views of the surrounding countryside.

Maps
The IGM 1:50,000 sheet *Volcán Llaima* (Section G, No 75) covers the entire area of the walk. This map does not show most of the hiking route, but is otherwise accurate and very useful.

Days Required
A shorter and simpler version of this trek can be done as a long return day walk from Laguna Conguillío. This trip is best lengthened to a more leisurely two days by making a camp on the lookout ridge above Laguna Conguillío.

For experienced parties the trek can be extended by an additional three to four days by continuing through the Sierra Nevada to the Termas Río Blanco. Unless you get a lift from the termas it will still be necessary to trek out via either the Río Blanco or the road to the main Curacautín-Melipeuco route.

Standard
Due to its cool climate, hiking trips into the parks' mountains are limited to the period from early summer (November/December) to mid-autumn (March). At Guardería Laguna Conguillío there is an excellent visitor's centre with displays on local flora and fauna. A resident ranger is available to advise you on present conditions.

The first part of the route (Stage 1) follows a marked and well-maintained path up a forested ridge into the Sierra Nevada. This track is steep in some places but should not present any routefinding difficulties.

The optional second section (Stage 2) is an unmarked and mostly trackless route leading several km around the northern slopes of the Sierra Nevada. Here the terrain is dissected by several deep gullies where snow may lie well into the summer. Stage 2 follows along the edge of the tree line at 1600 metres and is very exposed to westerlies. It should, therefore, only be attempted in fine weather by strong parties with good routefinding ability.

Volcán Llaima itself is best climbed from the skiing refugio on the mountain's south-western slopes (access via Temuco and Vilcún). Ice axe and crampons are essential, but it is not possible to hire such equipment out at the park.

Stage 1 is rated easy to moderate. The untracked section onward to the Termas Río Blanco is rated difficult. From the start of the trek to the Termas Río Blanco the distance is 14 km. From here the walk out to the Curacautín-Melipeuco road is a further 19 km.

Accommodation & Supplies
Apart from good overnighting facilities at Laguna Conguillío, the park has no refugios open for walkers, and it is essential to carry a tent. On the shores of Laguna Conguillío, not far from the Guardería Laguna Conguillío, is the modern Los Ñirres campground. Los Ñirres has tent sites (US$7) and 10 overnight cabins (US$25) with hot showers. There is another free campground two km east from the guardería on the right.

In season (January/February) a small store by the water at the Los Ñirres campground sells a few simple supplies. Any important provisions should be bought beforehand, preferably in Temuco or Curacautín.

Access
The trek begins at the eastern end of Laguna Conguillío, some 130 km east of Temuco by road via the towns of Cunco and Curacautín. Curacautín is most easily reached from Temuco by five daily buses passing through the villages of Lautaro and Agua Santa. From Victoria (65 km north of Temuco) several buses also run daily to Curacautín via Tres Esquinas. In summer only there are several buses per week from Curacautín to Melipeuco. These pass through the park en route.

If you do the extended version of the trek to Termas Río Blanco there are two alternatives for walking out: you can follow the road or head down the Río Blanco. If you are following the road you come out at the main

Curacautín-Melipueco route after 19 km. From here you can flag down passing buses back to Curacautín. Apart from locals and occasional logging trucks there is little traffic on this road, and hitchhiking is very unreliable. The route via the Río Blanco is a good horse track that services a few small farms in the valley. The track eventually comes out at the surfaced road from Curacautín to Lonquimay and Melipeuco.

Stage 1: Laguna Conguillío to Sierra Nevada
(6 km, 3½ to 5 hours)

There are no streams until you get to the end of this thirsty section, so make sure to fill your water bottle before setting out. From the park information centre head 2½ km east along the road to the south-east corner of Laguna Conguillío, and pick up an old signposted road leading off to the left.

The road soon becomes a path, and heads north-east for 1½ km onto the forested slopes above the Estero El Claro. In wide switchback curves, ascend onto the long and pronounced ridge above the lake. Follow the ridge-line north through beautiful araucaria forest for two to three hours, passing a wooden bench looking out over the lake. The vegetation gradually goes over into ñirre scrub and the ridge becomes narrower and rises more gently. Another 30 to 45 minutes on, you reach the southern end of the Sierra Nevada and the path disappears into the untracked country above the tree line.

Camp Sites After leaving Laguna Conguillío there are no camp sites with water until you reach the Sierra Nevada. Here reasonably sheltered tent sites can be found on the ridge in the scrub a short way below the tree line. Fetch water from the stream that descends the open slopes a short way to the north-west.

Stage 2: Sierra Nevada to Termas Río Blanco
(7½ km, 7 to 11 hours)

This more difficult section should be attempted by experienced parties in fine weather only.

Cross the stream and head onto a low ridge leading north. Follow this up for one km to above the vegetation line, before making your way around north-west across steep loose slopes and large snow patches. An indistinct col in the western range of the Sierra Nevada is reached after 2½ to 3½ hours. From here there are superb views of Laguna Conguillío below and Volcán Llaima immediately opposite, as well as other more distant peaks.

Descend to the Estero El Sapo on loose slopes directly below the col. In early summer the deep upper gully is filled by deep snow, which may allow an easier crossing of the fast-flowing stream. Once across, head up the adjacent steep embankment of loose powdery earth. Move up the bare ridge and continue around to the north below the craggy peaks of the Sierra Nevada until the route drops through grassy slopes to reach another stream, three to four hours from the lookout col.

Cross the stream and climb a short distance around to the right, from where you get a good view down the Valle Río Blanco. Start heading east down the steep slopes via an open strip in the dense scrub. Continue into the forest where vague route markings on trees lead down a steep ridge narrowly separating two streams. Descend for one to 1½ hours before dropping down to the stream on your left. Crossing wherever you have to, follow downstream to a wide alluvial wash above the Río Blanco. To get to the Termas Río Blanco head 300 metres to your right (north) and cross the stream. Look out for route markings taking you back uphill into the forest to an old timber building by a clearing.

The Termas Río Blanco are on private property and the building is normally kept locked, but may be occupied at weekends. Another established thermal spring nearby, the Baños El Toro, is apparently open to the public. The Baños can be reached via a one-km track that heads up the steep slopes of roble forest above the south bank of the Río

Blanco. The head of the enclosed valley is dominated by the crags of the Sierra Nevada rising some 1500 metres above the Río Blanco.

Camp Sites Little sheltered camping is available on the entire traverse route through the Sierra Nevada. There are poor camp sites on rocky and uneven ground around the two larger streams passed on this section. There is good camping at the Termas Río Blanco.

Stage 3: Termas Río Blanco to Curacautín-Melipeuco Road

(19 km, 5 to 7 hours)
Wade the glacial waters of the Río Blanco, and follow the road 7 km down through rich grazing country. An ancient steam-driven sawmill is passed on your left shortly before you reach the Río Negro on a wooden bridge. Pick up a trail leading one km down the north bank of the stream to its confluence with the Río Blanco. From here on the trail is well-transited and easy to follow. The route services many small farms in this pleasant valley, and ends at a surfaced road. This is the main route from Curacautín to Lonquimay and Melipeuco.

Camp Sites Quite good sites can be found in places along the Río Blanco for most of its course. Camp a discreet distance away from farmhouses.

Parque Nacional Huerquehue

Huerquehue is a small national park in the northern Lake District of Chile. Situated 35 km from the popular tourist town of Pucón, the park almost touches the eastern shores of Lago Caburgua.

The region is extremely active volcanically. This is not much in evidence within the park itself, but past eruptions have left a thick layer of volcanic ash covering the ground over much of the Huerquehue area. There are

a surprising number of thermal springs which can be found in the surrounding countryside. The natural undeveloped Termas de Río Blanco can be visited as part of the trek.

Huerquehue (pronounced 'where-kay-way') is a corruption of a Mapuche word, *huilquehue*, meaning 'place of the thrushes'. The name refers to the Chilean zorzal (*Turdus falklandu*), a native bird which inhabits this densely forested area. Among other birdlife in the park is the ubiquitous chucao, whose chuckling calls resound throughout the undergrowth of the forest floor. The area is also home to two woodpecker species, the carpintero negro (*Campephilus magellanicus*) and the carpintero chico (*Dendrocopus lignrius*).

As in much of the northern Lake District, the araucaria or monkey puzzle tree dominates the more elevated areas, often forming pure stands. These beautiful conifers fringe the lake shores and stand out like giant umbrellas on the ridge-tops.

Carpintero Negro

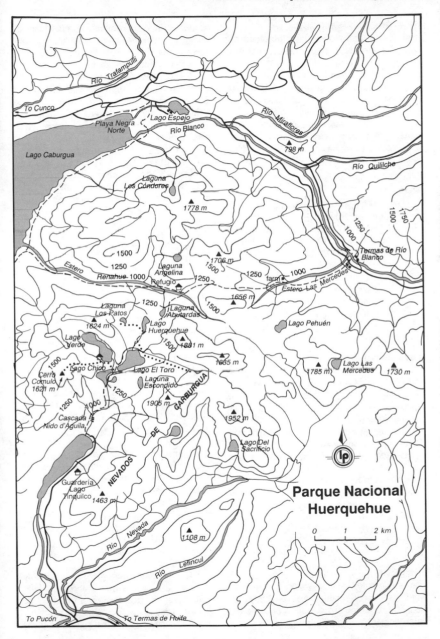

Parque Nacional Huerquehue

CENTRAL HUERQUEQUE

This route combination into the charming central part of the park is an excellent introduction to the Araucanía.

The central part of Huerquehue consists of a tiny subalpine plateau at 1300 metres above sea level. Set amongst dense temperate rainforest are numerous lovely lakes of varying size. Craggy ranges enclose and partly shelter the plateau, making this gentle area a delight to explore. Some of the higher peaks almost reach 2000 metres.

Maps

Almost the entire Huerquehue area is covered by the Chilean IGM 1:50,000 series sheet *Nevados de Caburgua* (Section G, No 96). For general orientation an adjoining sheet, *Lago Caburgua* (Section G, No 95), may also be of value. Although topographically very accurate, these maps do not show the hiking route described below, nor the location of huts etc.

In Pucón it may be possible to borrow and photocopy CONAF maps of Huerquehue.

Days Required

There are a few different ways of doing the trek, so various walking times are given.

A simple return trek from Lago Tinquilco up to the lakes in the central part of the park can be done in just two days. If you intend continuing on as far as the Termas de Río Blanco and coming back the same way to Lago Tinquilco allow at least four to five days.

The trip from the other direction, starting at Playa Negra (Norte) on Lago Caburgua, is best done in four or five days.

Playa Negra (Norte) should not be confused with the other better known Playa Negra at the southern end of the lake.

Standard

The track notes assume you will begin the walk at Lago Tinquilco and backtrack to finish at the same place. This is because the approach from Lago Tinquilco gives direct access to the most interesting central part of the park. Those with more time should consider doing the trek in the other direction from Playa Negra (Norte).

Most of the walk follows well-maintained tracks with intermittent route markings. The 2½-km stretch from Lago Huerquehue to Estero Renahue is, however, less often used, and may be overgrown in places. Here careful navigation is called for.

If you begin the walk from the other direction at Playa Negra (Norte), on Lago Caburgua's northern shore, you must trek up the Río Blanco. Doing the walk this way does not involve backtracking, and would actually be preferable if Playa Negra (Norte) were not such a remote spot. The route from Playa Negra (Norte) follows a good dirt road up the valley until arriving at the Termas de Río Blanco.

The Estero Renahue refugio is a run-down outstation dwelling. It offers primitive shelter only and will scarcely keep you dry in poor weather. There is a small cluster of houses in the vicinity of the Termas de Río Blanco, but no accommodation for walkers. The longer versions of the trek, therefore, can only be done safely by hiking parties who carry their own tents.

The section from Lago Tinquilco to Lago Huerquehue is graded easy. The rest of the trek is easy to moderate. The total distance from Lago Tinquilco to Playa Negra (Norte) is 32 km.

Accommodation & Supplies

There are two refugios within the national park at Estero Renahue and Lago Verde. Refugio Lago Verde is a modern and well-constructed wooden hut with sleeping capacity for six people (plus a few more on the floor) but is generally kept locked when CONAF staff are away. To stay there it is necessary to ask for the key at Guardería Lago Tinquilco.

The most convenient town to base the trek from is Pucón where there is accommodation in all price ranges. Apart from perhaps one or two farms along the Lago Tinquilco road which advertise home-made *kuchen*

(German-style cakes) and other simple refreshments, supplies cannot be bought in the area. The best places to stock up in are Pucón and Villarrica.

Access

The walk starts 35 km from Pucón at the Guardería Lago Tinquilco, which is also the administration and information centre for Parque Nacional Huerquehue. The closest you can get to the park by public transport is Paillaco, situated some seven km before Guardería Tinquilco.

In summer, there are two local buses from Pucón to Paillaco every day. These leave in the early and the late afternoon from the Buses Regionales terminal on Calle Palguín. Also in summer, tour bus operators run day excursions to the Termas de Huife. These buses pass the turnoff to the park and sometimes include a trip to the park as well.

It is also well worth asking at the CONAF office in Pucón (on Calle Fresia, just north of O'Higgins) if you could get a ride out to Huerquehue with one of their vehicles. The park is a popular destination for day-trippers from Pucón, and hitchhiking there is usually a reasonable proposition during the busy holiday period. There is a moderate admission charge payable at the entrance gate to the park. Private vehicles may be left for shorter periods at the Lago Tinquilco guardería, or for a fee, at the small farm at the north-eastern end of Lago Tinquilco.

Trekkers intending to walk in the other direction will have rather more difficulty getting to Playa Negra (Norte). From Temuco two buses daily make the 2½-hour trip out to the small town of Cunco. There a taxi can be chartered to Playa Negra (Norte). The 45-km trip via Lago Colico and Puerto García costs around US$25.

In January youth summer camps are held near Playa Negra (Norte), and during this period you might be able to thumb a ride. From the southern end of Lago Caburgua, where there is a modest tourist development by the white sand beach, it may be possible to hire a boat up to the Playa Negra (Norte).

Stage 1: Guardería Lago Tinquilco to Refugio Lago Verde

(6½ km, 3 to 5 hours)

From the park administration building follow the dirt road around the eastern side of Lago Tinquilco. At the north-eastern corner of the lake this passes a small holiday farm which runs a private carpark for tourists as a sideline. One hour from the guardería, cross a bridge and proceed up the true right (western) bank of the stream through a grassy clearing.

Find the start of the track at the top of this cleared area, and begin an initially gradual climb through the forest. Half an hour up from Lago Tinquilco the gradient steepens, and you pass Cascada Nido d'Águila. This is a lovely waterfall set amongst ferns and moss. Cross a brook coming down from the left out of the forest. The terrain levels out a bit as the path moves around to the east. After 40 to 50 minutes, just before you begin to head more sharply upwards again, a short side-track goes off to the right for five minutes to some tumbling mossy cascades.

The path now swings back to take a northerly direction and begins a one to 1½-hour climb up a steep ridge where switchback curves allow height to be gained steadily. Now and then, where the forest of coigües and mañíos opens, there are some nice views of Lago Tinquilco behind. Soon after the land has flattened out, cross the very small stream just below where it leaves Lago Chico and immediately flows over a high waterfall. Here there is a painted orientation map of the park mounted on a metal sheet beside the trail.

Continue around the soggy east side of Lago Chico for 10 minutes until you come to a signposted fork in the track. To get to the Lago Verde refugio follow the left-hand path for 15 minutes. The modern wooden hut is located near the south-eastern shore of the beautiful elongated Lago Verde. Unless already occupied, it is necessary to collect the key at the Guardería Lago Tinquilco before you ascend. Although the refugio was constructed primarily for use by CONAF personnel, trekkers are generally permitted to stay there. It may be full during the busy summer holiday period but is otherwise normally kept locked.

Sidetrips The delightful central part of Parque Nacional Huerquehue around the three larger lakes makes a nice area to spend a day or so exploring.

Cerro Comulo can be climbed by following a track branching west off the main path about half way between the refugio and Lago Chico. This ascends a mostly gentle ridge through the forest to the summit, but the trail is poorly marked and can be hard to follow (five hours return).

Another trail from Refugio Lago Verde goes north, crossing a ridge and a small stream to the beautiful Laguna Los Patos, but due to vigorous overgrowth may be all but impassable. This tiny lake is perhaps better reached from Lago Huerquehue (see the description which follows after Stage 2). Various anglers' tracks also lead around the shores of Lagos Chico, Verde and El Toro.

Camp Sites The CONAF-operated campground by Lago Tinquilco near the guardería has 10 sites for hire, but you can also camp in the meadows by the stream at the northern end of Lago Tinquilco. Higher up there are many excellent places to pitch tents around the lakes (see the following description). Reasonable spots can be found by the water 200 metres around the northern side of Lago Chico. The west shores of Lago Verde also offer good camping.

Stage 2: Refugio Lago Verde to Refugio Estero Renahue
(5½ km, 3 to 4½ hours)
Head back down to the signposted track intersection and turn left to head over a low rise after which Lago El Toro comes into view. The path moves around the often steep western edge of the lake, passing a small inlet at its north-west corner, and soon comes to a second stream flowing into Lago El Toro at the lake's northern end, one to 1½ hours from Lago Verde.

Unless you want to camp, do not cross.

Pick up a track that leaves the lake shore and begins ascending north a short way from the steam. This track passes through stands of araucarias before it reaches the lovely Lago Huerquehue after 40 to 50 minutes.

Backtrack about 100 metres to just below the lake where an indistinct route heads off east alongside a boggy strip for a few minutes. This first moves up for 25 minutes onto a low watershed ridge and then gradually swings around to take a north-easterly direction. Descend the gentle slopes leading down through the forest into a tiny valley to reach Laguna Abutardas after half an hour.

The tiny lake is rounded via its eastern side. Keeping to the right of the stream, the route emerges from the forest shortly after you leave the lake and begins descending a steep ridge that leads into the valley of the Estero Renahue. In places vigorous bamboo regrowth obscures the way and this may make the going harder.

About two thirds of the way down, the route starts moving off to the right to head down across the slope towards the junction of two streams below.

If coming from the other direction, pick up the track to Lago Abutardas about 200 metres downstream from here. It is also possible to join the route by heading 600 metres down the left (ie south) bank and then following the stream up.

Cross 150 metres above where the two arms flow together to form Estero Renahue. Located between these, one to 1½ hours from Lago Abutardas, is the refugio. Constructed in the traditional split-log style so common in southern Chile, the hut stands in a lovely spot on lush natural lawns surrounded by craggy ridges.

From here it is possible to trek down the Estero Renahue and along the shores of Lago Caburgua to Playa Negra at the lake's southern end, a trip taking at least two days.

Sidetrips It is possible to reach the tiny Laguna Los Patos by following a poor route from Lago Huerquehue. From about halfway along the west side of the lake head due west for 800 metres. There is also good camping in the forest around the lake.

Camp Sites Camping is recommended at any of the four lakes mentioned in this section, as well as by the Estero Renahue refugio. The narrow southern end of Lago El Toro offers very good camp sites by the sandy shores below the track. At Lago El Toro's northern end, cross the inlet stream to some idyllic camp sites on a tiny peninsula of araucarias. The three lakes Huerquehue, Los Patos and Abutardas also offer very good camping virtually anywhere around their shores.

Stage 3: Refugio Estero Renahue to Termas de Río Blanco
(7 km, 4 to 5½ hours)
Linking Lago Caburgua with the Río Blanco, a pronounced trail comes up the valley, passing near the hut on its way. Follow this path over to meet the other branch of the stream, and heading up its southern side cross the slopes made bare through fire. The gradient steepens a bit as you re-enter the forest after 30 minutes. Now moving almost directly eastwards, continue through another burnt-out area of forest for a further 45 minutes to 1¼ hours. Soon after this the steep terrain eases off as you near the long narrow saddle.

Follow occasional blazings on trunks as you pass through beautiful stands of mature rainforest. Here the near absence of underbrush produces a open 'park' landscape. Keeping well to the southern (right) side of the pass, contour about one km. In places the volcanic ash subsoil has eroded so quickly that the track resembles a deep trench.

Begin descending a broad ridge. Further down there are more patches of burnt forest, and you start to get a better view of the tiny valley of the Estero Las Mercedes below. Where this meets another brook coming down from your right, cross the left branch and proceed along the bank for 20 minutes to a farmhouse.

A wide path leads down to the water. Wade the very shallow stream and head out across grassy slopes for 30 minutes to where the forest fringes the cleared pastures. Continue on the right bank of the estero, crossing a brook on a bridge made of small logs. The path drops down gently through rich rainforest and crosses Río Blanco road, which is then followed down to the river itself.

The Termas de Río Blanco are located on the north bank of the stream immediately opposite the normal camping area, which is about 350 metres above its confluence with the Estero Las Mercedes. The Termas de Río Blanco are reached via a suspension bridge a few minutes downstream from the campground. Totally undeveloped and rather inconspicuous, they consist of a few simple pools of varying warmth dug out of the earth a few metres from the icy waters of the Río Blanco. The locals use the thermal springs regularly and can point them out to you.

Camp Sites Between Refugio Estero Renahue and the Río Blanco there are no especially suitable sites, and camping is only recommended at the Termas de Río Blanco.

Stage 4A: Playa Negra (Norte) to Lago Espejo
(4 km, 2 hours)
Stage 4A and Stage 4B are for trekkers starting out at Lago Caburgua and doing the walk in the opposite direction to that described in the rest of the track notes. Almost the entire stretch follows unsurfaced roads, but there is not much traffic.

Playa Negra (Norte) is situated about 1½ km south of the most northerly tip of Lago Caburgua. If you arrive by vehicle, follow a road down 700 metres past neglected orchards to the lakeside. In summer the area is popular with holiday-makers, who often camp right on the shore itself. Typically for much of the Chilean Lake District, the beach is composed of black volcanic sand.

Behind the beach, pick up a shortcut track heading east above the lake. This can be followed for one to 1½ hours as it moves away from the shore to cross swampy flats shortly before coming out at the road. Continue on for a further 20 minutes to the lovely

Lago Espejo, passing a picturesque homestead on the adjacent shore.

Camp Sites Playa Negra (Norte) can be a rather crowded place in the holiday season, but offers pleasant camping. More secluded spots can be found by the main inlet stream to Lago Espejo, about three-quarters of the way around the lake's shore.

Stage 4B: Lago Espejo to Termas de Río Blanco
(9 km, 5 to 7½ hours)
There are many small farms within the catchment area of the Río Blanco. Consequently the major streams along this route may be contaminated and water should be sterilised before drinking.

Leave Lago Espejo and proceed for 20 minutes to where the Río Blanco comes into view. Staying on the northern bank of the river, follow the road upstream for a further 4½ km. After 45 minutes to 1¼ hours you come to a major sidestream, the Río Miraflores.

Occasional farmlets are passed, mostly on the opposite side of the river. The vegetation in virtually all of the lower valley has been devastated by fire. The subsequent regeneration has left impenetrable thickets of quila and other quick-growing species covering the steep hillsides. After 1½ to 2½ hours, at a point where the valley begins to narrow, the road comes to the Río Quililche. This is a second large sidestream flowing into the Río Blanco from the north.

Here you come to two bridges. To the right a wooden bridge crosses the Río Blanco; straight ahead another spans the Río Quililche. As the two alternatives come together further upstream, either way may be taken. However, the going is probably easier if you continue along the north side of the Río Blanco for 1½ km to where yet another bridge crosses. Once on the south bank of the river continue for 1½ to 2½ hours below the steep slopes, crossing the Estero Los Mercedes immediately before you arrive at the Termas de Río Blanco.

Camp Sites The campground adjacent to the Termas de Río Blanco offers excellent camping and trekkers should aim to stop here. Acceptable spots can also be found sporadically by the river along the lower section of the Río Blanco road. Dense vegetation often blocks access to the stream. Once past Río Quililche the valley closes considerably and camping places are harder to find.

Parque Nacional Villarrica

The oldest national park in Chile (created in 1925), the 610-sq-km Parque Nacional Villarrica lies near Pucón, the popular Chilean tourist town on the shores of Lago Villarrica. The park stretches along the line of an interesting volcanic range south-east from Volcán Villarrica to Volcán Lanín on the Argentine border. Parque Nacional Villarrica is essentially a highland range of volcanic origin, and its lowest point is around 900 metres above sea level.

The major attraction and most obvious feature of the park is Volcán Villarrica. This beautiful mountain has a classic volcanic cone, and at 2847 metres towers over the surrounding countryside. Despite its continuing activity, Villarrica is the most climbed peak is southern Chile.

Volcán Villarrica has erupted repeatedly during the last century. The most recent major eruptions were in 1971 and 1984. The first of these two eruptions destroyed the small township of Coñaripe and only just spared Pucón. The volcano puts out a trail of smoke visible from all over the northern Lake District and, at night, the summit has an eerie glowing orange halo.

The slopes of Villarrica are covered by numerous recent and older lava flows. These show the fascinating battle of natural forces, as the local vegetation struggles to survive against recurring intense volcanic activity. Volcán Villarrica is being developed into one of Chile's premier ski resorts. Several new chairlifts are being installed, and the Refugio Villarrica has been renovated.

To the south-east in the centre of the park around the extinct Volcán Quetrupillán lies an interesting volcanic plateau rising above the tree line. Volcán Quetrupillán exploded to create its now wide and open form, reflected in its Mapuche name which means 'small volcano'. A number of attractive alpine lakes lie within this stark lunar landscape of lava flows, scoria rock and pumice. Lovely virgin Valdivian forests of araucaria and mixed southern beech cover the lower country up to 1600 metres.

AROUND VOLCÁN VILLARRICA

This round-the-mountain trek semi-circumnavigates the conical Volcán Villarrica. The ascent of Volcán Villarrica itself is an unforgettable experience, and can easily be done on your first day.

Maps

One Chilean IGM sheet scaled at 1:50,000 covers the entire walk: *Pucón* (Section G, No 104). Unfortunately the summit of Volcán Villarrica is left uncontoured, and the map does not indicate the track or other important features such as skilifts and refugios. Certain areas covered by lava flows are inaccurately depicted. Two neighbouring sheets, *Villarrica* (Section G, No 103) and *Liquiñe* (Section G, No 113), may be useful for additional orientation.

CONAF produces a single-sheet map of the park showing trekking routes. Although not freely available, you can look at this map in the CONAF office in Pucón on Calle Fresia.

Days Required

If you do the ascent of Volcán Villarrica, allow at least four full days to complete the trek. Slower parties will require at least one day more.

The trek can be combined with the Villarrica Traverse, increasing the walking time by a further four or five days.

Standard

The route follows a rough track through difficult volcanic terrain just above the tree line. Recent lava flows and fields of broken scoria often make the going strenuous. In the central section of the trek, the track all but disappears and you must find your own way across the open sandy slopes. Except for the final stage, the entire walk is very exposed to the elements. The route is fairly straightforward, and serious navigation is not called for.

Unless you take skis, the trek is best done from early November and early May. Early in the season, however, snow may still cover large areas of the route, and during the early summer some of the larger streams will require careful wading. Summer weather (December to February) can be surprisingly hot. The ground is always porous and well drained, and finding water can be difficult as many streams flow underground lower down. Many of the smaller meltwater streams stop running overnight. If you camp by small streams be sure to collect water for the next day before retiring. Keep your water bottles full for the long and thirsty sections between streams.

The best way to do the walk is probably anticlockwise. This allows you the highly recommended option of climbing Volcán Villarrica the day before setting out. Unless you have some experience in easy to moderate snow and ice climbing, the climb is best done with a guided party from one of the several outdoor tourist operators in Pucón. In addition to well-insulated boots, crampons and ice axe are necessary to make the ascent. This equipment is of no use on the trek itself, and guided parties should leave hired climbing gear with the mountain guide after descending in order to avoid returning to Pucón.

The volcano continuously emits sulphur dioxide and other noxious gases. Near the crater's inner rim be careful to consider sudden wind changes. Lemon juice squeezed into a handkerchief held over the face makes breathing the fumes more bearable (but only slightly).

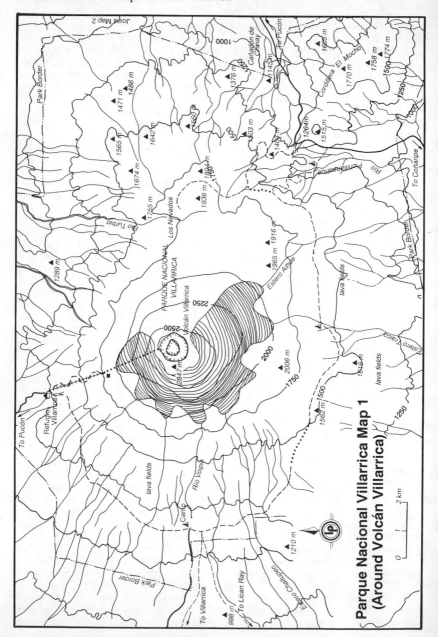

Parque Nacional Villarrica Map 1
(Around Volcán Villarrica)

The trek and climb are both rated moderate. The total distance of the trek is 39 km.

Accommodation & Supplies
There are only two refugios along the route, so the trek cannot be done without a tent. The Refugio Villarrica is located at the start of the trek on the volcano's lower slopes below the skilifts. Refugio Villarrica is a large building that caters mainly for skiers in winter. The Refugio Chinay is situated on the Coñaripe-Palguín road near the end of the walk, and is a small wooden building with bunk space for two people. Also near the end of the trek is the Termas de Palguín hostería, where there is mid-range accommodation with all meals (US$20 per night). There are no washing facilities at the Termas de Palguín, apart from the mineral springs themselves.

Most trekkers visiting Parque Nacional Villarrica will base themselves in Pucón or the town of Villarrica. All necessary supplies can be bought there.

Access
The trek begins at the carpark below Refugio Villarrica, some 12 km from Pucón. No public transport exists, but taxis can be hired out to the park for around US$15 one way. Several local outdoor tourist companies organise guided ascents of Volcán Villarrica. In the summer season a number of guided parties may do the climb each day. The full cost is about US$20, which includes transport to and from the mountain. You can walk to the start of the trek in three to four hours. Hitchhiking is a reasonable prospect whenever tourist traffic can be expected.

The trek ends at Palguín-Coñaripe road. As no public transport exists from here you will probably have to walk at least as far as the Termas de Palguín. For this reason the long final section to Palguín Bajo (on the road to Puesco) is also included in the track notes. There is some tourist traffic to the Termas de Palguín from Pucón, and you may be able to get a ride.

A nominal fee is charged at the portería for entry to the park.

Stage 1A: Ascent of Villarrica
(10 km return, 6 to 9 hours return)

The ascent of Volcán Villarrica is highly recommended. Although technically very straightforward, the climb requires good fitness. Crampons, ice axe and stout footwear are essential. Inexperienced climbers should make the ascent with one of the many local mountain guides. Do not attempt the climb in poor weather.

Follow the winding road up past the Refugio Villarrica to the bottom of the skilift that goes up the volcano's lower slopes. A well-trodden path leads up beside the line of steel poles. After climbing through unstable volcanic sand for one to two hours you reach the end station of the lift, situated just on the permanent snowline.

Make your way directly upwards (or slightly east of south) over a wide sloping névé. Unless there has been a recent heavy snowfall or you are doing the ascent out of season, the tracks left by other climbing parties are usually easily followed. The route crosses the glacier where there are no crevasses, and should be kept to as closely as possible. After midday the snow is likely to be soft and slushy, making the going very tiring. Climb a final steep icy section just before you arrive at the crater rim, three to five hours from the upper skilift station. Approach the rim cautiously to avoid being overcome by the acrid fumes.

Pudú

Inside the crater molten magma boils out of openings in the volcano's core. During occasional periods of increased activity, red-hot lava may even spurt up to near the rim. To get a good look into the crater, head down left to a kind of saddle and ease forward carefully towards the edge. From the summit there are superb views of virtually every major peak in the northern Lake District.

Return via the same route only. The descent is an almost unbroken glissade and scree slide, and should be more rapid (and enjoyable) than the climb.

Stage 1B: Refugio Villarrica to Estero Voipir

(9 km, 6 to 8 hours)
Pick up the unsignposted track 200 metres above the refugio. Construction of new skiing facilities has disturbed the first section of the track, which constantly crosses a newly-built road.

Where the road ends, head south-west through areas of alpine grassland and barren slopes below the snow-capped summit. Marked only by sporadic cairns, the track skirts the regenerating tree line of mainly ñirre scrub. Make your way across several lava flows of black rock and numerous streambeds (mostly dry). Difficult broken terrain makes progress slow. The beautiful Lago Calafquén comes gradually into view as you move around into a southerly direction. The track finally dips down into pleasant lenga forest to reach the small Estero Voipir a short way on.

Camp Sites There is an official campground inside the park by the road to Refugio Villarrica. Camping is allowed by the refugio, but running water may be difficult to find. A better spot to camp is further up the road just off to the right above a small stream (boil the water). Semi-sheltered camp sites can be found along much of the route wherever streams are flowing (water may have to be fetched from higher up the slope). Estero Voipir is a small but permanently running stream and makes a good camp site.

Stage 2: Estero Voipir to Estero Traico

(10 km, 4½ to 7 hours)
Wade the small stream and after filling up your canteen continue around through the forest. After 30 to 40 minutes you reach a signposted track junction. The right branch leads down to Villarrica, so proceed left. A short way on you come to a second fork where a route down to Lican Ray departs. The track now ascends steadily south-east to reach the Estero Challupen. Fill up on water here as all the streams ahead are subterranean until you get to Estero Traico.

Cross the stony river wash and head 200 metres upstream to where the path climbs the steep and loose river embankment on your right. There are spectacular views of the western side of Volcán Villarrica, from which numerous glaciers descend. Continue through beautiful mixed araucaria and lenga forest for one to 1½ hours. The track rises once again, following a course above the upper limit of the trees. To the distant south, the snows of Volcán Choshuenco come into view. Numerous crisscrossing animal trails make the track itself harder to follow, but routefinding is relatively simple due to the open country.

Make your way through a series of small canyons to reach another lava flow. Sidle around above this, and move up steadily left to where the vegetation grows only sporadically. The majestic Volcán Lanín now dominates the horizon to the south-east. Head across the bare terrain of black volcanic grit to pass through the obvious saddle between a bald red knoll on the right and a rocky glaciated outcrop much higher up. The track becomes more distinct here, and is followed east to reach yet another major lava field of apparently recent origin.

There is no definite route leading through this one km wide band of volcanic rock. The best place to cross seems to be higher up, where the lava is less broken and there are more open areas. Make for the grassy ridge to the left of some stands of araucarias. The going is strenuous and very hot in sunny weather, but the different rock shapes formed during cooling are very interesting. After 45

Top: Lago Cucao, Parque Nacional Chiloé
Bottom: Local house, Reserva Nacional Río Simpson

Top: Cordillera Castillo, Reserva Nacional Cerro Castillo
Bottom: Upper Valle Parada, Reserva Nacional Cerro Castillo

minutes to one hour you arrive at the Estero Traico. Early in the season this milky swift-flowing stream may be tricky to cross.

Camp Sites After leaving Estero Challupen, there is little suitable camping along the route until you get to the Estero Traico. There are nice semi-sheltered camp sites above the Estero Traico on grassy terraces on the western side of the stream. Firewood is very scarce.

Stage 3: Estero Traico to Río Pichillaneahue Camp
(8 km, 3 to 5 hours)
Rejoin the route at the grassy ridge on the other side of the stream. Keep to the lava side for some 300 metres before heading down to the right onto a grassy flat. Cross a dry creek bed, where the forest line ends sharply in an almost pure stand of araucaria trees. Move across the sparse grass plain towards the base of the bare red ridge ahead. After 1½ to two hours you reach another permanent stream of obvious glacial origin, the Estero Aihue.

Wade the stream and climb the loose eroding embankment. The way now becomes better defined, following a course 200 metres from the tree line. Ease gradually around to the north through pleasant isolated clusters of araucarias. A short way on, the path moves down into the forest, passing through a dead forest of short white trunks. A cut and well-graded track rapidly descends in steep zig-zags to arrive at the banks of the Río Pichillaneahue, 1½ to 2½ hours after leaving the Estero Aihue.

Camp Sites The Río Pichillaneahue is the recommended camp site. Here many excellent spots exist within the beech and araucaria forest, mainly on the true left bank of the river. There is also reasonable camping along the banks of the Estero Aihue, but sites are rather exposed and there is no firewood. Another good camp site can be found at a small stream near a tiny stand of araucarias, 30 to 45 minutes on from the Estero Aihue.

Stage 4: Río Pichillaneahue to Termas de Palguín
(12 km, 4½ to 6½ hours)
Although there is no bridge, the Río Pichillaneahue can be forded without major difficulty. Follow the path downstream along the east bank for one km. Climb left onto a low ridge before dropping down to reach the Palguín-Coñaripe road. If walking from the other direction, look out for the signposted track on your right after descending one to 1½ hours.

Continue left up through the forest. The road soon begins climbing steeply in a series of switchbacks that lead up to a pass in the range at 1264 metres. From here a path signposted 'Nevados' leads up to a plateau area on the north-eastern side of Volcán Villarrica.

The road descends into the Cañadón de Chinay in more sharp curves, and passes the Refugio Chinay 2½ to 3½ hours from the Río Pichillaneahue. The rustic wooden refugio is situated beside an attractive meadow, and has bunk space for two people. Follow the road down past the Guardería Chinay on the park boundary to arrive at the Termas de Palguín after a further two to three hours. The Termas de Palguín hotel offers reasonably priced accommodation, but apart from the mineral springs there are no bathing facilities. Meals and light refreshments are available.

The road below the Termas de Palguín is noticeably better maintained. A two-km return sidetrip can be made to a waterfall, the Salto El León, via a signposted turnoff 15 to 20 minutes down from the termas. The road down the valley is fringed by lovely mixed beech forest and passes many farms to arrive at Palguín Bajo three to four hours on. From here there are local buses roughly hourly to Pucón.

Camp Sites There is excellent camping around the Refugio Chinay. No other camp sites are recommended.

VILLARRICA TRAVERSE
This superb high-level route follows the

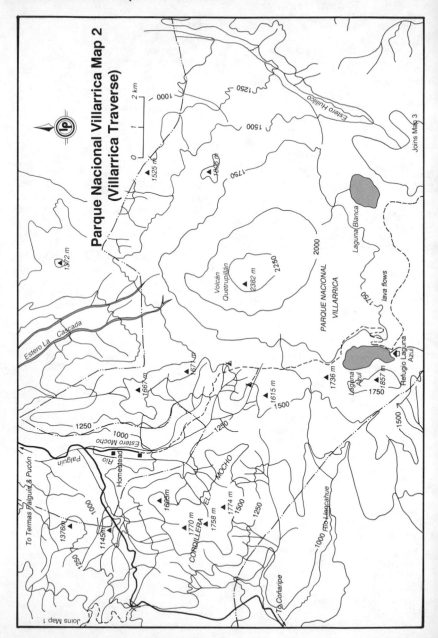

Parque Nacional Villarrica Map 2
(Villarrica Traverse)

broad range extending south-east from Volcán Villarrica towards Volcán Lanín, and passes through country exhibiting many of the park's interesting features. In its central area the range forms a broad volcanic plateau intersected by small calderas and lava flows. The altitude of the plateau varies from about 1700 to 2000 metres, and its rocky treeless landscape is fringed by rainforests enriched by beautiful stands of araucarias. The trek offers continually changing panoramas of the surrounding countryside of the northern Lake District.

Maps
Three 1:50,000 Chilean IGM sheets cover the area of the park: *Pucón* (Section G, No 104), *Curarrhue* (Section G, No 105), *Liquiñe* (Section G, No 113) and *Paimun* (Section G, No 114). These maps do not show the track or Laguna Blanca, but are otherwise topographically accurate. Unfortunately *Paimun* had still not been printed at the time of writing.

Days Required
The walk can be done in a leisurely four or five days. An additional day for sidetrips or rests is time well spent. It is possible to combine the Villarrica Traverse with the Around Volcán Villarrica trek, increasing the walking time by a further three or four days.

Standard
The trek follows a relatively good path for almost the entire distance. In the central section high and very exposed terrain well above the tree line must be crossed. Here deep winter snow remains well into November, and bad weather or low cloud can quickly move in to make navigation difficult.

The range's aspect tends to catch passing showers and summer thunderstorms and good rainwear is important. The route is marked by paint on rocks and trees, and on the higher slopes with wooden or bamboo stakes. Strong winds and deep snow tend to push over the marker stakes – re-erect them where necessary.

The recommended way to do the trek is

east to west, as the route is generally easier to follow in this direction. However, doing the walk in this direction involves slightly more climbing (unless you have transport to the Termas de Palguín), and will probably mean having your gear searched by the customs in Puesco.

There are resident guardaparques at the Guardería Chinay, near the beginning of the walk, and at Puesco. Those who intend to return to Pucón are advised to leave all details at the CONAF office there.

The Villarrica Traverse is graded moderate. The total distance is 41 km.

Accommodation & Supplies
There is only one refugio along this route. This is the Refugio Laguna Azul, an airy wooden shack that offers valuable but limited protection. A sturdy mountain tent is thus essential. At the start of the trek is the Termas de Palguín hostería, where there is mid-range accommodation with all meals (US$20 per night). There are no washing facilities at the termas, apart from the mineral springs themselves.

Most trekkers visiting Parque Nacional Villarrica will base themselves in Pucón or the town of Villarrica. All necessary supplies can be bought there.

Access
The trek begins at the Termas de Palguín, some 12 km from Palguín Bajo on the road to Coñaripe. In season there are organised tours out to the Termas de Palguín from Pucón approximately weekly. The fare by taxi from Pucón is around US$20. Regular local buses to Curarrehue and Puesco go past the turnoff at Palguín Bajo, from where the pleasant walk up to the Termas can be made in three to four hours.

It is also possible to do the trek after crossing from Argentina. There are eight buses per week from San Martín de los Andes and Junín de los Andes, normally passing the Termas de Palguín turnoff in mid-afternoon. Make sure the driver knows where you want to get off. Remember that the importation of most raw agricultural products into Chile is strictly prohibited, so if coming from Argentina be sure to carry only processed and packaged foodstuffs for the walk.

The trek ends at Puesco on the international road across Paso Mamuil Malal (or Tromen). There is a border post in the village, where you should present your papers after finishing the walk. From Puesco there is one local bus to Pucón daily at around 2 pm. You can also normally pick up a bus coming from Argentina, but it is not permitted to join a bus heading across the frontier unless you have already booked and are on the passenger list.

Stage 1: Termas de Palguín to Upper Mocho Camp
(10 km, 5 to 7 hours)
From the termas, walk one to 1½ hours uphill to a fork in the road, recognisable by the signpost 'Guardería 3 km'. Take the left branch which soon crosses the Río Palguín on a wooden bridge, and follow upstream along the banks of the Estero Mocho. Then continue past a stately homestead on your right to reach a cottage on the edge of a burnt clearing.

Leave the road and pick up a path a short way behind the cottage. This leads into the forest below fire-charred slopes. Ignoring numerous diverging tracks created by timber getters, stay close to the stream until you come to some red-painted blazings on trees indicating the correct route. The path climbs away from the Estero Mocho to a small indistinct ridge. Cross a tiny stream (the last running water until you reach the Upper Mocho Camp), and sidle left through lichen-covered araucaria forest to meet a wide spur. The ascent alternates between strenuous steep sections and gentle rises, and progress is good. The track arrives at some grassy camp sites 2½ to 3½ hours after beginning the climb. The Upper Mocho Camp is situated at around 1600 metres where several streamlets converge just below the tree line.

Camp Sites There are few reasonable camp sites along this section until you get to the tiny stream 30 to 45 minutes up from Estero Mocho. The Upper Mocho Camp is the most recommended spot.

Stage 2: Upper Mocho Camp to Refugio Laguna Azul
(7 km, 3 to 4 hours)
Head up to the grassy slopes. The magnificent puffing summit of Volcán Villarrica dominates the skyline to the north-west. Follow a line of cairns roughly south, passing an interesting round bluff on your right. The path makes its way over the open volcanic plateau to cross a westwards-flowing stream descending from the exploded crater of Volcán Quetrupillán.

Do not take the track leading down the left bank of the stream (this connects with an old trail that goes down the Río Llancahue). The route ahead is indicated by conspicuous red and yellow paint markings leading up the slope. The path heads around to the right beside a dry stream bed to pass through a small gap after 1½ to two hours. Although not quite visible, Laguna Azul lies in the deep trough just below.

Drop down the sandy slopes and begin heading south-east, some way to the left of the abrupt cliffline past large boulders. The track avoids the difficult terrain by moving left over a bare ridge to a sizable lava field, before turning right to descend in zig-zags to the southern shore of Laguna Azul. Continue around tiny sand beaches and cross the lake outlet on stepping stones. The revegetating rock on the left is part of the lava flow which created the lake by blocking off the stream.

The Refugio Laguna Azul is situated a few minutes' walk up the grassy slopes overlooking the picturesque lake. Another access track comes up out of the forest to the saddle below the refugio. The roughly 2½ by four metre shelter is well ventilated by gaps between the halved logs of its walls, and although it lacks a chimney a fire can be lit inside.

Refugio Laguna Azul makes a good base to climb Volcán Quetrupillán. This can be done by returning to the highest point of the track above the lake, and following scoria

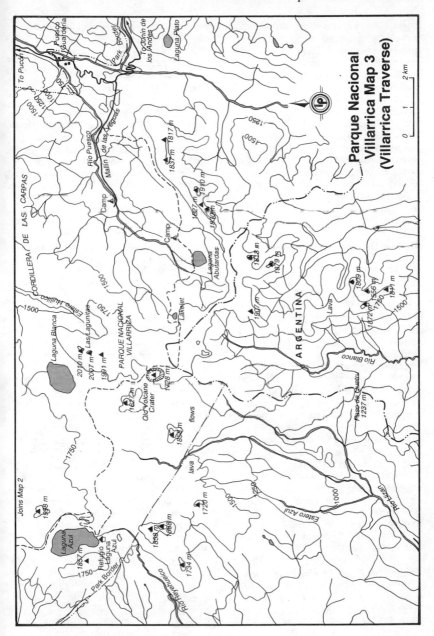

Parque Nacional Villarrica Map 3 (Villarrica Traverse)

ridges up to the volcano's rim at around 2000 metres. The crater has a permanent filling of glacial ice and snow. There are good views towards the south and south-east. This side-trip is recommended only to experienced parties.

Camp Sites The only good camping before Refugio Laguna Azul is well off the main path via the track down the stream you cross just before beginning the ascent to the small gap. Here sheltered camp sites can be found on a lovely clearing amongst stands of araucaria trees. Camping around the Refugio Laguna Azul is very scenic, though rather unsheltered. Most trekkers probably set up their tent inside the refugio.

Stage 3: Refugio Laguna Azul to Laguna Blanca
(6½ km, 3 to 4 hours)
Head back across the outlet stream to the lava field. Walk 100 metres alongside this until stake markers lead via a simple route through the stabilising volcanic rubble. Continue upwards beside the broken black rock to a second flow of lava. Make your way across this in the same fashion.

Climb onto the low ridge on the other side. The ridge can be followed up and around to the right to where a wide expanse of glacial-volcanic debris appears. Avoid this area by keeping to the right and move around the bare slopes to reach a small stream after two to three hours. Head 500 metres up across the silt wash to a large circular yellow and red paint marking and pick up the track again. This leads north-east over sandy hills into the undrained basin in which Laguna Blanca lies, just above 1600 metres. To get to the lake shore, leave the track and cross the rocky barren plain on your left. The lake is set in a dramatically desolate position below Volcán Quetrupillán.

Camp Sites Before Laguna Blanca there are no camp sites at all. The lake itself offers poor exposed camping only. A few large boulders provide some shelter, and previous campers have built a makeshift rock wall to protect their tents. There is no firewood (and don't burn marker stakes).

Stage 4: Laguna Blanca to Laguna Abutardas
(8 km, 3½ to 5½ hours)
Return to the path and walk a short way east into a tiny dry valley. The track follows the winding valley roughly south to reach a lava flow after 45 minutes to one hour. Although many marker stakes have fallen over, these can be followed around a low ridge forming the rim of a very small crater on your right.

Continue 20 to 30 minutes south, then swing around the bare slopes and head due east. Volcán Lanín constantly juts up in the background as you traverse above small valleys on the east of the continental divide. Drop down to a small stream wash and move diagonally left up to a tiny col. From here the path zig-zags down into a gully full of round lava boulders and heads down the left side. The gully soon opens out, leading down to the vegetation line past a marshy pond on the right after two to three hours. Across to the north-west is the interesting Cordillera de las Carpas, named for the peaks' resemblance to the original tent form.

A low cliff separates this valley head from the forested stream below. Look for the path on the left side, and climb down easily through the rocks. Make your way to the right below the cliffline past several waterfalls. The path heads through scattered ñirre scrub and soon gains the broad ridge separating two branches of the upper Río Puesco. From here you can see Laguna Abutardas in the valley on the right.

Follow the ridge down for 250 metres, before picking up a well-cut track that descends steeply through the forest to the open spongy meadow on the lake's north-western side. The charming Laguna Abutardas lies at around 1450 metres and is enclosed by ranges on either side. To reach the forested lakeside cross the outlet stream.

Camp Sites The generally high exposed terrain and lack of water makes camping along all but the last part of this stage inadvisable. At Laguna Abutardas nice camp sites can be found at the edge of the forest a short distance down the outlet stream, or on drier areas around the lake shore.

Stage 5: Laguna Abutardas to Puesco
(9 km, 6 to 9 hours)
Pick up the track near where the outlet stream leaves Laguna Abutardas. The path rounds the lake's forested northern shore, and moves down gently through clumps of bamboo to reach a small stream after 30 to 40 minutes. Head a short way up right to a long strip of boggy grassland interspersed with ñirre scrub. Make your way 250 metres diagonally across the clearing to some red-painted tree blazings indicating where the path re-enters the forest.

Follow the gradually descending path onto the forested slopes on the right side of the valley. The track passes through an old wooden gate after 1½ to 2½ hours, just before it climbs slightly to a lookout above the Río Puesco. From here drop down steadily north towards the river, coming out at a disused vehicle track after 45 minutes to one hour. If coming from the other direction, look out for a roundish rock outcrop on your left 150 metres on from a stream bridge, 1½ to two hours up from the international road.

Turn right along the old road and continue through abandoned farmland. The road first descends a way in steep switchbacks, then follows south-east close to the 1000-metre contour line to reach the international road after one to 1½ hours. Head left downhill in sharp curves to arrive at Puesco village after another 45 minutes to one hour. From Puesco, walk up the road for one to 1½ hours. Red-painted tree blazings indicate the track on your right, just above the sign 'Precaución Pendiente Fuerte'. Present yourself at the aduana office and explain that you are not coming from Argentina. From Puesco there is one local daily bus to Pucón leaving at around 2 pm. More frequent buses coming from Argentina can also take you to either Curarrehue or Pucón.

Camp Sites There are good camp sites near the stream 30 to 40 minutes below Laguna Abutardas. After that there is little camping until you get to the old Río Puesco road. Continue right along the road to find various camp sites beside small streams. Some other very nice riverside sites amongst stands of araucarias can be reached by walking west (ie left) along the road for 30 to 40 minutes. At Puesco ask permission to camp by the stream near the Carabineros building.

Other Treks in the Araucanía

PARQUE NACIONAL NAHUEL BUTA – CHILE
(1 to 3 days)
Nahuel Buta is located in the Coast Range (Cordillera de la Costa) 35 km west of Angol and was established to protect one of the last great araucaria forests of the Chilean Araucanía. The park is fairly small but some 20 km of walking tracks make overnight trips a possibility.

Maps
The Chilean IGM 1:50,000 sheets *Elicura*, (Section G, No 36) and *Los Sauces* (Section G, No 37) cover most of the park.

Access
From Angol by daily bus.

PARQUE NACIONAL TOLHUACA – CHILE
(1 to 2 days)
Tolhuaca is situated 44 km north of Curacautín in the northern Araucanía. Short trails lead around the park from the guardería at Laguna Malleco but the hiking is fairly limited. Within the park is the spectacular 50-metre Salto de Malleco (waterfall).

Maps
The Chilean IGM sheet *Laguna Malleco*

(Section G, No 52) covers all of the park, but trails are not shown.

Access

Curacautín can be reached by daily buses from Temuco, but there is no regular transport out to the park.

PARQUE NACIONAL LANÍN – ARGENTINA (LAGO QUILLÉN TO LAGO MOQUEHUE)

(4 to 6 days)

This trek leads through relatively remote country in the northernmost sector of Parque Nacional Lanín. A track leads north from the east end of Lago Quillén following a track around the eastern side of the Cordón de Rucachoroi before dropping down to meet a road on the south shore of Lago Rucachoroi. From here the route heads north-west up the Arroyo Calfiquitra and across a watershed at Mallín Chufquén before again descending to Lago Ñorquinco via the Arroyo Coloco.

At Lago Ñorquinco a road continues north-west around the lake shore into the Arroyo Remeco valley and up to a pass, then heads north-east down a wide valley to Lago Moquehue. This trek requires good routefinding ability as the trail is overgrown in places.

Maps

Two old Argentinian IGM 1:100,000 sheets, *Lago Ñorquinco* (Neuquén, No 3972-23) and *Quillen* (Neuquén, No 3972-29) cover the area (but not the track) of this walk.

Access

From Junín de los Andes there are daily buses to Rahué, from where it is 30 km to Lago Quillén.

Lake District

The luxuriant rainforests of the Lake District contain the greatest diversity of plants and animals found anywhere in Patagonia. The Lake District's outstanding scenery includes large glacial lakes, volcanic plateaus, fresh clearwater streams and wild mountain passes, making this area a real delight to explore.

Of particular interest are ancient forests of the alerce tree, a conifer that reaches gigantic proportions, and the pudú, a native midget deer species. The area's obvious appeal and easy accessibility have helped it become the premier trekking region of Chile and Argentina, and this is reflected in the number of Lake District treks in this book.

Parque Nacional Lanín

The 3790-sq-km Parque Nacional Lanín is a long thin strip of land stretching south through the Andes of Neuquén Province in the Argentine Araucanía and Lake District. Until the late 19th century the vast area of the park was inhabited by the Pehuenche people. The lifestyle of this large Mapuche tribe was integrally linked with the annual harvest of *piñones* (or pine nuts) from the once widespread montane forests of coniferous araucaria trees. Two Indian reserves within the park, at Rucachoroi and Curruhuinca, are all that remains of the former Pehuenche lands.

Parque Nacional Lanín is virtually the only area on the Argentine side of Araucanía where the so-called *bosque valdiviano* is found. This rich mixed forest type has species of southern beech not found further south, such as raulí (*Nothofagus alpina*) and roble (*N. obliqua*). These beautiful trees dominate the lower forests of the park. The forest occupies a typical zone of climatic transition. Precipitation levels drop away sharply from up to 4500 mm in the moist temperate rainforests in its mountainous western sectors to as little as 1000 mm near the dry plains bordering the eastern fringes of the park. A key geographical feature of Parque Nacional Lanín are some five major lakes of recent glacial origin that stretch west from the Patagonian steppes to deep in the Cordillera, the largest of which is the 105-km-long Lago Huechulafquén.

ASCENT OF VOLCÁN LANÍN
Volcán Lanín towers over the northern Lake District, rising from a base plain of around 1100 metres to reach a height officially given as 3776 metres. The mountain is the last of three cones that form an interesting volcanic range extending east from Volcán Villarrica in Chile, and gives its name to the Parque Nacional Lanín. Lanín lies directly on the border, and its north-western side, about one-sixth of the volcano's bulk, is actually Chilean territory.

Viewed from any other direction than the east, Volcán Lanín appears almost impossible to climb. The upper third of the volcano

Puma

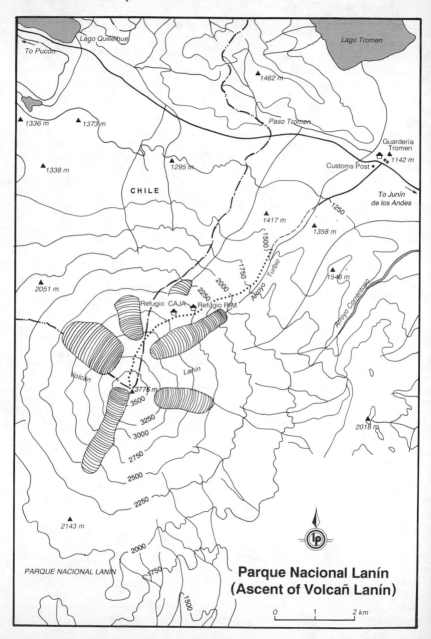

Parque Nacional Lanín
(Ascent of Volcań Lanín)

is covered by a thick cap of heavily-crevassed glacial ice. Nevertheless, the ascent of Lanín is strenuous yet relatively straightforward, and this is probably the highest summit in Patagonia attainable without ropes.

The Mapuche word *lanín* can be loosely translated as 'the extinguished one'. Unlike its near neighbour Villarrica, whose smouldering summit is clearly visible from its higher slopes, the perfectly cone-shaped Volcán Lanín is indeed no longer active. The mountain's great height creates a marked rain shadow to its east, where dry tussock grasses and ñirre woodland mark the beginning of typical Patagonian steppes. As the porous volcanic soil retains little moisture, the tree line is low, and never exceeds 1500 metres. The slopes around the base of Lanín itself are covered by beautiful lenga and araucaria forests.

Maps

The best map available is the Chilean IGM 1:50,000 sheet, *Paimun*, (Section G, No 114). This map provides good topographical information on all of Volcán Lanín, but does not show the location of huts, ascent route or the correct position of glaciers. This sheet is also useful for the Villarrica Traverse trek in Chile. The Club Andino de Junín de los Andes has reasonable sketch maps covering Lanín's usual ascent routes.

Two ancient Argentine IGM 1:100,000 sheets, *Volcán Lanín* (Neuquén, No 3972-28) and *Quillen* (Neuquén, No 3972-29) also cover the wider Lanín area. The detail on these sheets is very poor so their use is not recommended.

Days Required

The recommended walking time is three days return. This allows for a late start on the first stage of the trek, spending the night in one of the two refugios on the mountain. The summit can be climbed on the second day, and the return to Guardería Tromen made the day after that. Very fit hiking parties sometimes do the climb in two days by making a complete descent from the summit on the second day.

Standard

The trek involves an ascent from around 1100 metres above sea level to the 3776-metre summit of Volcán Lanín, an altitude difference of some 2600 metres. Due to its height, the route is very exposed to the elements. This includes the penetrating summer sun as much as the chill winds likely to be encountered near the summit. There is also a theoretical possibility of altitude sickness (see the special Health section in Facts for the Trekker). In addition to standard weather protection, trekkers should carry sunglasses, a hat and suncream.

The steep and loose earth makes a frustratingly unstable walking surface. To avoid slipping, careful placement of every step is called for. To protect your shins and prevent small rock fragments filling your boots, gaiters are recommended.

Trekkers should be physically fit and have some experience in mountainous terrain. The route traverses Lanín's north-easterly side where snowmelt is always fastest. Earlier in the season (usually up to mid-December), however, there may still be snow on the upper volcano. A good cover of old snow stabilises the slopes and can make the ascent easier, but for such conditions you should carry (and know how to use) an ice axe and crampons.

The route described below follows the Espina del Pescado, a narrow ridge providing the most direct access. Although often strenuous, a well-worn path can be easily followed until you reach the higher slopes. Here there are sporadic cairn markings, bamboo stakes and occasionally splotches of paint on rocks, but for much of this section it is necessary to find your own way.

Theoretically, permission to climb Volcán Lanín must be obtained from the the military authorities in Junín. In practice this seems to be unnecessary however, although having an army permit may be helpful if military personnel happen to be staying in the Refugio RIM. It is important that you sign in at

Guardería Tromen before you set out and that you also inform the ranger on your return. The resident ranger makes regular ascents of the the mountain and is up-to-date on current conditions. For advice and more information on conditions and numbers of climbers currently on the mountain it is best visit the Parque Nacional Lanín administration centre situated on the Plaza de Armas in San Martín.

The route is rated moderate to difficult.

Accommodation & Supplies

No accommodation is available near to the start of the climb. The nearby tourist cities of San Martín or Junín are the best bases from which to climb Lanín. There is free camping behind the Guardería Tromen, but except for a few poor sites near the Refugio RIM (an option if the hut is overcrowded), the volcano's exposed and mostly quite steep slopes are definitely no place for tents.

There are two free, unstaffed refugios on Lanín, both roughly halfway up the mountain. The refugios provide good shelter, but are otherwise extremely basic. It is essential to carry your own means of cooking and a (warm) sleeping bag. At 2450 metres is the Refugio RIM, a military-built hut with capacity for up to 10 persons. Some 30 to 45 minutes away at 2600 metres, is the Refugio CAJA. Built and owned by the Club Andino de Junín de los Andes, this smaller refugio has space for about six people. The ascent of Volcán Lanín is a popular excursion among Argentinians, and in the peak holiday the number of climbers on the mountain may exceed the huts' (comfortable) capacity.

It is not possible to buy provisions at Tromen, so you must bring whatever you need from San Martín or Junín. If coming from Chile, buy your provisions in Pucón or Villarrica.

Access

This trek begins at the Guardería Tromen, four km from the frontier to Chile on the international route across Paso Tromen. The Argentine border post is opposite.

The bus companies JAC, IGI-Llaima and Impresas San Martín together have eight services per week in either direction along this road. These generally run between Temuco and San Martín de los Andes via Pucón and Junín de los Andes. Buses heading in both directions leave early in the morning, and normally arrive at the first border post around 11 am.

The climb is conveniently located for people crossing into Argentina from Chile, who can disembark at Tromen. The ascent of Volcán Lanín can also be done as a return excursion from San Martín de los Andes. If you do this, it might be worthwhile arranging with the bus company to have a seat reserved for the trip back out, even if you have to pay a bit extra.

For trekkers intending to cross into Chile after the climb, the situation is more problematic, as boarding a bus to Chile in Tromen is not usually permitted unless you are on the official passenger list. In either San Martín or Junín you may be able to make arrangements to join a bus on its way across the border a few days later. The road is remote and carries little traffic, so hitchhiking is not recommended.

Stage 1: Guardería Tromen to Refugio CAJA via Espina de Pescado
(6½ km, 4 to 6½ hours)

This direct and more straightforward route is preferable to the longer Sendero de las Mulas, and provides access to both refugios.

After signing in at Guardería Tromen, pick up the rough dirt road starting from behind the whitewashed gendarmería building and follow this through an attractive forest of lenga. Head roughly south-west for two km, before swinging around north-west through a plain of volcanic sand to reach the Arroyo Turbio after 30 to 45 minutes.

Continue upstream across the gravel wash towards the volcano, jumping the few small channels of the Arroyo Turbio. This is the last running water until the first refugio, so fill a canteen. You will notice a low yet striking ridge that snakes around to the right above the stream, some 500 metres ahead. Known as the Espina de Pescado, this is a long and narrow 'spine' of lateral moraine giving a direct route to both huts on the mountain.

Head straight for the Espina de Pescado, picking up a track that leads up through thinly vegetated moraine rubble onto the ridge itself. Follow the track along the line of the Espina de Pescado, which steepens and curves slightly to the right. After one hour a graded path departs off to the right. This leads to the Sendero de las Mulas, (a longer route for pack animals which comes out at the Refugio CAJA).

Do not try to ascend the well-trodden scree slope coming down onto the sendero right of the Espina de Pescado. This is extremely loose and difficult to climb, but makes an excellent descent route. Just keep to the ridge-line.

The ridge now becomes more craggy, and in places there is loose and unstable rock, calling for careful footwork. Occasionally, minor detours to the right are necessary to negotiate rocky outcrops on the ridge. After 45 minutes to 1¼ hours the route comes alongside a long, broken-up glacier. Continue for a further one to two hours to reach the red and orange painted Refugio RIM.

Partly sheltered from the westerly winds by a high rock rib, the refugio is built on ground left almost level after the recession of the nearby glacier. There are two double bunks in poor repair, with space for up to 10 persons on the floor. There are poor camp sites on the rocky ground behind the hut. In the afternoon, meltwater can be collected from the nearby glacier. Take care not to get too close to where the ice falls away abruptly, and tread cautiously on dirt-covered ice. Be sure to save enough water for the next day.

Just above the refugio, pick up a vague trail leading up beside the glacier, and follow this up to where the rock rib disappears. The route continues up for 100 metres, before leaving the ridge-line and heading right through an area of broken-up rock rubble. The tin-roofed Refugio CAJA is a on a low flat ridge on the far side of this area. There is space for about six persons. Collect water from glacial snows just around to the west.

Camp Sites For those staying at Tromen, camping is usually permitted behind the Guardería Tromen (ask the resident ranger first). More secluded sites can be found on the first section of the route where it crosses the Arroyo Turbio. Near Refugio RIM there are a few camp sites on levelled-out rocks below the rock rib, but these are sheltered from westerly winds only. There are otherwise no safe or recommended camp sites anywhere else on this ascent route.

Stage 2: Refugio CAJA to Lanín Summit
(7 to 11 hours return)

This section requires a climb of over 1100 metres on extremely unstable scoria slopes, with a return to the hut the same day. Do not try for the summit unless weather conditions are good. Allow yourself plenty of time. *Carry enough water with you to last the whole day!*

From the refugio head up the slope towards some large snow patches right of the cliffs above the glacier. In places you may have to cross short sections of permanent snow. The gradient is initially easy. Look out for cut bamboo stakes indicating the way, and less frequent red paint markings on rocks.

The route passes between two larger snowfields, about 400 metres over from the glacier. Here you begin ascending more steeply. The ground becomes looser, often giving way as you step. Interesting layers of volcanic rock have weathered unevenly to produce very low ridges leading up the slope. These are much more stable and if winds are not too strong may make easier climbing.

Although strenuous, the route is now straightforward. In the last stages before you reach the summit, a scramble up over rock ledges leads up past the impressive seracs of a glacier which descends westwards. Follow a few rock cairns left onto the small permanent snowfield leading up to the summit. Untypical for a volcano, Lanín does not end with a wide caldera. The tiny summit area is capped by glacial ice which falls away sharply on the south side. Sometimes small crevasses open up and, particularly in early summer, extreme care should be taken on the summit.

Llaima, Villarrica, Tronador and many other major peaks of the Lake District and Araucanía are visible from the summit of Lanín. Directly north and south are the large lakes Tromen and Huechulafquén, and a number of beautiful smaller lakes on the north-west slopes of the volcano.

Do not attempt to descend any other way than via the ascent route, as there are large and heavily-crevassed glaciers on all other sides. Walk slowly and carefully as the loose rock is even more liable to slide with heavy steps from above. Once down, be sure to report back at the Guardería Tromen before you leave.

QUEÑI CIRCUIT

The Queñi circuit is a relatively undemanding but enjoyable walk starting at the western end of Lago Lácar in Parque Nacional Lanín, 47 km west of San Martín de los Andes. Unlike other walks in this book, most of the route goes via old 4WD tracks, but these are extremely rough in places and little transited.

The trek circumnavigates the 1855-metre Cerro Chachín, and passes by secluded farms in the Chachín Valley and on Lago Nonthué. In the central part of the walk the valleys are richly forested and enclosed by snowcapped crags. With stands of raulí, roble, lenga, ñirre and coigüe, most of South America's native beech (Nothofagus) species are present. A small amount of selective logging is carried out within the Queñi area, though this is scarcely visible. Bamboo is also harvested locally and, particularly in late summer and autumn, bundles of scorched canes can sometimes be seen stacked up on lake shores, left for later collection.

Thermal springs are a special feature of the area, and can be found at two locations along the circuit. The Termas del Lago Venados are very slow flowing, and the water is probably warm enough for summer bathing only. However, the completely undeveloped Baños de Queñi are probably the highlight of the walk. The baños are a

series of hot baths of various temperatures that lie hidden amongst the trees.

Maps

The entire walk is covered by Argentine IGM 1:100,000 sheet, Hua Hum, (Neuquén, No 4172-4). Dating from the 1940s, this old map does not show the route of the central part of the trek. The Chilean IGM produces a 1:50,000 sheet, Baños de Chihio (Section H, No 8), which overlaps to cover this central area. It shows topography far more clearly, and although the route is not indicated, this map may be of some use. The Guardería Queñi has a large scale sketch map on display which shows the route.

Days Required

The trek is a circuit that is best completed in three leisurely days.

Standard

This gentle trek follows partly overgrown vehicular tracks through two valleys connected by a very low watershed. This is a low elevation route that always remains well below the tree line and is therefore quite sheltered. For this reason the trek can be done as early as October or as late as May, when other walks are out of condition, but the ideal time is mid autumn (April) when the native deciduous beech forests are at their most colourful.

Only a basic level of physical fitness is required, and even inexperienced trekkers should have little difficulty with routefinding. The small Río Chachín must be waded a few times, and early in spring may be a bit more difficult to cross.

The walk is rated easy. The Queñi circuit has an overall length of 29 km.

Accommodation & Supplies

There are no real walker's refugios in the Queñi sector of Parque Nacional Lanín, so it is necessary for all parties to carry a tent. There is, however, a private refugio for anglers located on Lago Queñi which may be open at times throughout the summer season. Convenient accommodation for

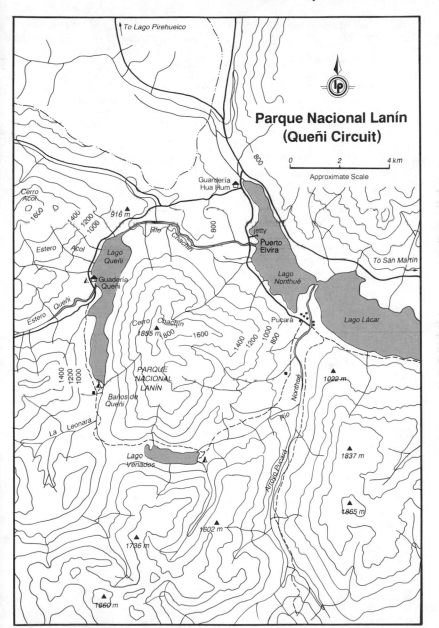

Parque Nacional Lanín
(Queñi Circuit)

travellers can be found in San Martín de los Andes, which is the most suitable base for the trek.

There is no store at the start of the walk in Hua Hum, so bring everything you need with you. San Martín has two supermarkets where all necessary supplies are available. If coming from Chile via Lago Pirehueico, your last (if limited) opportunity to stock up is in the village of Choshuenco.

Access
The circuit commences at the Gendarmería Hua Hum, on the international road between San Martín de Los Andes and Lago Pirehueico in Chile. The walk is ideally located for people on their way across the border, and at Hua Hum there is no problem boarding buses for Chile after you have finished the trek. There are two ways of getting to the start of the trek.

In the summer season, there is one bus to Lago Pirehueico at 7 am every day except Sunday. Buses leave from the San Martín terminal and arrive at Hua Hum around 9:30 am. On its return journey to San Martín the bus passes through Hua Hum at about 11:30 am.

One tour boat operator runs summer day trips to Puerto Elvira, two km from Hua Hum on Lago Nonthué. These leave from the San Martín wharf around 9 am and arrive about midday. It is possible to arrange to rejoin the tour at a specified later date.

Stage 1: Guardería Hua Hum to Lago Venados
(12 km, 4½ to 6 hours)
If arriving by bus, get off at the gendarmería building in Hua Hum and head 50 metres further along the road to Chile. Turn left at the road signposted 'Guardería' and head across the bridge. The guardería is on the right above the Lago Nonthué, 500 metres from the international road.

After signing in, continue along the road around the shore of the lake, passing many tiny pebble beaches. Forty minutes on, the road comes to Puerto Elvira, where the landing jetty for tourist launches from San Martín is located. Cross the Río Chachín and follow the road around the lakeside through a pretty meadow with scattered wild rosebushes.

The road rises and falls slightly where steeper sides meet the lake. Small farms occupy the flat land around tiny stream deltas. Two to three hours from Guardería Hua Hum the road comes to Pucará, a small village by the Río Nonthué. Turn off to the right onto a narrow vehicular track, about 100 metres before you reach the schoolhouse.

Follow the track gradually up for 30 minutes, first through light forest and then through an attractive clearing to ford a sidestream of the Río Nonthué. Passing a makeshift shack on the right, continue on into the forest. The track moves steadily away from the river, passing to the right of a low hill. Many old logging trails lead off the main track, but keep to the most transited way which is the correct route.

After climbing gradually for a further 45 minutes to 1¼ hours, the track rapidly descends to riverflats covered by ñirre woodland. Cross the young Río Nonthué and head directly up the valley. There are views of the craggy ranges on either side. Where the track makes a sharp curve to the right and re-enters the forest, look for a path which continues straight ahead. This leads down to the sandy eastern shores of Lago Venados.

Camp Sites At the start of the trek there are excellent sites by Lago Nonthué, just down from the guardería (boil lakewater). Once you leave the lake behind there is only poor camping in the damp forest, so you should plan your camp for Lago Venados. Excellent spots can be found both on the lake shore or in more sheltered places in the forest.

Stage 2: Lago Venados to Baños de Queñi
(5½ km, 2½ to 4 hours)
Go back to the main track and follow this across the lake's outlet stream. A few paces on you pass a tiny thermal spring on the right. Usually too cool and muddy for bathing, the

pool is easily detected by its luxuriant weed growth and sulphurous smell.

The track now moves back into the forest and climbs well above the steep-sided Lago Venados. There are very few views of the lake due to the dense forest, and in places bamboo leans over the track. The track imperceptibly crosses above a low watershed and after 1½ to 2½ hours and drops down to the Río Chachín.

Ford the icy river and follow its gravelly banks downstream. Recross after a short way and again another 15 minutes on. The track now leaves the river and leads through dense bamboo thickets, reaching the Baños de Queñi after 40 to 50 minutes.

A warm-water stream crossing the track indicates the presence of the thermal springs. In the forest just above, a 'bath' with space for three or four persons has been dug out and dammed with rocks. Do not wash with soap or detergents as these pollute the water.

Camp Sites After leaving Lago Venados there are no suitable camp sites until you reach the Río Chachín, where possibilities exist along the banks. There is reasonable camping by the river near the Baños de Queñi, or near the main track beside Lago Queñi. More sheltered and scenic spots can be found on the south-eastern shore of Lago Queñi. From the baños take the first track off to the right, and follow this for 10 minutes to the inlet stream.

Stage 3: Baños de Queñi to Guardería Hua Hum
(11 km, 5 to 8 hours)
Continue on for a few minutes to Lago Queñi, and begin heading around the western side of the lake. The track dips and rises continually through the evergreen coigüe forest for two to three hours, then begins descending a ridge into an extended area of pleasant clearings alongside the lake. A tourist lodge is located on a sheltered inlet. A further 40 to 50 minutes on the Estero Queñi is crossed on a wooden bridge.

Some 500 metres on the Guardería Queñi is passed. This is not a refugio for trekkers,

but it is possible to camp nearby. Due to logging activity numerous tracks diverge into the nearby ranges. The road follows a course about 20 metres above the lake, crossing a multitude of tiny streams.

After one to two hours the Estero Acol, a large stream feeding the Río Chachín, is crossed. Turn right where a logging road comes down the river's true left bank to intersect with the main track. The road now becomes noticeably better. Passing a few small farms you begin gently rising into the forest to reach a fork signposted 'Cascada' after one km.

The waterfall is a worthwhile 40 to 50 minute return sidetrip. Follow the road to where another sign indicates the start of a trail on the left. Cross a footbridge to descend a stepped path leading through coigüe forest to a cliff ledge. The lookout gives a spectacular view of the Río Chachín thundering out of narrow chasm.

Continue on up through cleared land, passing another farmlet on the left. Turning left at the intersection, descend until the road comes out on the Lago Nonthué road after two to three hours. Head back north 200 metres to the Guardería Hua Hum. Be sure to let the ranger know you have returned before you leave the area.

Camp Sites There is no suitable camping until shortly before you reach the area around Estero Queñi. Here numerous possibilities exist in clearings by the lakeside. Further on there are only occasional poor camp sites in the forest beside the road, and trekkers should aim to arrive back at Lago Nonthué before nightfall.

Parque Nacional Puyehue

The 1070-sq-km Parque Nacional Puyehue lies some 100 km east of the Chilean provincial city of Osorno. Puyehue's name (pronounced 'pooh-yay-way') comes from a

Mapuche word meaning 'place of the puye', a small native fish abundant in the freshwater lakes and rivers of the Lake District. Volcán Puyehue and a fascinating broad volcanic plateau stretching out to its north-west are the central features of the park.

The park's close proximity to the higher mountains along the continental divide produces a very wet climate, even by the southern Lake District standards. Precipitation levels on Puyehue's western edge start at around 4000 mm in Anticura and Aguas Calientes and rise considerably in the ranges to the east. Typical for the Lake District, luxurious temperate rainforest covers the lower areas of the park. Rich forests fringe the slopes below Volcán Puyehue, where species such as the fragrant ulmo (*Eucryphia cordifolia*) are abundant. The extremely moist conditions also favour vigorous quila thickets and there are even examples of the coniferous ciprés de las guaitecas.

PUYEHUE TRAVERSE

The 2236-metre Volcán Puyehue is the highest point in the park and lies on the border of the national park (although some maps show it outside the park). The volcano experienced a major eruption in 1960 but has remained dormant since then. Since the local vulcanologists reckon with a major eruption every 30 or so years, Puyehue is now considered overdue! Great quantities of pumice and volcanic ash have been spewed out to cover the once forested slopes, and in places the trunks of trees long buried by previous eruptions can be seen protruding from the now eroding hillsides. Fires resulting from the last eruption have also destroyed much of the forest close to the volcano, and recolonisation has occurred only slowly. Isolated streams of solidified black lava are further evidence of sporadic volcanic activity.

The entire area remains intensely active, and various volcanic phenomena can be observed in a wild and unspoilt setting. In numerous places steaming fumeroles (*azufreras* or volcanic steam vents) break through the ground spreading deposits of sulphur crystals over the surrounding area.

Geysers gush out amongst pools of perpetually boiling water and bubbling mud pits. Thermal springs provide naturally heated bathing high above the tree line.

Maps

Two Chilean IGM 1:50,000 sheets cover this walk: *Volcán Puyehue* (Section H, No 27) and *Riñinahue* (Section H, No 17). The hiking route and many roads as shown on the latter map are incorrect. There are also some other general topographical errors, and areas of local thermal activity (fumeroles, etc) are not indicated.

Days Required

As a return trek from Anticura, the Puyehue area can be visited in three relatively short days. The extended Puyehue Traverse to Riñinahue is best done in about four days. For the more experienced, at least one additional day might be added to explore some of the interesting but trackless expanse of volcanic country on the north-western side of the Puyehue Plateau.

Standard

The best months to do the trek are December to April, but trips at least before and after this are possible if weather and snow conditions permit. The area is ideal for skiing trips from the beginning of June to the end of October and large patches of winter snow often lie in places well into November. There is a guardería and visitor's centre at Anticura where you can get up-to-date information on the hiking conditions.

The recommended walk is from Anticura to Riñinahue, but the trek can easily be done as a return trip based at Refugio Volcán Puyehue. The route follows a relatively good and well-trodden track for the entire distance. The central part of the route crosses very exposed and unvegetated terrain rising to well above 1500 metres. Loose pumice (a very light volcanic rock) at times makes the going tiresome. Pumice is easily shifted by wind and water which makes the trodden path a bit more difficult to follow. Above the tree line, bamboo stakes have been mounted

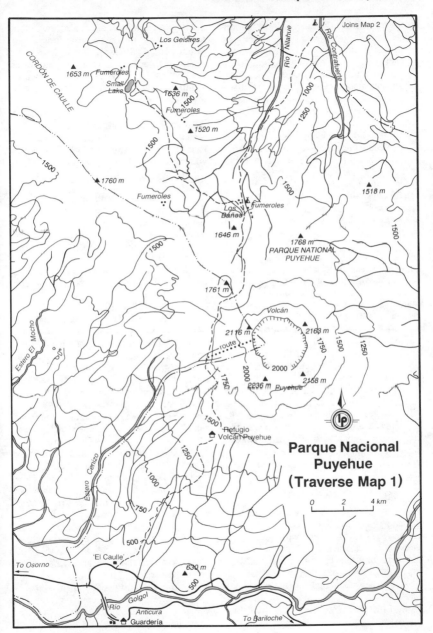

Parque Nacional Puyehue (Traverse Map 1)

to mark the way. Unfortunately, these marker stakes are often removed for firewood by irresponsible trekkers.

South to north is definitely the best direction in which to walk, as starting out from Riñinahue makes routefinding more difficult. The trek is rated moderate and has a total distance of 74 km.

Accommodation & Supplies

There is only one refugio along the route, so if you want to do the whole traverse as far as Riñinahue it is necessary to carry a tent. This is the well-built Refugio Volcán Puyehue on the first stage of the trek. The hut is generally kept locked, but in summer there are frequent visitors. In order to stay there you should arrange to collect the key from the resident guardaparque at the Guardería Anticura. If you intend hiking out to Riñinahue, you may be able to arrange to leave the key hidden outside the refugio when you go.

Opposite the Guardería Anticura at the start of the walk is an up-market hostería (about US$30 per night). There are also 10 modern five-person cabins at Anticura and a campground (but no hot showers; US$4 per site) run by CONAF. At the small township of Riñinahue where the trek ends there is one hostería (US$4).

Supplies cannot be bought in Anticura so bring everything you need for the trek. The most convenient place to by provisions will probably be Osorno. If you plan to start the trek immediately after arriving from Argentina, bear in mind that many raw agricultural and dairy products are not allowed to be imported.

Access

The walk starts from the Guardería Anticura, 22 km past Aguas Calientes on the highway (Ruta 215) linking Osorno with San Carlos de Bariloche in Argentina. From Osorno take the once-daily (except Saturday) local bus that goes via Aguas Calientes to Pajaritos. The bus leaves from opposite the municipal market at around 4 pm, and arrives in Anticura in just over 1½ hours. The same bus returns early the next day at 7.30 am.

Many international buses also travel this road via Osorno en route around Lago Nahuel Huapí to Bariloche in Argentina. There are three or four weekly departures to Bariloche (and vice versa) from Puerto Montt, Valdivia and sometimes even directly from Santiago.

The traverse of Puyehue finishes at Riñinahue, on the eastern shore of Lago Ranco. This route is well serviced by at least four buses passing through Riñinahue village each day en route to Osorno and La Unión.

Stage 1: Guardería Anticura to Refugio Volcán Puyehue
(10 km, 4 to 6 hours)

After signing in at the guardería, walk two km north-west along the highway, crossing two bridges. A short way on from the second bridge take the dirt road with a large gate on your right. The road makes a curve around to the right to reach a small farmstead ('El Caulle') after 15 to 20 minutes. Follow on through the farmyard and look for the start of the path on the left 150 metres on.

The obvious but unsignposted trail leads up through clumps of blackberry bushes to cross a green pasture area after 20 to 30 minutes. Head right a way before you begin to climb a sometimes steep ridge into the lush rainforest, where the fragrant native ulmo tree grows abundantly. The track continues steadily upwards to reach a small stream, 1½ to 2½ hours from the last farm.

Make your way up the naturally eroding slopes on the right side of the stream, where the unstable volcanic earth allows only low vegetation cover. A short distance on, move east over another low ridge to a second stream and continue ascending. The final section leads up steeply into a pleasant lenga forest, before you come out onto grassy alpine slopes. Contour around left 300 metres to arrive at the refugio after a further one to two hours.

Refugio Volcán Puyehue is situated just on the tree line in a lovely spot in view of the volcano. The refugio has six bunks, a fireplace and a toilet below. It is normally kept locked. An empty woodshed close by is a reasonable alternative if you do not have a key. To fetch water follow the main path on a short way down to a small stream. The water usually flows underground due to seepage, but listen for a permanent trickle spring coming down from the opposite bank. Avoid collecting water from anywhere below the hut because of the chances of contamination (boil it if you do).

Camp Sites At Anticura fees are charged per tentsite at the CONAF campground, but there are no showers. There is also a private hostería (with up-market prices) opposite the Guardería Anticura. After leaving Anticura, there is a poor camp site by the first stream you come to, about half way up. After that no other camp sites can be recommended until you reach Refugio Volcán Puyehue. Good sites can be found around the refugio where the forest fringes the alpine meadows.

Stage 2A: Refugio Volcán Puyehue to Campamento Los Baños

(9 km, 3½ to 5 hours)
Follow the track north-east across grassy slopes. The track ascends quickly to the bare western side of Volcán Puyehue. From here you get an excellent panorama of the major volcanic peaks to the south: Osorno (the magnificent cone to the south-west), Puntiagudo, Casablanca and Tronador (the high irregular ice-covered mountain to the south-east). Lago Puyehue stretches out below to the west.

Make your way north-west through lava and scoria rock, roughly contouring along the slope. The route is marked by intermittent stakes. Volcán Puyehue can be climbed by heading up an obvious ridge just south of the first large glacial stream you come to, 45 minutes to one hour from the refugio. There is no track, but this straightforward route leads up easily to reach the ice-filled crater after 30 to 45 minutes.

Deep snow may cover the upper slopes well into December. Snow-corniced cliffs drop away into the crater, so be careful where

you tread. From the rim there is a superb view of the country to the north-west.

Crossing a number of smaller meltwater streams, head gradually around towards the north-east onto the barren pumice-covered Puyehue Plateau. Look out for occasional marker poles leading gently down the side of a dry stream. Navigating carefully, head left over the loose sandy banks to cross a flat plain. Continue through an area of grey rounded dunes until you come onto a low ridge to the right of a green gully. Follow the ridge down past a small group of fumeroles, before dropping down to the stream.

Los Baños are a short way ahead on the east (or true right) side of the stream. Two pools have been dug out of the earth immediately below where the boiling water gushes out. The water temperature is far too high for bathing, so dilute the bath with water from the cold stream. The hot spring is rather acid and will quickly dissolve weeks of built-up grime. Do not drink the water or stay in the baths too long. The immediate area has various other volcanic features, such as hidden geysers and fumeroles, which are interesting to explore.

Camp Sites If the humidity and sulphurous smell does not bother you, there are many semi-sheltered camp sites right by the stream. Firewood is very scarce and must be laboriously collected from the slopes above, where the remains of trees killed by various eruptions can be found. Other camp sites can be found by crossing the steam and following the track 20 to 30 minutes to the Río Nilahue (see Stage 2B).

Stage 2B: Campamento Los Baños to Los Geisires

(14 km return, 5 to 7 hours return)
This easy sidetrip to a small field of geysers and other interesting thermal activity is a must. The return walk can be done as a day walk from Los Baños.

Head north-west across the bare pumice dunes, passing fumeroles on the adjacent slopes of Morro Los Baños to your left. After

20 to 30 minutes the path crosses a side-stream just before reaching some camp sites by the Río Nilahue. From here continue a short way from the river, crossing two more small sidestreams, and gradually ease around to the right along a dry watercourse.

The track becomes indistinct here, but make your way north over a short flat section towards the obvious tiny valley flanked by low bare hills on the far side. Pick up the track again and walk a few minutes on until you reach the main branch of Río Nilahue. Wade the shallow stream and continue up the western bank of a mostly dry creek bed. Steam puffs from a few scattered fumeroles can be seen on the slopes to your right. As you near the upper valley, the path crosses the stream bed to follow a sandy ridge over a low flat pass. A small undrained lake (not shown on IGM or CONAF maps) lies immediately below in a depression.

Drop down to the lakeside (where there is some wreckage) and head 750 metres north around the shore to the far end of the muddy wash plain. Look out for cairns indicating where the path continues and climb away steeply to the top of a high ridge overlooking the lake.

In the distance, slightly east of north, a steaming area of thermal activity is visible. Various easy routes can be followed through the eroded terrain to reach to the geyser field 30 to 45 minutes from the lake. A few hours can be spent exploring this fascinating area of bubbling mud tubs, effervescent pools and geysers. For your own safety and to preserve the delicate formations be very careful where you tread. It is best to return via the same route.

Camp Sites There is little sheltered camping along this section. Reasonable camp sites can be found at the small sidestream 20 to 30 metres on from the baños and at the Río Nilahue crossing. Camping near the small lake is very exposed. At Los Geisires semi-sheltered sites can be found, but the volcanic fumes can be unpleasant.

Stage 3: Campamento Los Baños to Lower Río Contrafuerte
(14 km, 5 to 7½ hours)
Backtrack 10 to 15 minutes to 100 metres past the first small patch of fumeroles by the track above the stream. Look out for bamboo marker poles leading over the highest pumice ridge between the two upper branches of the Río Nilahue. Begin descending northwards high above the cascading eastern stream across slopes of chaura bushes overlooking the head of the densely forested Nilahue valley.

After 30 to 45 minutes the path drops down right very steeply to cross the river, before climbing the opposite bank onto a long-disused road. Continue for five to 10 minutes through some semi-sheltered camp sites by the track, where alpine lenga forest is slowly regenerating after previous fires. The road is often badly eroded or overgrown, and the path constantly moves off and back onto the route.

Head down into the trees and continue the long descent. The track winds its way interminably through beautiful lush rainforest via a broad ridge separating the Río Nilahue from the Río Contrafuerte to your right. The going is straightforward but rather monotonous due to the thick vegetation. After two to three hours the path edges right to easily cross the Río Contrafuerte, before returning to the left bank 150 metres on.

Follow on 30 to 45 minutes past a spectacular cascading gorge of the Río Contrafuerte. As the gradient eases the track becomes increasingly muddy and wild pigs (*jabalís*) have left occasional wallowing pools. Continue in the same fashion as before for a further two to three hours, until you finally come out near the Río Nilahue at a clearing covered with nalca plants. Make your way 10 to 15 minutes through a cleared area until you reach a road. The road can be followed around left a short distance to some attractive riverflat meadows with scattered blackberry bushes.

Camp Sites Good camp sites can be found just above the tree line below Campamento

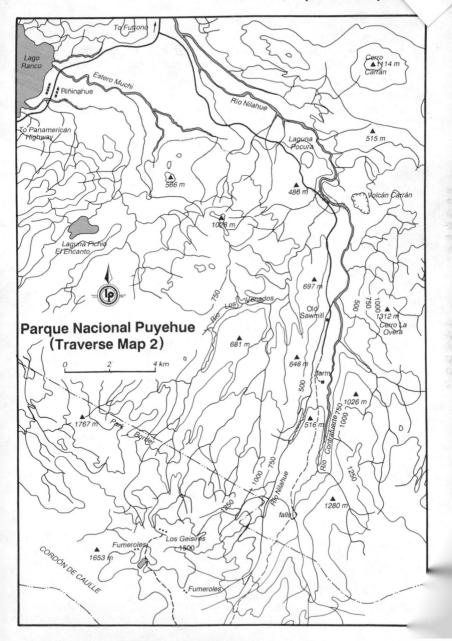

Parque Nacional Puyehue
(Traverse Map 2)

Los Baños. There is more sheltered (though less scenic) camping where the track meets the Río Contrafuerte at about half-way down. Camping in the forest itself is very damp and there is no running water. At the end of the section, potential camp sites by the Río Nilahue road are excellent, but in places vigorous blackberry growth makes it hard to get to the river.

Stage 4: Lower Río Contrafuerte to Riñinahue
(27 km, 8 to 12 hours)
Follow the road along the Río Nilahue through a number of stock gates. Heavy logging trucks and other vehicles have left the road muddy in places, but progress is good. Pass an old sawmill and cross the bridge to climb away steeply through forest and patches of cleared grazing land. After three to four hours the road crosses the Río Los Venados bridge, just up from where the river enters the Río Nilahue. Continue past more small dairy farms and the picturesque Laguna Pocura on your right.

The lower valley is open and more populated and developed. The road leads through the small settlement of Quirrasco after two to three hours, and follows the Río Nilahue to intersect with the Riñinahue-Lago Ranco road (ask locals about the shortcut to the main road via some small lanes between fields). Turn left and make your way to Riñinahue. The small township has one hostería and is quite well serviced by buses.

Camp Sites Along the first part of this section numerous good tent sites can be found in the forest or clearings off the road. At Riñinahue, camping is possible at the south-eastern corner of Lago Ranco. Ask permission first before camping on private property.

Other Treks in Parque Nacional Puyehue

PAMPA FRUTILLA
(2 to 3 days)
Pampa Frutilla is an attractive subalpine plateau situated almost directly west of Volcán Casablanca. From near the guardería at Anticura a closed 4WD track rises gradually south-east through the rainforest, passing a newly constructed CONAF refugio a short way off the road several km before Pampa Frutilla. From here trekkers with good routefinding ability can ascend eastwards via the open volcanic ridges to Volcán Casablanca (see the description which follows).

Maps
Two Chilean IGM 1:50,000 sheets, *Volcán Puyehue* (Section H, No 27) and *Volcán Casablanca* (Section H, No 36).

VOLCÁN CASABLANCA
(1 to 2 days)
Volcán Casablanca is a relatively low (2240 metres) volcano. From the ski lodge, Refugio Antillanca, a road can be followed uphill to the carpark and lookout. Volcán Casablanca is best climbed from Crater Rayhuen in an easy half day return. Trekkers with good navigational skills should be able to descend west from Casablanca's summit, following bare ridges to Pampa Frutilla (see the preceding description).

Maps
Volcán Casablanca (Section H, No 36).

Access
In summer, buses from Osorno run only as far as Aguas Calientes, some 18 km before Antillanca.

Condor

Parque Nacional Vicente Pérez Rosales

The 2200-sq-km Parque Nacional Vicente Pérez Rosales is the largest in the Chilean Lake District. The park fronts the Argentine border where it meets the even more sizable Parque Nacional Nahuel Huapí, and together with the adjoining Parque Nacional Puyehue this area forms the largest tract of trans-Andean wilderness in the Lake District.

Vicente Pérez Rosales completely takes in Lago Todos los Santos. Apart from Lago Pirehueico some distance to the north, Lago Todos los Santos is the only one of the major low-level lakes on the Chilean side that stretches deep into the Andes. This is because the lake is not at the termination of a former glacier's path (like Lago Llanquihue) but lies within a deep glacial trough. It has a distinctly glaciated 'fjord-like' form and is surrounded on all sides by some of the highest and most prominent peaks of the southern Lake District. Todos los Santos is also unique among the larger lakes because there are no roads to disturb its steep and densely forested shores.

At the north-western rim of the park a long arc-shaped volcanic range extends from the perfect conical form of Osorno to volcanoes Puntiagudo, Cenizas and Casablanca. Volcán Osorno and Volcán Puntiagudo are both visible from watercraft on Lago Todos los Santos.

TERMAS DE CALLÁO

The relatively remote Termas de Calláo lie hidden behind Volcán Puntiagudo in the Valle Sin Nombre. The Termas de Calláo are delightful natural hot springs that emerge from the ground just beside the small Río Sin Nombre, a river which flows into Lago Todos los Santos. Blending into the dense temperate rainforest along the river are a number of small enclaves of freehold land run as small family farms.

The heavy rainfall and the relatively mild conditions supports lush vegetation, making this sector of the park a paradise for birds, of which parrots and honey-eating humming-birds are especially plentiful.

Maps

Two Chilean IGM sheets cover this walk, *Volcán Casablanca*, (Section H, No 36) and *Peulla* (Section H, No 44). These maps both show the walking track, though there are omissions and errors regarding the exact route. An adjoining sheet, *Cerro Puntiagudo* (Section H, No 35) includes the final three km section of the trek, but is unnecessary and out of print.

Picaflor gigante

Days Required

The trek can be done in three easy days, but at least one additional day should be spent enjoying this most attractive area.

Standard

The trek takes a low-level route along two river valleys and reaches its highest point at

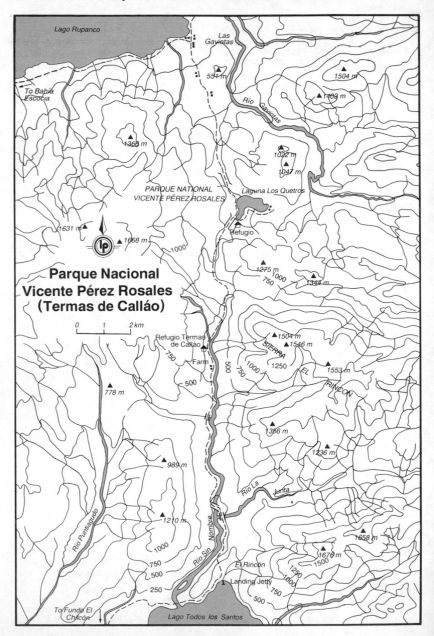

a forested pass of around 800 metres. Due to its low elevation and relatively sheltered aspect, the Termas de Calláo can be visited from late spring until late autumn (late October to early May) when other walks may be out of condition. However, the summer months (December to February) are the recommended time to do the trek.

The walk follows generally good foot and horse trails for the entire distance. These serve as the only access to isolated farm enclaves inside the park, and are well transited. All larger streams are bridged and the path is generally kept in condition by the local inhabitants. In some places cattle pads confuse the route, but navigation is fairly straightforward. The unstable volcanic earth on some steeper sections has caused the path to erode away steadily so it resembles a deep trench, but this presents little difficulty for trekkers.

At the Guardería Petrohué at the western end of Lago Todos los Santos there is a CONAF information centre which is worthwhile visiting before you cross the lake to the start of the trek.

You are strongly advised to do the trek in a south-to-north direction. This is because there is no reliable way of getting out from El Rincón (on the remote northern shore of Lago Todos los Santos) once you arrive.

The trek is rated easy. The total walking distance is 37 kilometres.

Accommodation & Supplies

There are two refugios along the route. At the Termas de Calláo is a superb hut constructed from native timbers by a local farmer for CONAF. The Refugio Termas de Calláo has bunks for six people, a wood stove and running water. A fee of US$4 is charged to stay here. There is another primitive but sturdy three-sided refugio at Laguna Los Quetros which is free. Although it is possible to do the trek without a tent, this is not recommended.

At Petrohué, Hostería Petrohué offers tourist-style accommodation (from US$30 per night). The Familia Küscher on the other side of the river has cheaper lodgings. There

is also an organised CONAF campground with facilities (US$4 per site) and a newly renovated refugio.

At Lago Rupanco it may be possible to find cheap accommodation for a night at one of the dozen or so dwellings around Las Gaviotas. At Bahía Escocia there is a tourist lodge for anglers and $2\frac{1}{2}$ km on, in Puerto Rico, there is a campground. At El Islote, 13 km further along the road on Lago Rupanco, there is another hostería and campground.

Farm produce such as eggs, cheese and fruit jams can usually be bought at farms along the route (most notably from the first farm you come to, five to 10 minutes downstream from the Termas de Calláo). There is a small store at Petrohué that mainly sells snacks and takeaways. For all other supplies Puerto Montt and Puerto Varas (on Lago Llanquihue) are the most convenient places to buy provisions.

Access

The trek begins at the El Rincón, situated in an inlet about halfway across Lago Todos los Santos on the lake's northern shore. There is no regular direct transport, but there are several other possibilities.

The simplest way to get to El Rincón is to charter a boat. This is easiest from Petrohué, on the west side of Lago Todos los Santos, than from Peulla, on the lake's remote eastern shore. Petrohué can be reached directly by many daily buses leaving from Puerto Montt or Puerto Varas. Enquire at the CONAF information office or ask around at the landing jetties for anyone willing to carry you across the lake. The trip by private boat takes about two hours and will probably cost around US$20.

It is also possible to reach El Rincón by catching one of the several daily ferry boats that run across Lago Todos los Santos between Petrohué and Peulla. Arrange with the captain to be dropped off at Punta Verde, a small cluster of farms some four km opposite El Rincón on the southern side of the lake. From Punta Verde you must arrange to be rowed across. The people of these isolated farms around the lake shore are accustomed to their privacy, and although friendly and helpful, would rather not be disturbed too often by backpackers. Where possible avoid causing them inconvenience. Remember, once at El Rincón the only way out is the route described below.

The walk finishes at Puerto Rico, a village near the south-eastern corner of Lago Rupanco. From Las Gaviotas or Puerto Rico it may be possible to charter a boat (or hitch a ride) across Lago Rupanco, but continuing on by foot will probably be best. The regional bus company Piedras Negras runs one daily bus from Puerto Rico to Osorno. This departs very early in the morning and takes about 2½ hours to reach Osorno. There is one later bus from El Islote, seven km on from Puerto Rico. Check bus departure times in Osorno or Puerto Montt before you set out.

Stage 1: El Rincón to Refugio Termas de Calláo

(9½ km, 3 to 4 hours)
From the landing jetty walk one minute uphill to a wide trail running across the slope. Turn right and continue a past a signpost a short way on. The path leads up north-east through lovely grassy meadows overlooking Lago Todos los Santos to meet the Río Sin Nombre after 20 to 30 minutes.

With the loud whitewater river on your left, follow the track 1½ km through temperate rainforest to reach a precarious suspension bridge crossing a sidestream of the Río Sin Nombre. Cross by the bridge (or wade through the usually shallow water of Río La Junta), and make your way 10 to 15 minutes upstream to another suspension bridge spanning the Río Sin Nombre itself.

Cross the rickety bridge (one person at a time), and head on upstream along the river's steep-sided western bank. The path dips and rises before coming to a sturdy third bridge across a large sidestream after one to 1½ hours. Continue through pretty clearings in the forest, where there are occasional glimpses of the volcanic plug summit of Volcán Puntiagudo to the west. The track passes traditional farm cottages sealed with

wooden shingles, to arrive at the Termas de Calláo after a further 40 to 50 minutes.

The Refugio Termas de Calláo is a superb hut with a wood stove for heating and cooking, bunk space for six people, wonderful wooden and bamboo furniture and even running water. Use of the hut is no longer free, and you must pick up the key at the closest farm five to 10 minutes downstream along the path (farm produce is also sold here). The thermal baths are just down from the refugio in a little shed by the river. There are two private interior tubs and a sheltered tub outside carved out of an alerce trunk. The water is piping hot and very relaxing. There is no charge for using the baths themselves. The scenic valley is enclosed by high densely rainforested granite peaks on either side, and makes an excellent spot to stop an extra day.

Camp Sites The best camping near El Rincón is on the scenic flats where the Río Sin Nombre enters Lago Todos los Santos, 15 to 20 minutes west around the lakeside via a good trail. Further up the track, fair camp sites can be found in occasional small clearings by the river where the riverbanks are not too steep. At the Termas de Calláo, the best place to camp is in the sheltered area below the refugio.

Stage 2: Refugio Termas de Calláo to Laguna Los Quetros

(6 km, 4 to 5 hours)
From the refugio proceed two km up the valley along the west side of the river. Crossing several minor tributaries, the path goes through a series of fire-cleared areas with charred stumps and patches of regenerating bamboo. Where the main Valle Sin Nombre swings around abruptly towards the east, head north-west into a small side valley. A recent landslide on an adjacent mountainside has exposed a sheer rock face.

Follow the path uphill for 20 to 30 minutes to reach another small stream. Cross on stepping stones and continue northwards below a ridge well left of the stream. The heavily eroded and often steep track leads over a slight saddle, three to four hours from the Termas de Calláo in tall montane rainforest.

Heading north-east the path steadily drops down to reach burnt clearings around the southern shore of Laguna Los Quetros. To reach the lake make your way 500 metres on cattle pads leading through the remaining scattered trees. There is an old three-sided shack here which provides basic shelter. On the far side of the little bay is a farmhouse where you can ask to borrow a rowing boat.

Camp Sites There is excellent camping at the south-west corner of Laguna Los Quetros. The only other good camp site is where the path crosses the small stream in the side valley leading up to the saddle.

Stage 3: Laguna Los Quetros to Puerto Rico
(23 km, 7 to 10 hours)
Pick up the trail on the west side of Laguna Los Quetros and climb high around its steep shore. The path moves back into forest of fragrant-leafed laurels and ancient gnarled mañíos to cross a low and indistinct pass after 30 to 45 minutes.

Continue roughly northwards and begin dropping down. In places erosion has cut severely into the loose volcanic soil, and the track resembles a deep trench. As you reach steeper and more open slopes lower down there are excellent views towards Lago Rupanco. After descending for 1½ to 2½ hours the path comes out onto a large undulating meadow with scattered idyllic farms surrounded by high peaks. The Río Gaviotas thunders down through gorges to your right.

Head one km across the open grazing land and climb a short way left of a rounded hill. From here you can look down directly to the tiny village of Las Gaviotas at the south-east corner of Lago Rupanco. Follow a broad track down through several gates, passing farm gardens and small cherry groves to arrive at Las Gaviotas after a further 30 to 45 minutes.

It is possible to charter a motor boat from here 12 km across Lago Rupanco to Puerto Rico (or another nearby settlement). There is

also a well-used walking route along the coast of Lago Rupanco to Puerto Rico.

At Las Gaviotas pick up the trail by the shore, and follow this west past isolated farmlets. There are good views of Volcán Casablanca to the north-east. The track reaches Bahía Escocia after 2½ to 3½ hours, where there is a tourist fishing lodge. Continue 2½ km to the cluster of houses known as Puerto Rico. From there are two early buses each day to Osorno.

Camp Sites Camping is not recommended on the first part of the walk from Laguna Los Quetros to Las Gaviotas. There are numerous potential camp sites in sheltered bays along the Lago Rupanco shore line, especially in the central section. Always seek permission before camping on private land.

Other Treks in Parque Nacional Vicente Pérez Rosales

VOLCÁN PUNTIAGUDO LOOKOUT
(1 to 2 days)
Puntiagudo is a spectacular sharp volcanic plug whose distinctive form makes it easily recognisable from many places in the southern Lake District. From Bahía Escocia near the south-eastern corner of Lago Rupanco a track leads south via a steep spur to a lookout point on the prominent volcanic ridge coming down from Puntiagudo's north-eastern side.

Maps
Two Chilean IGM 1:50,000 sheets, *Cerro Puntiagudo* (Section H, No 35) and *Volcán Casablanca* (Section H, No 36) cover this trek but do not show its route.

VOLCÁN OSORNO – REFUGIO PICADA
(1 to 2 days)
From Petrohué on Lago Todos los Santos a marked track leads around the north-eastern slopes of Volcán Osorno (2652 metres) to the

Refugio Picada. Ascents of Osorno are usually made from the Refugio Teski Club (see Other Treks in the Lake District at the end of this chapter).

Maps
The Chilean IGM 1:50,000 sheet *Petrohué* (Section H, No 44) covers area of the walk but does not show the path.

TRONADOR – RÍO PEULLA
(1 to 2 days)
From the Casa Pangue Carabineros post (see Paso de las Nubes trek, Stage 3A) a glacier on the northern slopes of Monte Tronador can be reached via an eight km route along the east bank of the Río Peulla. This is a mainly trackless but relatively easy route that can be done as a sidetrip by parties doing the extended version of the Paso de las Nubes trek.

Maps
Chilean IGM 1:50,000 sheet *Monte Tronador* (Section H, No 46).

Access
By ferry to Peulla, then walk or bus to Casa Pangue.

RALÚN TO LAGO TODOS LOS SANTOS
(2 to 3 days)
This is an easy walk leading up the Río Reloncaví and over the low Puertozuelo Cabeza de Vaca (pass) to Lago Cayutúe, then on to Ensenada Cayutúe on Lago Todos los Santos. The land fronting Ensenada Cayutúe is private property and camping isn't allowed there.

Maps
Two Chilean IGM 1:50,000 sheets, *Petrohué* (Section H, No 44) and *Cochamo* (Section H, No 53), cover the trekking route.

Access
Ralún is about 95 km east of Puerto Montt by road and can be reached by daily bus or ferry.

Parque Nacional Nahuel Huapí

The 5570-sq-km Parque Nacional Nahuel Huapí lies to the west of the popular tourist centre of Bariloche in the southern Argentine Lake District. The mountains around San Carlos de Bariloche are probably the most developed area for winter sports and hiking in South America. The park has many excellent alpine refugios, which are largely managed by the Club Andino Bariloche.

The 557-sq-km Lago Nahuel Huapí forms the hub of the park. With its numerous fjord-like branches, Lago Nahuel Huapí itself is probably the finest example of the many large glacial lakes in the greater Araucanía. At around 750 metres above sea level, the lake is nevertheless the lowest point in the park. Due its relative elevation and distance from the Pacific (about 180 km) the Nahuel Huapí area has a cool and drier 'continental' type of climate. On its eastern side Nahuel Huapí fringes the dry Patagonia steppes.

The park is a wonderfully scenic area of forests and lakes set among impressive craggy ranges. The park's wild rugged interior is easily accessible via an extensive network of marked and well-maintained tracks. Forests of deciduous lenga (*Nothofagus pumilio*) are the typical vegetation, and grow in the valleys interspersed with areas of mallín country where the local drainage is poor.

Nahuel Huapí (pronounced 'na-well-wuppie') is from the Mapuche language and means 'island of the tiger'. The area of the modern-day park formed a large part of the Mapuche heartland, and tribes lived around the eastern shores of the great lake. There are several low Andean passes in the park, such as the Paso Vuriloche (near Pampa Linda) and the Paso de Pérez Rosales, which linked the many local Mapuche tribes on either side of the Cordillera. These passes were later used by Christian missionaries as a safe route to Chiloé.

Established in 1922, Nahuel Huapí is the

oldest of Argentina's national parks. The park's original title was simply 'Parque Nacional del Sur' and comprised a vast tract of land first granted to the pioneering explorer Francisco Perito Moreno for his services to the Argentine Boundary Commission. Perito Moreno donated it back to the nation on the condition that it be turned into a national park, and Nahuel Huapí is still easily the largest national park in northern Patagonia.

NAHUEL HUAPÍ TRAVERSE

This hut-to-hut route close to Bariloche takes in some of the finest country in the Lake District, and is one of the most popular walks in Argentina. The traverse crosses the rugged and interesting ranges (which average around 2000 metres) in the eastern sector of the park north of Lago Mascardi.

The area lies well east of the continental divide and receives somewhat lower precipitation levels due to the rainshadow effect of mountains further west. For example, Puerto Frías on the border with Chile has annual rainfall averages of around 4000 mm, while the Cerro Catedral area receives under 2000 mm. As a consequence the mountaintops are barren and sparsely vegetated above 1600 metres and there are no real glaciers left on this eastern side of the park. In places intense frost shattering has formed large scree slides on the higher slopes.

Maps

Two Argentinian IGM sheets scaled at 1:100,000 cover the area: *Llao-Llao* (Neuquén, No 4172-22), and *San Carlos de Bariloche* (Neuquén, No 4172-23). Produced in 1947, these maps have many topographical errors, but show the locations of the older refugios and parts of the hiking route. The Club Andino Bariloche sells quite a useful sketch map showing all tracks and walking routes in the area. Ideally you should carry both.

Days Required

The full traverse can be done in four to five days. A further one or two days will allow

you time to rest or do short sidetrips. Many shorter variations of the trek can also be done. These include the so-called Circuito Catedral (three days), the Circuito Chico (one long day, or two short days) and the exit route via the Arroyo Goye (four days). A description of these alternatives follows.

Standard

Many sections of this trek are well above the tree line. The route's relatively high altitude generally makes it unsuitable for all but very experienced parties until around the beginning of December, though in places deep snow may remain well into January. The area is somewhat sheltered by the mountains to the west (chiefly Volcán Tronador), and the weather tends to be just a bit more settled than on the adjacent side of the Andes. Even so, many parts of the route are very exposed to the elements. If conditions are poor you should wait for the weather to improve.

The route follows well-trodden and well-marked tracks for most of its length, and routefinding is relatively straightforward. The exception to this is the central section between Refugio Jakob and Refugio Segre, where the going is particularly strenuous and navigation demands considerable care and experience. Many other tracks intersect with the traverse route, allowing you to shorten or vary the walk as you like. On all stages of the trek it is possible to walk out in one day. In places loose rock and scree slopes must be climbed, and gaiters will make the trip more comfortable.

By far the best direction in which to do the trek is clockwise from Villa Catedral. At Villa Catedral skilifts can be used to get up into the mountains before you start walking. This saves about three hours and makes the first stage far less strenuous.

Apart from the section from Refugio Jakob to Refugio Segre (Stage 3A, rated difficult), all sections are of a moderate walking standard. The total length of the traverse is 39 km.

Accommodation & Supplies

There are five refugios along the route,

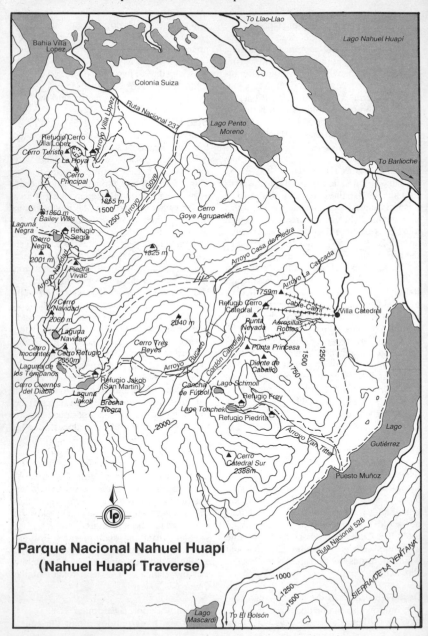

Parque Nacional Nahuel Huapí
(Nahuel Huapí Traverse)

Top: Laguna Elefantita, Reserva Nacional Tamango
Bottom: Moorland, Parque Nacional Los Glaciares

Top: Cerro Fitz Roy, Parque Nacional Los Glaciares
Bottom: Cerro Fitz Roy, Parque Nacional Los Glaciares

making it is possible to do the trek without a tent. However, for greater safety and in case huts are overcrowded, you are nevertheless advised to carry a tent. There are also good camp sites along all sections. Overnight fees at refugios are around US$4. Meals and simple refreshments are usually available from the refugios. Most of the refugios are closed during the colder months.

The most practical base for the trek is Bariloche itself, where there is an enormous range of accommodation in all price ranges. Bariloche also has several large and modern supermarkets and is the best place to buy supplies.

Access

The trek begins at Villa Catedral, a ski village some 20 km from Bariloche. Regular tourist buses (Transportes Mercedes company) run out to Villa Catedral. From here two alternative cableways can be taken up Cerro Catedral to the start of the trek (Stage 1A): the Aerosillas Robles, and the Cable-Carril/Aerosilla Lynch. The single fare up costs about US$7.

The walk ends between a small bay in Lago Perito Moreno and Colonia Suiza, 22½ km west of Bariloche on Ruta Nacional 237. The No 10 bus to Bariloche passes here four times a day.

Stage 1A: Villa Catedral to Refugio Frey (via Lynch Cableway)

(9 km, 4 to 5½ hours)
The Lynch cableway carries you most of the way up the Cerro Catedral. Then ride the shorter chairlift to the scenically located Refugio Lynch. A four km track underneath the cableway can be followed for two to three hours to this refugio. There are no overnight facilities for trekkers at Refugio Lynch, but you can buy refreshments.

Follow yellow paint markings south along the ridge, passing a meteorological station and rocky outcrops. The path rises a short way to reach Punta Nevada after 20 minutes, then drops 100 metres or so into a col. Here the path from the Aerosillas Robles climbs

up beside the Diente del Caballo spur to join the main trail at the right.

Head up over Punta Princesa. The ridge-line turns to a south-westerly direction, with the Valle Rucaco below on your right. A short distance on, a large broken boulder blocks the way. Pass this by descending around to the right. Continue along the craggy and steep-sided range, for 1½ to two hours until you arrive at the Cancha de Fútbol. In clear conditions this more open spot offers fine views of surrounding peaks, most particularly the 2388-metre Cerro Catedral Sur (to the south-east) and Volcán Tronador (due west).

Follow a track left 200 metres down through a rock gully. Here deep snow may make the going dangerous early in the season. The path quickly leads down to the Laguna Schmoll. Head to your right around the lake and cross the tiny outlet stream. Continue down initially steep slopes to Laguna Tonchek, making your way around the lake's northern shore to the far end. The Refugio Frey is reached after 40 minutes to one hour.

The attractive two-storey stone refugio lies on the vegetation line at 1700 metres. There is sleeping capacity for 40 persons, and cooking facilities are available. Meals and refreshments can be bought. Refugio Frey is normally open from December until the end of March, when the surrounding granite crags attract many rock climbers.

Camp Sites The only places where camping is possible are around Laguna Schmoll and Laguna Tonchek. Sites are very exposed and there is little firewood.

Stage 1B: Villa Catedral to Refugio Frey (via Arroyo Van Titter)

(11½ km, 4 to 5½ hours)
Purists will prefer this alternative route, which does not use mechanical means of ascent. The walk is a bit more strenuous than Stage 1A, but is better sheltered. The scenery is very pleasant. The route is also the usual second leg of the so-called Circuito Chico trek.

From the carpark, take the vehicular track 200 metres to where a signpost indicates the start of the path to Refugio Frey and Lago Gutiérrez. Follow the wide trail south through the ñirre scrub as it contours below Cerro Catedral, crossing tiny streams and avoiding small boggy areas. After 1½ to two hours a small lookout is reached, from where you have a wonderful view out over Lago Gutiérrez. Continue for a further 15 to 20 minutes until you get to the signposted track junction. The left path goes to Ruta Nacional 528 at the south-eastern end of Lago Gutiérrez (three to 4½ hours).

Turn right and head into the enclosed valley of the Arroyo Van Titter. Follow trail markings upstream for one km to cross the river on a fallen log. The tiny Refugio Piedrita is reached after 20 to 30 minutes climb through the forest. This remarkable refugio belongs to the local Club Andino Esloveno, and is constructed underneath an overhanging boulder. Refugio Piedrita is not normally open to the public and is likely to be locked.

Continue up 500 metres to where the valley divides into two branches. Follow the path up initially steep slopes into the western branch of the stream to arrive one to 1½ hours later at Refugio Frey (see the earlier description).

Stage 2: Refugio Frey to Refugio Jakob (or San Martín)
(7 km, 4½ to 6 hours)
Return via Lagunas Schmoll and Tonchek to the Cancha de Fútbol. Follow an arrow painted on a rock indicating the track to Refugio Jakob. Drop down 500 metres via steep scree slopes to reach the Arroyo Rucaco after descending 30 to 45 minutes. Follow the red paint markings up the valley through an extensive area of alpine moors, then cross a number of small streams in the lenga and ñirre forest. The path remains on the true right (ie southern) bank some distance from the river. Water bottles should be filled here as there is no water until you reach the next valley.

After the forest disappears, make your way up through the increasingly bare slopes towards the head of the valley. A strenuous 250-metre ascent through more steep scree leads you onto the broad ridge that connects Cerro Tres Reyes with Brecha Negra. There are superb views from here, with the refugio on Laguna Jakob clearly visible below to the south-west.

Descend west through a wide and long scree slide into the valley of the Arroyo Casa de Piedra. After 45 minutes to one hour you reach the mallín on the north-east side of Laguna Jakob. Head around the northern edge of the moor to cross the lake's outlet stream. Proceed up the valley to arrive at the Refugio Jakob (or San Martín) a few minutes on.

The timber and stone refugio lies at 1600 metres, and can sleep 25 people. There is a kitchen for trekkers and a simple kiosk.

Camp Sites Excellent camp sites can be found in the forest in the upper Valle Rucaco. Similarly, there is good camping around Lago Jakob, especially at the western end of the lake. Campers should remember it's their responsibility to prevent forest fires and to carry out all rubbish.

Stage 3A: Refugio Jakob (San Martín) to Refugio Segre
(8½ km, 6 to 8 hours)
This section of the trek follows a high-level route much harder and more hazardous than other stages. It should not be attempted unless weather conditions are very good. Early in the season (usually at least until mid-December) snow may make the route impassable without crampons and ice axe.

Head up the valley from the refugio, around the northern side of Laguna Jakob on the marked trail to Laguna de los Témpanos for 20 to 30 minutes. Before reaching the higher lake, the path goes over a rocky spur. This comes down from Pico Refugio on your right. Carefully study the course of the route from below.

Following occasional cairns, begin climbing north along the spur. After 20 to 30 minutes you come to the first of three abrupt rock faces visible from the refugio. Head a short way left to where a tiny stream emerges from a gully. Either make your way up a track through loose rubble in the gully, or ascend on the rock at your right. Continue upwards until you come to the ridge at an area of rock debris below twin towers. From here there is a panorama of the surrounding mountainscape.

Taking care when negotiating patches of old snow, head north-west along the ridge. After a short distance, a rocky pinnacle blocks the way. Avoid this by descending around to the right, and traverse the slopes below the rock face. Continue through a stony area of gully cracks towards an obvious gap in the craggy range ahead, 2½ to 3½ hours from Refugio Jakob (San Martín).

Move over onto the loose scree slopes on the eastern side of the range above Laguna Navidad. This leads to a low point in the main ridge-line between Cerro Inocentes and Cerro Navidad. Head 500 metres up a spur to reach the summit of Cerro Navidad. The Refugio Segre and Laguna Negra are just visible from here, a fraction east of north at about 20°.

Head 400 metres down the ridge on the northern side of Cerro Navidad. A track on your right then leads north-east down more steep and unstable slopes into the narrow and enclosed *cañadón*, or small canyon, at the head of the Arroyo Navidad. Crossing the cascading stream wherever necessary, follow the unmarked trail down the valley. A tiny sidestream flows in from a gully on the south-east side of Cerro Negro. Soon after re-entering the forest, 45 minutes to one hour on, you pass through a boggy area on the eastern side of the stream. Continue for another 30 to 45 minutes to reach the path coming up the Arroyo Goye. An overhanging bivouac rock, Piedra Vivac, is located near the junction of the two streams.

Cross Arroyo Goye below where the Arroyo Navidad enters, and begin heading upstream. Red paint markings are again followed. Rising over 300 metres, the path climbs steadily in steep switchbacks to reach

Laguna Negra in 45 minutes to one hour. The Refugio Segre is located just above the rocky south-eastern lake shore underneath Cerro Negro, in the spectacular glacial cirque filled by the Laguna Negra. The interesting stone and concrete structure has bedspace for some 40 trekkers. The refugio is not usually open before mid-November or after the end of April.

Camp Sites After leaving Laguna Jakob, no camp sites exist along the route until you reach the lower part of the Arroyo Navidad. There is good camping here, and also a short way up from the stream junction before the land becomes too steep. Camp sites by Laguna Negra are fairly exposed, and firewood is scarce.

Stage 3B: Refugio Jakob to Puerto Perito Moreno

(12 km, 4 to 6 hours)
This is the normal access to Refugio Jakob, and is the quickest exit route from that refugio. The walk down the Arroyo Casa de Piedra is also the third and last stage of a popular circuit around Cerro Catedral.

Pick up the well-transited path from below the refugio, and descend for 30 to 45 minutes to cross the stream. Continue down the extremely steep slope in a series of switchback curves (known locally as Las Serpentinas), where an iron stairway must be negotiated. After 45 minutes to one hour the gradient becomes much gentler, and you enter a long forested strip.

Head downstream for another 1½ to two hours to a suspension bridge across the Arroyo Casa de Piedra. After crossing, proceed along the river flats through more lenga forest. After 1½ to two hours you arrive at an inn, from where a short road leads out to Ruta Nacional 237. The No 10 bus to Bariloche passes by four times a day. Six km on to the right is Puerto Perito Moreno, from where Transportes Mercedes bus line runs a twice-hourly service to Bariloche.

Camp Sites Excellent camp sites can be

found all along the lower Arroyo Casa de Piedra.

Stage 4A: Refugio Segre to Refugio Cerro Villa López
(8 km, 4½ to 6½ hours)
Follow the red paint markings around the broken-up north side of Laguna Negra. There are a few uncomfortable sections to negotiate. Head for a low point in the ridge at the termination of the valley between Cerro Bailey Wills and Cerro Negro. At first follow the lake's tiny inlet stream, before moving left and gently climbing 150 metres to the pass. This is reached 45 minutes to one hour after leaving Refugio Segre.

Proceed north up the wide rocky spur towards Cerro Bailey Wills. Before reaching the main (eastern) summit, sidle left into a high pass between the mountain's two peaks. Looking out for red paint markings, drop down north-east through loose rubble into the valley that begins below the pass. A small brook is then followed down and around to your right to reach the head of a bigger side valley after 30 to 45 minutes (this is the northern branch of the Arroyo Goye).

Avoid the area of boggy moorland by moving around the upper side of the valley. Continue for one to 1½ hours in a north-easterly direction, heading out of the light forest to climb up beside a gully of rock debris. The very steep slopes lead up to an indistinct col in the ridge that connects Cerro Principal with Cerro Turista to your left. The short and easy sidetrip up to the 2050-metre Cerro Turista (marked on IGM maps as 'Cerro López') is recommended. Follow the spur north-west to the 2050-metre summit, where a lookout offers a fine panorama over Lago Nahuel Huapí (one hour return).

Descend north-east for 200 metres into an interesting round depression. Known as La Hoya, this is a small glacial cirque. The path passes a tiny lake at the lower end of La Hoya, before heading down eastwards through a rocky gully to arrive at Refugio López after 20 to 30 minutes. The privately-owned refugio is a very large two-storey construction with modern amenities and sleeping capacity for up to 100 persons. Refugio López is the most popular and accessible refugio on this walk, and is set in a particularly scenic location looking out over the Valle López to Lago Nahuel Huapí.

Camp Sites The best camping along this section is in the upper Valle Goye after descending from the first pass crossing. Look for sites in the low forest around where two tiny streams converge. It is also possible to camp on the riverflats about one km below the Refugio López (boil all river water taken downstream from the refugio).

Stage 4B: Refugio Segre to Campamento del SAC (Colonia Suiza)
(10 km, 4 to 5 hours)
This is the usual access to Refugio Segre. The walking is easy and very pleasant, and the route is recommended as a shorter alternative to the full traverse.

From Refugio Segre descend very steep switchbacks to the track junction near Piedra Vivac. After crossing the Arroyo Goye, follow markings down the valley along the almost flat riverbanks. The path stays close to the river, passing through lovely mixed beech forests to reach an old sawmill after three to four hours. A short vehicle track is then followed through two gates for 15 to 20 minutes to arrive at Ruta Nacional 237.

Immediately opposite is the Campamento del SAC, a popular campground with modern facilities. The No 10 bus to Bariloche passes here four times a day. If hiking from the opposite direction, take the signposted road 100 metres before you come to the Arroyo Goye bridge.

Camp Sites There is excellent camping by the Arroyo Goye virtually anywhere downstream from the Piedra Vivac track junction.

Stage 5: Refugio López to Colonia Suiza
(3½ km, 1½ to 2 hours)
This very short section is often done as part of the fourth day. Many trekkers simply head down the road from Refugio López, but

taking the path is probably quicker and makes a nicer walk.

From below the refugio, follow the road 700 metres to where a marked and well-trodden trail leads off to the left. The path meets the road again a short way on, but the road soon heads away to the right. Crossing two tiny sidestreams, continue through the forest on the east side of the Arroyo Villa López. Finally, descend some steepish switchbacks before you come out on the Ruta Nacional 237. Hiking parties coming from the other direction can pick up the path near the road bridge, 22½ km from Bariloche.

PASO DE LAS NUBES

The Paso de las Nubes route passes alongside the mighty Monte Tronador. At 3554 metres above sea level (at least according to Argentinian maps), this great mountain massif stands almost 1000 metres above its nearest rivals throughout the Lake District. Monte Tronador lies at the edge of the park on the Chile-Argentine frontier and dominates all views to the west.

The actual geological origin of the mountain has been the subject of some argument. The area's original Mapuche inhabitants apparently believed Tronador to be an extinct volcano, and European settlers maintained this view. However, the mountain does not have anything like the typical form of a volcano, and some leading geologists and climbers have had cause to question Tronador's supposed volcanic beginnings.

The mountain's complicated three-peak summit appears as an irregular massif composed of large névés and icefalls. Some 60 sq km of Monte Tronador's surface is covered by glaciers, the only such icefields in the park. Tronador takes its name from a Spanish word meaning 'the thunderer', a reference to the noise caused by repeated snow and ice avalanches.

Although the mountain creates a rainshadow effect to the east, the ranges close to the international frontier are high precipitation areas. Dense rainforests cover the lower slopes and the proximity of Monte Tronador seems to create a locally cooler and intensely wet microclimate.

Maps

The Argentine IGM 1:100,000 sheet *Llao-Llao* (Neuquén, No 4172-22) completely covers this area. This map (also used for the Nahuel Huapí Traverse trek) is very much out of date and gives poor topographical detail. The location of the hiking route is not shown correctly. A good sketch map of the area can be bought at the Club Andino Bariloche. A Chilean IGM 1:50,000 sheet, *Monte Tronador* (Section H, No 46), includes a good part of the frontier area on the Argentinian side as well as most of the road to Peulla, and is quite useful.

Days Required

The average walking time from Pampa Linda to Puerto Frías is two full days, but at least one additional day is recommended. The overnight sidetrip to the Otto Meiling refugio lengthens the walking time by another two days. Extending the trek by continuing on to Peulla requires one long day. Trekkers arriving at Pampa Linda by tourist bus will generally set off well after midday.

Standard

The trek follows a much transited but often poorly marked path for most of the way. In the central section the route crosses the 1335-metre Paso de las Nubes, where snow may lie well into January. Apart from a short section on top of the pass, the route is completely within the shelter of the forest. In places waterlogged ground and fallen trees often make the going slow.

From Pampa Linda a return sidetrip can be made to the Refugio Otto Meiling on a ridge of Monte Tronador. This highly recommended sidetrip follows a relatively straightforward route up a disused road. Carry a stove as firewood is scarce at most camp sites along the way.

From Puerto Frías many trekkers continue on into Chile via a good dirt road to Peulla on Lago Todos los Santos. This isolated 27-km section across the Paso de Pérez Rosales

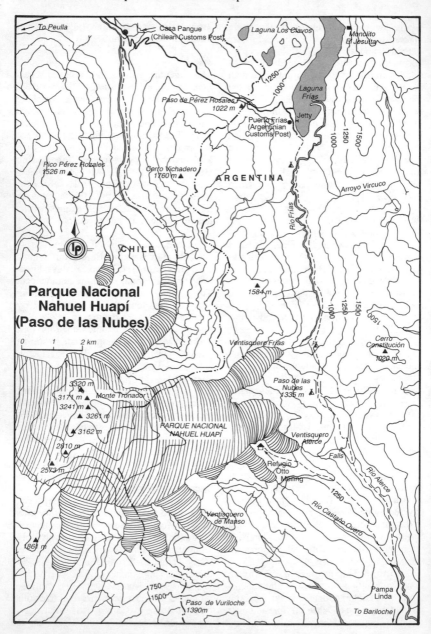

Parque Nacional Nahuel Huapí (Paso de las Nubes)

is not accessible to outside traffic, and is transited only by a regular bus service and occasional border control vehicles.

The walk can be done in either direction, although for transport reasons south-to-north will probably be the most convenient. As this is a frontier area, be sure to carry proper identification. The trek (including the Refugio Otto Meiling sidetrip) is graded moderate. The total walking distance from Pampa Linda to Puerto Frías is 21 km.

Accommodation & Supplies
Except for the Refugio Otto Meiling which is on an optional sidetrip route, there are no refugios for walkers along the Paso de las Nubes route, and all hiking parties must therefore carry a tent.

At the start of the trek the small Hostería Pampa Linda has medium-priced (approximately US$15) accommodation. There is also a modern campground at Pampa Linda (approximately US$5 per site).

Puerto Frías at the beginning of the international road has no accommodation either, but for those continuing on to Chile there are three or four simple-style pensiones at Peulla (on Lago Todos los Santos).

A few simple items are available at Pampa Linda, but no other supplies are available along the way. Bariloche is the best place to buy your provisions. For trekkers continuing on to Peulla, remember that raw agricultural products and dairy foods may not be taken across the border into Chile. The only possibility of buying provisions in Puella is a tiny shop at the back of the Hotel Peulla (rooms from about US$20). There are also several pensiones in Peulla where meals are served.

Access
The trek begins at Pampa Linda, 85 km by road from Bariloche via Villa Mascardi. The best way to reach Pampa Linda is to take an organised coach tour. In summer, various companies run daily excursions to Pampa Linda. Tours normally leave at 8 am from Bariloche and arrive at around 1 pm. The return fare is about US$12, which usually includes a boat trip across Lago Mascardi.

Hitchhiking to Pampa Linda is only advisable in the busy tourist season.

The walk finishes at Puerto Frías. From here a tourist boat across Laguna Frías connects with a bus to Puerto Blest on a branch of Lago Nahuel Huapí. At Puerto Blest a second boat must be taken across Lago Nahuel Huapí to Llao-Llao, where another bus completes the final leg to Bariloche. The combined cost of these fares comes to around US$15.

There is also an alternative exit route into Chile that takes you from Puetro Frías to Peulla. An expensive (US$13) bus service operates along the little transited 27 km international road linking these tiny settlements. Remember that it is prohibited to bring most unprocessed agricultural foodstuffs into Chile. From December to February there are several daily ferry boats from Peulla to Petrohué. The last boat departs around 3 pm. The trip across Lago Todos los Santos costs about US$7 and takes 2½ hours.

Stage 1A: Guardería Pampa Linda to Refugio Otto Meiling
(22 km, 7 to 10 hours return)
The Guardería Pampa Linda is situated off the main road 200 metres to the right. After signing in, follow an old vehicle track roughly north for 30 to 45 minutes through open meadows and areas of tall coigüe forest to the Río Castaño Overo. Cross the stream on a makeshift footbridge and continue a short way ahead to a (possibly unsignposted) track junction.

Take the left branch which heads northwest along the the route of the disused vehicle track. The old road (not correctly shown on the Argentine IGM map) soon begins a steady ascent of the slopes on the north side of the valley. Look carefully for where steep shortcuts leave the bulldozed track to cut off long switchback curves. Two to three hours after crossing the Río Castaño Overo the path comes out at the crest of a ridge coming down from Monte Tronador. There is a level area here providing an ideal resting spot.

Make your way up the broad ridge through

fiirre and lenga scrub. The well-marked path sidles between rocks along the left side of the spur, before climbing steeply right to arrive at the Refugio Otto Meiling after a further two to three hours. The large reinforced concrete building has been built in a depression and does not become visible until you are quite close.

Refugio Otto Meiling stands at around 2000 metres above sea level. The refugio has a capacity for 60 mountaineers and trekkers and offers meals and simple refreshments. Its location offers a superb panorama taking in Pampa Linda, the Paso de las Nubes and Cerro Catedral directly to the east. In summer, Refugio Otto Meiling often serves as the base for courses in snow and ice climbing run by the Club Andino Bariloche.

The descent is made via the same route.

Camp Sites At Pampa Linda there is an excellent campground with modern facilities. A reasonable fee is charged per person. A scenic but exposed camp site exists near where the path first reaches the top of the spur. Good sites can also be found lower down by the river.

Stage 1B: Pampa Linda to Paso de las Nubes
(11 km, 5½ to 7 hours)
Follow the old road three km north-west to the Río Castaño Overo. Cross the bridge and proceed past where the track to Refugio Otto Meiling departs left. Head along the western bank of the Río Alerce, ignoring trails that lead off across the stream. The old vehicle track continues through damp forest to peter out at an area of boggy mallín after 2½ to 3½ hours.

Wade the small river and pick up the path amongst light lenga forest. Passing a cascading water chute on your left, continue north into the pretty upper valley enclosed by peaks. Here the track zig-zags steadily up the steep slopes on the left to leave the forest. Look out for a large round paint marking on a boulder before making your way across moist alpine meadows to arrive at the top of the Paso de las Nubes after three to 4½

hours. The pass lies at 1335 metres and offers fine views of the snowy slopes of Monte Tronador and Cerro Constitución to the north-east.

Camp Sites The recommended camp sites are on scenic grassy meadows just below and on the south side of the pass. Be sure to choose a dry and well-sheltered site. Camping is also possible lower down almost anywhere in the damp forest along the river.

Stage 2: Paso de las Nubes to Puerto Frías
(9½ km, 4½ to 6 hours)
Drop down 300 metres to a natural lookout on the path. From here there is an outstanding view ahead towards Laguna Frías. Continue descending steeply through the forest to some rock cliffs. The cliffs look out onto the interesting Ventisquero Frías, from which a thundering waterfall emerges. Follow paint markings down through a series of gaps in the rock to reach the valley floor after 45 minutes to one hour.

Move right across the gravel wash and cross a tiny sidestream. Pick up the track below some camp sites in the trees and begin the long walk down the valley. Waterlogged ground lower down is avoided by maintaining a course along the base of forested slopes on the valley's east side (the Argentine IGM map incorrectly shows the track on the west side of the stream). The path finally crosses a wide area of wet bogland to reach Río Frías after three to four hours.

If there is no bridge here, continue downstream for 15 to 20 minutes and cross the river on a fallen tree trunk. Follow an old muddy track initially along the true left bank of the Río Frías before heading 1½ km north-west to the southern shore of Laguna Frías. There is a small landing jetty and an outpost of the Argentine Gendarmería Nacional here. Spectacular sheer-sided mountains rise up directly from the lake shore giving Laguna Frías a dramatic fjord-like appearance. Trekkers not going on to Chile can begin the long trip back to

Bariloche by catching a boat to Puerto Alegre (at the lake's northern end) from here.

Camp Sites There is very good sheltered camping in the forest opposite Ventisquero Frías. As these are very popular camp sites firewood can be hard to find. The next reasonable camping is at the bottom of the valley just after crossing the Río Frías. At the Laguna Frías camp on level sites just up from the boat jetty (boil the water).

Stage 3A: Puerto Frías to Peulla
(27 km, 7 to 10 hours)
Be sure to have your passport exit-stamped at the gendarmería building before setting out.

Follow the good dirt road around the south-west side of Laguna Frías. The road climbs steadily in switchbacks to reach the Paso de Pérez Rosales after 45 minutes to one hour. The pass lies in the lush rainforest at 1022 metres above sea level. From here a badly overgrown track leads three km south-west to the open higher slopes of Cerro Vichadero, where there is a run-down refugio just inside Chilean territory.

Begin the descent past tiny pampas and a small abandoned farmhouse on your left. The road gradually winds its way down through more dense forest of coigüe and arrayán to reach a border post of the Carabineros de Chile after two to three hours. This place (shown on the Chilean IGM map as Casa Pangue) looks out up the valley towards the spectacular snowbound northern slopes of Monte Tronador. From Casa Pangue there is a eight km route along the gravelly east bank of the raging Río Peulla to the snout of a receding glacier. This can be done as a one or two-day return sidetrip.

Follow the road three km downstream and cross to the south side of the Río Peulla on an impressive suspension bridge. The road heads west across the flat valley floor for 2½ to 3½ hours, before swinging around through a wide expanse of soggy grassland. Continue south another 1½ to two hours to the Chilean customs house just outside Peulla. Passports must be presented and luggage may be searched.

There are several moderately priced residenciales but no shops in Peulla. The tiny boat harbour is one km on from the village. In the tourist season (December to February) ferry boats return across the lake to Petrohué as late as 3 pm. The trip takes about 2½ hours.

Camp Sites There are some excellent camp sites on little meadows 10 to 15 minutes down from the Paso de Pérez Rosales. Camping is also possible in many places along the Valle Peulla. At Peulla itself there is a free camp site without facilities below the village at the lakeside. At Petrohué an organised CONAF campground charges a fee per tent site.

Other Treks in Parque Nacional Nahuel Huapí

The Club Andino Bariloche (CAB) and the Argentine SNPN can advise you on treks in the Nahuel Huapí area. The local publication *Las Montañas de Bariloche* by Toncek Arko also has many other good route suggestions.

BARILOCHE TO REFUGIOS NEUMEYER & ÑIRECÓ
(2 to 3 days)
This is an easy and very well-sheltered hiking area that can be visited directly from Bariloche. It makes a good option if the weather looks unstable.

From the main Ruta 258 a turnoff road heads south-west up the Arroyo Ñirecó, before heading into the broader side valley of the Arroyo Challhuaco. The road leads to Refugio Neumeyer, a well-equipped CAB hut, from where a variety of nice day walks can be done.

Where the road crosses the Arroyo Ñirecó a foot track turns off to the right (west). A path continues along the eastern bank of the stream to the Refugio Ñirecó located beside a mallín at the head of the Valle Ñirecó. From the refugio a rough and more difficult route leads west up to a pass and follows the range north for a way before descending via the Arroyo Melgurejo to the east shore of Lago Gutiérrez.

Maps
San Carlos de Bariloche (Neuquén, No 4172-23) or CAB sketch maps.

Access
Either walk from Bariloche itself or get a lift with a bus tour to Refugio Neumeyer.

BAHÍA LÓPEZ TO PUERTO FRÍAS
(4 to 6 days)
This a difficult trek is easily combined with the Paso de las Nubes walk. From the hotel at Bahía López on Lago Nahuel Huapí a good but lengthy track leads along the south-eastern shore of Brazo Tristeza. From the termination of Brazo Tristeza a route first heads north-west around the northern shore the two Lagos Anasagasti to where the small valley divides. From here a ridge leads west to the top of a range. The range is followed north to finally descend into the Valle Frías where the track to Puerto Frías is picked up.

Maps
Llao-Llao (Neuquén, No 4172-22), and *San Carlos de Bariloche* (Neuquén, No 4172-23) and CAB sketch maps.

Access
There are regular buses to Bahía López from Bariloche.

LAGO MASCARDI TO BAHÍA LÓPEZ
(5 to 7 days)
This is another fairly difficult but varied walk though the backcountry of Parque Nacional Nahuel Huapí. From the guardería at the north-eastern end of Lago Mascardi a track leads initially around the lake's western side before climbing away west to Laguna Llum. The path continues over the main ridge and descends to follow the lakeside to Lago Mascardi's north-western end.

Here the route follows the true right bank of the Arroyo Callvuco (or Azul) for 8 km north-west to Laguna Callvu (or Azul). From Laguna Callvu the route goes north-east via ridges around Cerro Cristal before dropping down to Laguna Lluvú (or CAB) where there is a refugio. From the lake a track leads down the Arroyo Lluvunco to intersect with a path leading north along the southern shore of Brazo Tristeza to Bahía López on Lago Nahuel Huapí.

There is another more difficult route possible from Laguna Lluvú (or CAB). This goes into a northern branch of the Arroyo Lluvunco and over the Bailey Wills range to connect with the Refugio Segre to Refugio Cerro Villa López route (see Stage 4A of Nahuel Huapí Traverse).

Maps
As above.

Access
Either by daily bus to El Bolsón or by tourist coach to Pampa Linda or Lago Fonck.

Parque Nacional Alerce Andino

Alerce Andino is situated in the *pre-cordillera*, or Andean foothills, on Seno Reloncaví some 25 km to the east of the Chilean Lake District city of Puerto Montt. Since the area's proclamation as a national park in 1984, a modest amount of development has taken place. Despite this, the area still attracts a surprisingly low number of visitors.

The relatively small (392 sq km) park is ostensibly a reserve for the majestic alerce tree, or lahuén (*Fitzroya cupressoides*), an extremely slow-growing native conifer. The relative inaccessibility of the area has prevented major exploitation of its valuable stands of giant alerces. Now saved from the foresters, the most ancient and massive specimens may exceed four metres in diameter and reach several thousand years of age. The alerce typically requires a very moist climate, and thrives in a smaller form even in the waterlogged soil around the shores of the many lakes within the park.

The close proximity to the coast gives the area a milder marine climate, but also high annual rainfall. Precipitation ranges from 3300 mm in the lower sectors to maximum levels of 4500 mm on the highest ranges, usually falling as snow above 800 metres in winter.

PANGAL–CHAICA TRACK
This route takes you into the central part of the park. Here, a rough plateau situated at between 500 and 700 metres is surrounded by low but heavily glaciated granite ranges reaching to around 1250 metres.

Dense evergreen montane rainforest covers all but the higher elevations, and in the tiny valleys a dozen odd small lakes lie nestled into temperate jungle and are a delight to explore. A particularly attractive feature of the rich life in the forests are the native hummingbirds, or *picaflores*, which thrive on the many nectar-bearing flowers found in the park. Due to their surprising lack of timidity, these delicate birds can often be observed from close range. The copihue, the national flower of Chile also grows abundantly throughout the forests, which are dominated by the ubiquitous beech and scatterings of other tree species such as tepa, tineo, canelo and avellano.

Maps
Two 1:50,000 IGM sheets cover the central part of the park: *Correntoso* (Section H, No 52) and *Lenca* (Section H, No 61). These maps do not indicate the hiking route, but are otherwise reasonably accurate (note that on these sheets the Río Lenca is incorrectly given as the Río Chaica and vice versa). The CONAF office in Puerto Montt can give you a map to look at showing tracks and the location of refugios.

Days Required
Whether or not you decide to do the trek right

through to Laguna Chaiquenes, or return to Guardería Río Chamiza, the trek takes about four days. A further half-day might be needed to walk out via the Río Chaica road to Lenca.

Standard
A generally well-maintained and marked path follows a lake-to-lake route into the heart of the park. Vigorous bamboo overgrowths lean over and obscure the track in places, but walkers should have little difficulty in finding their way. The final section of Stage 3 over the pass from Laguna Fría to Lago Triángulo is extremely steep (requiring ladders in places) and hard work, especially with packs.

Unfortunately, a vital two km section around Laguna Triángulo had still not been cut at the time of writing. This means that it is necessary to either backtrack, or make an extremely strenuous 'bush-bash' down to the lake shore and around its steep and densely forested side. There is a primitive dug-out canoe in Laguna Triángulo which might be used to ferry trekkers from one end of the lake to the other, but there is no guarantee that it will be at the convenient end when you arrive. It is difficult to say how long it will take CONAF to complete the track, but check with the ranger before setting out.

There are two ranger stations in the park. These are the Guardería Chamiza and Guardería Río Chaica on the southern and northern access roads.

Because of better transport connections and easier routefinding, the recommended walking direction is north to south, starting at Correntoso and continuing to Lago Chaiquenes. This will remain the case even after the completion of the track around Laguna Triángulo. The walk is rated easy to moderate, except for the presently untracked section around Laguna Triángulo which definitely deserves a difficult rating. The total walking distance from Correntoso to Lenca is 44 km.

Accommodation & Supplies
There is little or no visitor's accommodation

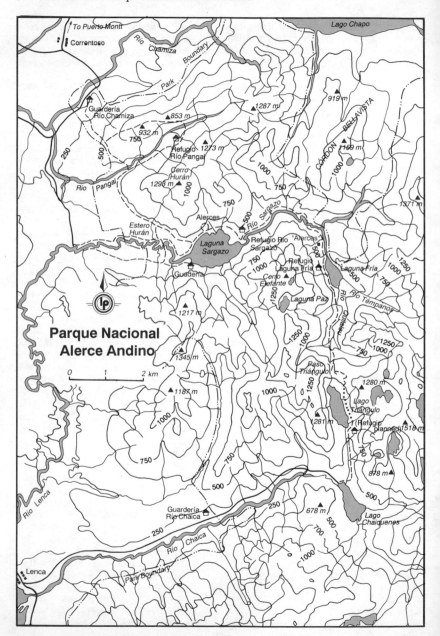

either near to the start of the trek at Correntoso or in Lenca, where the trek finishes. Puerto Montt will probably the most convenient place to base your walk from.

Correntoso is the last place from where supplies can be bought until you reach Lenca but Puerto Montt is definitely the best place to buy provisions.

The park has four refugios: at Río Pangal, Río Sargazo, Laguna Sargazo and Laguna Triángulo. The construction of another refugio is planned for the southern end of Laguna Triángulo. Except for the Refugio Río Sargazo, the refugios are kept locked, and it is necessary to arrange with the ranger to use them. Until the Lago Triángulo refugio is built, it will not possible to do the full trek to Lago Chaiquenes without a tent.

Access

The trek begins at the village of Correntoso, 25 km west of Puerto Montt. Two buses leave daily for Correntoso from the main terminal, taking about one hour to complete the journey. From here it is a short three-km walk to Guardería Río Chamiza in the northern sector of the park.

If you do the whole trek as far as Lago Chaiquenes, you will probably still have to continue a further 17 km on foot (unless you are lucky enough to get a lift) down the little-transited Río Chaica road. The road leads out to Lenca, a scattered village on Seno Reloncaví. The Carretera Austral passes through Lenca and provides access to coastal towns further south. Several regional buses pass through Lenca each day and take approximately 1½ hours to reach the main bus terminal in Puerto Montt.

Stage 1A: Correntoso to Refugio Río Sargazo (via Cordón Pangal track)

(10 km, 6 to 8 hours)

From Correntoso take the road branching left, which is signposted 'Salto'. The salto is really more a violent cataract than a true waterfall, and can be viewed from the Río Chamiza bridge. Guardería Río Chamiza is situated 600 metres downstream on the left side of the road. You should sign in here and can ask the resident guardaparque for advice.

The path heads left from the guardería across flat paddocks to behind a blue shack, before beginning a stepped ascent into the forest. After one to 1½ hours the track divides. The left path follows a high-level circuit route along the Cordón Pangal, leading back onto the main trail by way of an excellent new refugio above the Río Pangal. This two to three hour sidetrip is strenuous and almost entirely without views.

Continue upward a short way before dipping down to cross the small Río Pangal. The Pangal circuit rejoins the main track on the opposite bank 20 metres above the river. The path now contours the slopes below Cerro Hurán for one to 1½ hours, turning slowly around south-east. A trail is passed on the right, leading from the alternative access route via the upper Río Lenca.

The path now rises quickly to pass through a gap above Laguna Sargazo, from where you get the first glimpse of the lake. Descend to the shoreline, and join a prominent track leading around the northern shore of the lake. Follow this through the forest, where unobstructed views of Laguna Sargazo are few and far between. After 20 to 30 minutes a signposted trail heads off left. This is a short circuit leading up through some superb stands of great alerces and is a very worthwhile 40-minute sidetrip.

Make your way painstakingly on through a log-jammed section on the eastern shore of the lake, and pick up the track 20 metres to the right in the scrub. Head upstream for 10 to 15 minutes through senescent fruit trees near the Río Sargazo to arrive at the Refugio Río Sargazo. The small refugio is an old farm cottage with space for a maximum of eight people. The simple wooden shelter is in fair condition and is kept unlocked.

Camp Sites At the start of the trek there is a cheap campground by the Río Chamiza, 100 metres downriver from the bridge at El Salto. It is possible to camp by the Río Pangal, but nowhere else is recommended until you get to Laguna Sargazo. The only good camp sites on the lake are by the inlet stream (Río Sargazo) and the outlet stream (Río Lenca).

Stage 1B: Correntoso to Refugio Laguna Sargazo (via Río Lenca)

(13 km, 5 to 8 hours)

Despite it being longer in distance, this pleasant route is the quickest and most straightforward way to Refugio Laguna Sargazo.

From Correntoso follow the road to the Guardería Río Chamiza as described in Stage 1A. Follow the road two km across the Río Pangal bridge, turning immediately left at a crossroad. Continue for four km to where the road terminates by the banks of the Río Lenca. Head gently upstream through occasional clearings along the northern banks of the river, reaching the tiny Estero Hurán after one to 1½ hours. It is possible to continue along the riverbank until you get to Laguna Sargazo. Otherwise cross the stream and head uphill along a track for 30 to 45 minutes to intersect with the main trail. The remaining section to Refugio Río Sargazo is described above.

Camp Sites There is good camping all along the Río Lenca and on the eastern side of Laguna Sargazo.

Stage 2: Refugio Río Sargazo to Refugio Laguna Fría

(4½ km, 1½ to 2½ hours)

Head around the north bank of the Río Sargazo. The path gently rises to cross the stream on a log bridge after 45 minutes to one hour. Continue for 15 to 20 minutes to where a short track leads off right to a stand of magnificent alerces. An arrow near a log bench indicates the location.

Laguna Fría is reached after an easy 20 to 30-minute walk. Follow the track 300 metres around the western side of the lake to the Refugio Laguna Fría. The refugio has a fireplace and bunk-space for four persons, and is kept locked. Despite its name, Laguna Fría is fine for swimming. It is enclosed by various granite peaks visible only from the middle of the lake.

Camp Sites Camping is possible all along the river, but Laguna Fría is recommended. The best sites are at the southern end of the lake by a small pebble beach on the other side of an inlet stream (see information on camping beside the Río Quilaleu which follows the description of the next stage).

Stage 3: Refugio Laguna Fría to Laguna Triángulo

(5½ km, 6 to 9 hours)

Until the track planned for the section around Lago Triángulo is eventually constructed, this difficult stage should only be attempted by experienced and fit parties. The pass offers a spectacular view of Lago Triángulo and Lago Chaiquenes, and makes a good return day trek.

Follow the path around the western side of Laguna Fría. The path rises onto a very low ridge near the southern end of the lake, where a track departs off left to some camp sites on the other side of the Río Quilaleu. Head south into the valley of the Río Quilaleu. The path makes its way close to the river, crossing a number of sidestreams. Quila, the vigorous native bamboo, may have overgrown the track in places, slowing progress.

After 1½ to two hours, the gradient sharpens and you begin the very strenuous ascent to 'Paso Triángulo'. Fill up your water bottle at the stream emerging from a deep gully on the right, as there is no water from here on until you get to Lago Triángulo. The 400-metre climb is steep enough in places to have warranted the fixing of ladders. The pass is gained in 1½ to 2½ hours, and the exertion is rewarded by truly impressive vistas. Immediately below, Lago Triángulo lies in a deep fjord-like trough at the head of a valley, with massive blank granite walls rising directly out of the water on one side.

Do not be tempted to follow routes leading immediately downward, as the land falls away in a series of impassable cliff-ledges. Pick up the track leading left along the ridge-line, where at the highest point the volcanoes Cabulco and Osorno come briefly into view. The track dips into a fire-damaged saddle after 20 to 30 minutes, before dropping 500 metres south-west down extremely steep slopes to reach the northern end of the lake.

Camp Sites There is good camping all along the Río Quilaleu. After leaving the river only dry camp sites exist until you get to Lago Triángulo. At the northern end of the lake there are pleasant grassy sites on the shore (these are subject to minor flooding at times).

Stage 5: Lago Triángulo (North Side) to Lago Chaiquenes
(3½ km, 6 to 10 hours)
At the time of writing the planned track around the steep and very difficult eastern side of Lago Triángulo had still not been completed. The slopes are covered by damp rainforest, and endless moss-covered logs and deep gullies make the going extremely slow and exhausting. You will probably need the better part of a day just reach the southern shore of the lake. As well as a cleared track, a refugio is planned for the south-eastern corner of Lago Triángulo.

Beginning on the east bank of the Río Triángulo, the lake's outlet stream which flows underground for the first 15 metres, the track passes through forest of coigüe and bamboo thickets. The route stays close to the river, descending continually. Cross the river on a wooden footbridge shortly before you reach Lago Chaiquenes, then head 500 metres around the north shore to a small landing jetty and car park.

Camp Sites There is reasonable camping in the rainforest at the southern shore of Lago Triángulo or on the lake's narrow beach. At Lago Chaiquenes there are pleasant but slightly less scenic sites near the small boat jetty.

Stage 6: Laguna Chaiquenes to Lenca
(17 km, 3 to 4 hours)
The Río Chaica road to Lenca makes a very pleasant downhill walk. The Guardería Río

Chaica is on the right side of the road at the park boundary, four km from Lago Chaiquenes. Notify the ranger of your safe arrival on your way down. Lenca is on the Carretera Austral and there are buses daily to Puerto Montt.

Other Treks in the Lake District

VOLCÁN CHOSHUENCO
(2 to 3 days)
Choshuenco (2415 metres) and Mocho (2413 metres) rise from a small volcanic range south-west of Lagos Panguipulli and Riñihue in one of the more remote parts of the Chilean Lake District. A road to a small skifield on the lower south-western slopes can be followed to above the tree line from where there is off-track walking.

The higher slopes are covered by glaciers and only experienced trekkers equipped with climbing equipment are advised to visit this area.

Maps
The two Chilean IGM 1:50,000 sheets, *Choshuenco* (Section G, No 122) and *Neltume* (Section G, No 123) cover the Choshuenco area.

Access
Buses on the international route to Argentina via Lago Pirehueico pass near to the village of Choshuenco from where it is 23 km to the Club Andino de Valdivia ski refugio.

RÍO BUENO TO VALDIVIA
(4 to 6 days)
This is a long walk along the wild and sparsely settled Pacific coastline south of Valdivia. At the village of Trumao, six km south-west of La Unión, a weekly steam ferry can be taken down the Río Bueno to the tiny outpost of Venecia. From here the route follows paths and roads north through coastal rainforest, along sandy beaches and

across several rivers. A number of isolated fishing villages are passed on the way where basic supplies can be bought. The trek finishes in Corral at the mouth of the Río Valdivia from where there are boats upriver to Niebla and Valdivia.

Maps

Three Chilean IGM 1:50,000 sheets, *Corral* (Section G, No 117), *Chaihuin* (Section G, No 116) and *Rio Colun* (Section H, No 1) cover the trek, but do not always indicate the route.

BAHÍA MANSA
(1 to 2 days)
There is coastal walking accessible from the large provincial town of Osorno. Tracks lead south along the rocky seafront from Bahía Mansa past Maicolpué.

Maps

Chilean IGM 1:50,000 sheet *Bahía Mansa* (Section H, No 21).

Access
By daily bus.

ASCENT OF VOLCÁN OSORNO
(2 to 3 days)
The western slopes of Volcán Osorno are completely outside of the Parque Nacional Vicente Pérez Rosales. A service road leads off the main Puerto Octay/Puerto Varas road, two km north of Ensenada on the eastern shores of Lago Llanquihue up to the Refugio Los Pumas and on to the Refugio Teski Club at 1180 metres above sea level. At all times of the year the climb to the summit requires crampons and ice axe. Inexperienced climbers are advised to make the ascent of the volcano with a professional local mountain guide.

Maps

The Chilean IGM 1:50,000 sheet *Las Cascadas* (Section H, No 43) covers the west side of Volcán Osorno and most of the ascent route. The adjoining sheet *Petrohué* (Section H, No 44) is also very useful.

Central Patagonia

The Central Patagonian Andes are remote, often extremely wet and have considerable problems of accessibility. Despite this, trekkers adventurous enough to visit this thinly-settled region will be rewarded for their perseverance by its wild and untamed nature. This ranges from the remote seascapes of Isla Grande de Chiloé to the spectacular glaciated ranges of the mainland national reserves of Río Simpson and Cerro Castillo.

Typical Chiloén church

Parque Nacional Chiloé

Despite centuries of gradual colonisation, large parts of the great island of Chiloé remain as virtually untouched wilderness. The 430-sq-km Parque Nacional Chiloé, on Chiloé's windswept western side, offers attractive scenery of sandy beaches and coastal lagoons before a backdrop of densely forested hills.

In the language of the Cunco (a Mapuche people), Chiloé means 'land of the seagulls', a fitting symbol for the island, whose environment and culture are so intricately connected with the sea. Facing out towards the south Pacific, Chiloé's climate is decidedly oceanic. This often makes weather unstable and blustery, with sea squalls regularly moving along the coast. Annual precipitation levels in Cucao reach 2200 mm but this rises to 3000 mm in the low ranges of the island's interior. The coastal aspect does, however, moderate the temperatures considerably.

RÍO ANAY WALK

This treks takes you along the lovely sandy beaches that fringe the rainforest in the southern part of the park, where there is an interesting and extensive area of dunes. In the 1961 earthquake, the western coast of Chiloé subsided up to two metres. The stumps of trees killed after the resulting advance of the ocean can still be seen in many places along the shore.

Descendants of the indigenous inhabitants still live in a few small villages along the park coast, fishing and collecting edible kelp, called *cucho yuyo*, which grows abundantly in the waters of southern Chile. This tough seaweed grows in thick clusters on the surf-buffeted rocks, and strands grow to lengths of many metres.

The rich rainforests on the immediate coast contain species not always found further inland. The coigüe de chiloé (*Nothofagus nitida*), with its characteristic serrated diamond leaves and the arrayán (*Myrceugenella apiculta*) are particularly common trees. The bark of the arrayán contains a harmless reddish-brown pigment which is washed out by the area's frequent rains, staining the local streams the colour of tea.

The coipo *(Myocastor coipus)* can sometimes be spotted (or more likely heard) swimming in the coastal lagoons in the evenings. A great number of aquatic and marine birds such as native herons and pilpilenes also inhabit the area.

Coipo

Maps
The area is covered by two Chilean IGM sheets scaled at 1:50,000: *Río Anay* (Section H, No 86), and *Cucao* (Section H, No 95). These recent maps indicate the route fairly accurately to the Río Cole Cole, after which no path is shown.

Days Required
Three days is the minimum walking time for this trek. This allows you to reach the Río Cole Cole at a leisurely pace on the first day. From there the section north to the Río Anay can be done as a short day trek.

Standard
This route through the park's (southern) Sector Anay provides access to isolated coastal settlements. Well-marked paths around the rocky points link the beaches. The track ends at the Río Anay, and you must return to Cucao via the same route. Runners or other light footwear are preferable to heavy walking boots.

A modern information centre has been built at the guardería, just up from Lago Cucao. The CONAF office in Castro (on Plaza de Armas) is also helpful, and can advise you on other treks on Chiloé.

The trek is graded easy. The distance to Río Anay is 26 km (or 52 km return).

Accommodation & Supplies
There are two free CONAF refugios on the hiking route. These are situated at Río Cole Cole and Río Anay, and provide basic shelter for about eight to 10 persons. In Cucao village at the start of the walk there are at least two *residencial*-style places offering cheap accommodation.

You can buy foodstuffs, wine and other basic supplies in Cucao. In Castro, or one of the other larger towns on Chiloé, the range and prices are better.

Access
Parque Nacional Chiloé is divided into two sections separated by a large parcel of freehold land. The route described below is within the southern section known as Sector Anay.

The trek begins at the village of Cucao, 55 km from Castro. From Castro there are three daily buses to Cucao, leaving from the regional bus terminal. The trip takes two hours, and buses return to Castro a short time after arriving. There is little local traffic out to Parque Nacional Chiloé, and hitchhiking is not recommended.

Stage 1: Cucao Village to Río Cole Cole
(18 km, 5 to 7 hours)
From where the bus drops you off, head right one km through Cucao village and cross the sturdy suspension footbridge spanning the Río Cucao. Continue along the path fringed by native fuchsias and lupines for 10 minutes to the Guardería Cucao. Short walks can be made through a wide area of foreshore dunes to the adjacent beach, or around the northern side of Lago Cucao.

Follow the sandy vehicular track past several farms until you arrive at the Posta Salud building by the Río Puchanquín after 45 minutes to one hour. For a view of Lago Huelde (which you otherwise don't see) take

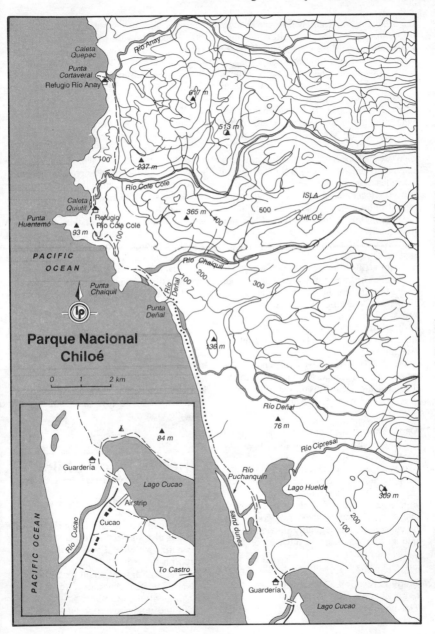

Parque Nacional Chiloé

the road leading right before the bridge. Work has been done to stabilise the sand dunes fronting the beach to save the lake from further coastal advancement.

Cross the bridge and follow what remains of the track for 30 minutes until to where it leads out onto the broad white sand beach. Move down to the firmer ground on the shore where the going is easier, and continue for two hours until you reach a small rocky point, Punta Deñal.

Wade the Río Deñal where it leaves a long lateral lagoon, and pick up a short stretch of track leading up over the point. This then descends to a lovely small beach on the other side. Continue 800 metres along the shore veering slightly to the right to find a bridge over the Río Chaiquil. After crossing, head left past several farmlets until you pick up a path to a playing field.

Climb into the forest behind Punta Chaiquil. The track winds around to contour along the cliffline. In places there are views of breakers crashing against the forest-clad rocks below. After one hour, the sheltered Caleta Quiutil comes into view, and the track descends from Morro Huentemó back to beach level.

Head 500 metres to the far end of the caleta where a signposted path leads to the refugio in the forest. This provides very basic shelter for about eight persons.

Camp Sites At the scenic north-western end of the brackish Lago Cucao there is a very pleasant campground with toilets and fireplaces. Reasonable fees are charged per site. No good sites exist along the shore until you reach the Río Cole Cole. Here there are lovely semi-sheltered spots at the northern end of the beach by the tiny lagoon. The brackish lagoon is regularly flooded by the tide so it is necessary to fetch water from further upstream.

Stage 2: Río Cole Cole to Río Anay
(8 km, 2 to 3 hours)
This short section can be done as a simple return day trek from Cole Cole.

Cross the Río Cole Cole suspension bridge and follow the path as it turns slightly eastward. The path swings back into a northerly direction after 20 minutes and follows the swampy course of a tiny sidestream through the beautiful rainforest of arrayán and tepu. Small logs have been laid down to stabilise the track, and very wet areas are bypassed on log platforms.

The path crosses a low watershed to meet another small stream flowing north. Follow mostly on the left side of this for 30 to 45 minutes until the path emerges at the Río Anay. The refugio is amongst bamboo thickets on the southern side of the stream at the lagoon outlet. It has a fireplace but no bunks, with room for about 10 persons.

Where the Río Anay enters the sea is a 10-metre wide lagoon. There is no bridge, and although narrow, the river is a very deep wade even at low tide. The lagoon can be swum easily if you wish to reach the lovely wild beach of Caleta Quepec.

Camp Sites There is no suitable camping between Río Cole Cole and Río Anay. Good camping exists at Caleta Quepec on the northern side of the Río Anay. The small lagoon where the Río Anay meets the beach is slightly brackish, and the nearest available fresh water is the last small stream you passed on the way.

Other Treks on Chiloé

NORTHERN (CHEPU) SECTOR
(2 to 3 days)
The northern part of the Parque Nacional Chiloé is also interesting, especially for its rich marine wildlife. From the locality of Chepu on the island's Pacific side a good track can be followed south along beaches and rainforested coast to a refugio and guardería at the Río Lar. Seal colonies inhabit the numerous rock islets just offshore.

Map
Chilean IGM 1:50,000 sheet *Chepu* (Section H, No 75).

Access
By bus from Ancud.

CENTRAL SECTOR
(4 to 5 days)
From the village of Piruquina (22 km north of Castro) a vehicle track leads west to a trail along the Río Grande. After initially following the river the route heads over the low Cordillera de Piuchén to an isolated beach and coastal lagoon at the mouth of the Río Abtao.

Maps
Two Chilean IGM 1:50,000 sheets, *Castro* (Section H, No 87) and *Río Anay* (Section H, No 86), cover this area but do not show the hiking route.

SOUTH OF CUCAO
(2 to 4 days)
From Cucao at the southern end of the national park rough roads and foot tracks can be followed south along the Pacific coastline to various sandy beaches.

Maps
The Chilean IGM sheet *Río Catiao* (Section H, No 104) covers this area.

Access
Transport is by bus to Cucao from Castro.

Volcán Chaitén

Volcán Chaitén is situated less than 10 km directly north-east of the small coastal township of Chaitén, opposite the island of Chiloé. The tiny extinct volcano nestles inconspicuously in a low ridge descending from the much higher and more majestic Volcán Michinmahuida by the Carretera Austral.

WALK TO THE CALDERA
This short walk takes you to the volcano's two-km wide caldera, in the centre of which there is a volcanic plug of recent origin. The plug is composed of broken lava rocks and rises some 400 metres above the crater. It is surrounded by a circular strip of mainly open grass meadows and this ring extends for most of the way around the caldera, providing a natural walking route. Around the crater the 150-metre rim forms a high wall broken only by the outlet stream which drains into the Río Chaitén. There are two small lakes and reportedly also some effervescent mineral springs within the crater.

The slopes of the volcano are covered with the luxuriant rainforest typical for much of the western coast of Chile. Along with all three of the evergreen coigües, tree species such as tepa and the beautiful mañío conifers dominate the vegetation. A variety of wildflowers can be found in the forest or growing under the benign conditions within the crater.

Maps
The entire area is covered by a single 1:50,000 sheet produced by the Chilean IGM, *Chaitén*, (Section H, No 110). This map does not shows the Carretera Austral or the route of the trek, but is otherwise reasonably accurate.

Days Required
The return trek into Volcán Chaitén takes one day in either direction. At least one additional day should be spent exploring the interesting area within the crater. Depending on transport you may have to get to the start of the trek on foot. This would lengthen the walk by about half a day for either direction.

Standard
This relatively straightforward but rough route rises some 700 metres through thick rainforest to the crater of the volcano. The trek is nevertheless rather strenuous, with many fallen trees and vigorous bamboo growth to slow you down, and is not to be underestimated. There is no real track, but a

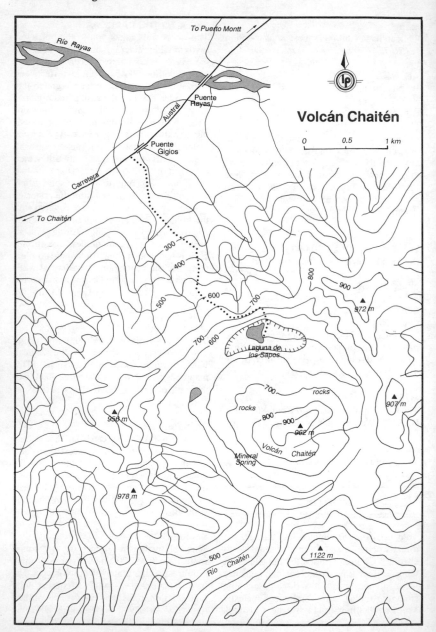

Volcán Chaitén

vague route should be discernible once you climb away from the bamboo on the initial section. The return is via the route of ascent.

A machete is recommended to clear thick vegetation from the track. The Club de Montaña in Chaitén, at Ignacio Carrera P, can give information on this and other walks in the area (see Carlos Alvarado García).

The trek is graded moderate to difficult. The distance from the Carretera Austral into the crater is four km.

Accommodation & Supplies

The local mountain club is planning to put up a small refugio in the caldera, but until this is built there is no shelter of any kind on the route. It is therefore essential for all parties to carry a tent. Chaitén has a good range of accommodation in the low to medium price range, and has two or three large food stores, a hardware shop and a small greengrocery.

Access

The trek begins 100 metres south of the Puente Gigios on the Carretera Austral, some 25 km north of the township of Chaitén. There is no local public transport to the start of the trek, although a minibus runs twice a week between Puerto Montt and Chaitén. Local and tourist traffic is growing, and hitchhiking (best in early morning) is a good prospect. The road offers pleasant scenery, and you can walk to the Puente Gigios in four to five hours. Camp sites can be found by the Arroyo Gigios upstream from the bridge.

Stage 1: Carretera Austral to Volcán Chaitén

(4 km, 3½ to 5 hours)
From the Puente Gigios walk 100 metres south-west along the Carretera Austral to a small sign marked 'Arroyo 76', and pick up the track among the leafy nalcas on the western side of the small stream. Cross a narrow ditch and follow blazings on trees leading into the forest. The track initially stays close to the stream, but gently rising and moving a short way to the right meets a second watercourse.

Make your way upstream through almost continuous thickets of bamboo above the steep banks. After 45 minutes to one hour, leave the stream and begin heading south-east up steep slopes (fill canteens beforehand as there is no water higher up until you reach the crater). Move more or less directly upwards, following occasional tree blazings. Many of these are only visible from above, so look downhill for orientation. Ascend for 45 to 60 minutes until you reach a ridge which falls away sharply on your left. From here there are views out through the trees to the perpetual snows of Volcán Michinmahuida and Lago Blanco on the Carretera Austral.

Head south up the ridge where many fallen logs and areas of thick vegetation make the going slow and strenuous. The route eases over to the right and comes to at the rim of the volcano after one to 1½ hours. Traverse left high above the crater for 700 metres, and descend a steep ridge leading down towards a lone coigüe tree on the open grassland at the north-eastern corner of 'Laguna de Los Sapos'.

A good day should be spent exploring the interesting area within the crater. It is possible to walk right around the largely open circular strip below the central mountain of denuded volcanic rock. The main peak is probably best climbed from ridges in the eastern part of the crater, and offers excellent views of Chaitén township on the coast and nearby Volcán Michinmahuida. An elusive spring of mineral water supposedly exists about one km down from the smaller murky lake on the inner slopes.

The return to the Carretera Austral is made via the ascent route. Take particular care on steep sections of track dropping down through bamboo thickets, where cut canes are sharp and very dangerous.

Camp Sites There is excellent camping within the crater on the east side of 'Laguna de los Sapos' (where the native frogs are very vocal at night). Below the second lake by the stream draining the caldera is also good. Lower down along the route, camp sites can also be found by the streams before you begin climbing.

Other Treks Around Chaitén

TERMAS EL AMARILLO TO LAGO ESPOLÓN
(4 to 7 days)
This is a very long route that leads to Futaleufú near the Argentine border. From the Termas El Amarillo (also known as Termas Vuelta y Vuelta) 25 km south of Chaitén, a rough route leads south-east via the Río Michinmahuida to Lago Espolón. This is a challenging route for experienced trekkers only.

PLAYA SANTA BARBARA
At a bridge 12 km north of Chaitén a short road off the Carretera Austral goes to Santa Barbara. Trails lead north along the beach front past former Chono caves and shell middens and rocky headlands. Camp sites can be found in the sheltered forest.

Reserva Nacional Río Simpson

The 408-sq-km Reserva Nacional Río Simpson is situated north-west of Coyhaique in Chile's IX Region. The reserve takes in the snow-capped ranges visible from the city, and offers pleasant and readily accessible hiking. The Río Simpson is named after an American palaeontologist who explored much of the Aisén area in the early part of this century. The Coyhaique-Puerto Aisén road follows the Simpson valley for most of the way as the river cuts through the Cordillera. The Río Simpson also cuts through the centre of the reserve, dividing it into two sectors.

The Río Simpson area is considerably sheltered by coastal ranges, while the rainfall in Puerto Aisén, directly west, exceeds 5000 mm. The local climate shows the gradual fall in precipitation levels that typically occurs with increasing distance east.

CERRO CATEDRAL
The northern sector of Río Simpson consists of a compact series of steep and glaciated granite ranges. These surround Cerro Catedral whose impressive citadel-like summit almost reaches 2000 metres. Small glaciers cling to the higher summits and several small glacial lakes lie in the forested valleys.

As in much of Chile's XI Region, fires have devastated a large part of the lower evergreen forest. Denuded slopes along the Río Correntoso are a reminder of the fire-sensitivity of the native vegetation. Deeper into the reserve's small valleys attractive forests dominated by the southern beech species lenga and colihue bamboo have remained relatively unscathed. The few remaining farms inside the reserve's boundary still graze cattle, but the park is gradually returning to its previous wild state.

Maps
A Chilean IGM 1:50,000 sheet, *Río Correntoso* (Section I, No 108), completely covers the area. This map does not show the track or local farms etc, but is otherwise quite topographically accurate.

Days Required
The optimal time to spend in the reserve is three or four days. This allows one long day hiking in to Refugio Laguna Catedral and another day to walk out.

Standard
The trek follows an often wet track providing access to a few tiny farms along the Río Correntoso. Cattle and horses have left the route very muddy and eroded in places and have caused constant branching of the track. The route is poorly marked but relatively straightforward. The best weather is experienced in February and March, but the trek can be done between November and late April.

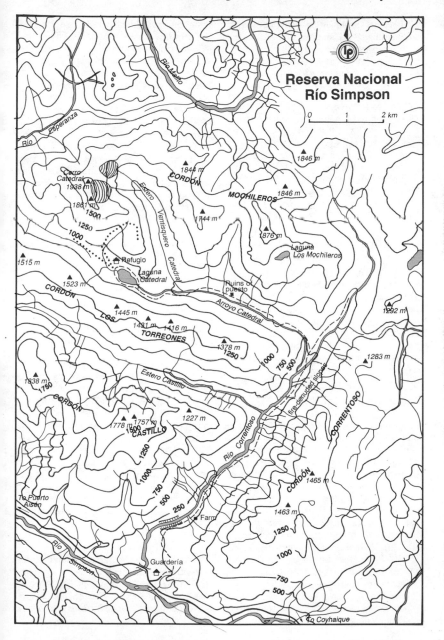

The park headquarters and information centre, situated 10 km west along the Aisén road, is worth a visit.

The walk is graded moderate. The return walking distance to Lago Catedral is 38 km.

Accommodation & Supplies

There is an old log hut at Laguna Catedral. This refugio has a leaky roof and provides basic shelter only, so it is highly advisable to carry a tent. The nearest accommodation is in Coyhaique, but there is a CONAF campground near the guardería on the Río Simpson road. There is no store near the start of the walk, so you should bring all you need from Coyhaique.

Access

The walk begins at the Puente Correntoso on the road to Puerto Aisén (Ruta CH 245), 22 km from Coyhaique. Some four buses run daily in either direction between Coyhaique and Puerto Aisén. The bridge is not well marked at the road so make sure the driver knows where you want to get off. Traffic is fairly constant and hitchhiking is a reasonably reliable alternative.

Stage 1: Puente Correntoso to Refugio Laguna Catedral

(19 km, 7 to 9 hours)

From the Puente Correntoso walk for five minutes to the east (towards Coyhaique) to where a signposted dirt road departs off to the left. The road leads up for 450 metres to the Guardería Correntoso. Leave all relevant details of your party here.

Head up through a farm gate and follow the broad track into light forest. The often very muddy and eroded path winds through low ridges for 45 minutes to one hour to meet the Río Correntoso at a safely fenced-off gorge. Follow the east side of the river one km to a puesto and small corral. Here the valley opens out slightly.

Proceed upstream across paddocks of regenerating coigüe trees and clumps of resilient colihue (bamboo). The path crosses

numerous small streams flowing down from the fire-devastated slopes at your right. Where a deep side valley meets the Río Correntoso on the adjacent bank, climb away to the right to avoid difficult terrain. The track continues through several stock gates and pockets of undisturbed forest to return to the river side after three to four hours.

Wade the small stream above its junction with the Arroyo Catedral. Head 400 metres up between the two branches where a small track leaves off north-west into the Valle Catedral near a tiny stand of deciduous lengas. Follow the path down onto forested riverflats and make your way upstream mostly on the northern bank. The path briefly fords and refords the stream to reach the ruins of an outstation one to 1½ hours on.

Continue 1½ km through pleasant lenga forest and make a final crossing just downstream from where the Estero Ventisquero Catedral enters. Here pick up an initially indistinct trail that leads off to the left and ascends gently beside a small clearwater stream. The path passes through a last gate and ascends past a waterfall to arrive at the Laguna Catedral after a further 30 to 45 minutes.

Follow the southern shore of the lake for 15 to 20 minutes around to the far end. A scrubby section must be negotiated before you get to the refugio in a clearing 150 metres back from Laguna Catedral. The refugio is in poor condition but offers basic shelter. Lying directly below the spectacular citadel-like summit of Cerro Catedral, this lovely spot provides a good base to explore the surrounding area. A lookout can be reached by following the inlet stream up north onto a ridge descending from Cerro Catedral. It is also possible to trek up the Estero Ventisquero Catedral.

Camp Sites Good camp sites can be found the central section of the Río Correntoso (boil water) and in many places along the banks of the Arroyo Catedral. At Laguna Catedral there is good camping on clover lawns near the hut.

Other Treks in Reserva Nacional Río Simpson

RÍO CLARO
(1 to 2 days)
The Río Claro is 10 km directly west of Coyhaique in the southern sector of the Reserva Nacional Río Simpson. The ranges surrounding this small river valley look down on the city and are easily explored. The reserve is also a CONAF sanctuary for the endangered huemul.

Maps
The Chilean IGM sheet *Coyhaique* (Section I, No 120) covers this area.

Reserva Nacional Cerro Castillo

The 1340-sq-km Reserva Nacional Cerro Castillo is situated between the Río Ibáñez and Lago Elizalde, a large elongated glacial lake set in the mountainous country southwest of Coyhaique (pronounced 'coy-ai-kay, meaning 'landscape of lakes' in the Tehuelche language) in Chile's XI Region. Cerro Castillo lies some 85 km south of Coyhaique at the southern end of the reserve, where it towers above the Río Ibáñez and the recently constructed Carretera Austral. The most prominent peak of the compact and spectacular Cordillera Castillo, the mountain's Spanish name comes from the many striking basalt turrets and craggy ridges which give Cerro Castillo its resemblance to a medieval castle. As a major landmark of the region, the 2675-metre peak of Cerro Castillo regularly attracts international climbers.

In spite of its relative accessibility, the area does not receive many visitors. During the warmer months a few *puesteros* (outstation cattlemen) live in the lower valleys, but move their animals down to lower ground as

the winter approaches. As in much of the Aisén region, uncontrolled burning has scarred a large part the reserve's periphery, yet the interior remains as relatively unspoiled wilderness.

IN & AROUND CERRO CASTILLO
The scenery along this walk is spectacular and varied. Typical features of the central Patagonian mountains can be seen. The forests are of mainly mixed beech species, and these cover much of the lower area. The tree line in most places reaches just over 1200 metres, and with increasing height the forest goes over into subalpine moorland or meadows abundant in wild berries. The high average precipitation in the ranges (around 3000 mm) produces numerous waterfalls. Glaciers cling precariously to craggy cliffs above alpine lakes clouded by moraine sediment. In the Valle Ibáñez to the south, the reserve borders abruptly on the dry windy steppes so typical of eastern Patagonia. Rainfall here is often as low as 1000 mm. Reserva Nacional Cerro Castillo is one of some five sanctuaries in Chile's XI Region established to protect the southern Andean deer, or huemul *(Hippocamelus bisulcus)*. Sadly, the numbers of this once common inhabitant of the southern Andes have dropped to alarmingly low levels, and the huemul is now an endangered species. Only a few of these graceful but generally shy animals remain in the Cerro Castillo area. The huemul is attracted by the remoteness of the central part of the reserve, where small herds graze in places where recent glacial recession has led to recolonisation by palatable plant species.

Maps
The Chilean IGM 1: 50,000 series covers the area of the trek in three sheets: *Lago Elizalde* (Section I, No 132); *Balmaceda* (Section I, No 133); *Villa Cerro Castillo* (Section J, No 10). Although most of the route described below is not shown on these maps, they are still very useful.

Days Required
Although it could be done in three days by

fit parties, allow a minimum of four days to complete this trek. For the more experienced, an optional sidetrip can extend the trek by around three days to make an excellent walk of six or seven days.

Standard

The trek follows an unmarked route of often indistinct stockmens' trails. As is common in areas subject to livestock grazing, the path becomes confused at times by endless branching and numerous scrubby sections have to be negotiated. Reasonably fit and experienced walkers should have relatively little difficulty in making their way through this country.

Careful navigation is important in the more rugged central section. There you will twice have to cross exposed terrain above the vegetation line, where prior to January some snow may be encountered. A number of alpine stream crossings must be undertaken. These are mainly glacier-fed streams that during sunny weather generally reach their highest level in late afternoon.

For more information about the route you can stop at the CONAF guardería, six km north of where the trek starts at Las Horquetas Grandes. CONAF also has its regional headquarters in Coyhaique on Avenida Ogana 1060 (on the left as you head south out of town; ☎ 21065).

The best direction in which to do this trek is north to south. The recommended starting point at Las Horquetas Grandes is almost 350 metres higher than Villa Cerro Castillo where the walk finishes. If you begin from the south end of the reserve the first day will be a bit more strenuous. Villa Cerro Castillo also makes a rather more convenient place to end the trek than the bend in the road at Las Horquetas Grandes.

The rating for all sections is moderate to difficult. The shorter version of the trek (walking out as described in Stage 4A) has a walking distance of 35 km. If you make the sidetrip to 'Campamento Nueva Zelandés' the total distance will be 48 km.

In August 1991, after being dormant for some 20 years, Volcán Hudson erupted vio-lently. The 2500-metre volcano is situated roughly 90 km north-west of the Reserva Nacional Cerro Castillo, and although no loss of life occurred, this major eruption caused considerable damage both to the environment and property. Volcanic ash was reportedly deposited over vast areas to the east extending well into Argentina. It seems likely that the Cerro Castillo area has received at least 50 cm of ash fallout (and quite possibly even more).

It's hard to say how long it will take for the reserve to return to normal, particularly if eruptions on this scale continue. With time, the volcanic ash will wash away or consolidate, but if there is enough of it ash can choke whole forests. Volcán Hudson is the source of the Río Ibáñez, and it seems inevitable that much of the local topography within its basin has been altered. A 25 km section of the Carretera Austral was either destroyed or obstructed by volcanic debris, and it may take some time for this to be repaired (check at the CONAF office in Coyhaique or at Guardería Puerto Ibáñez).

Accommodation & Supplies

There are no huts or trekker's refugios to speak of on any part of the trek, and it is essential that all parties carry a tent. The nearest accommodation is at the Pension El Viajero (US$2) in the small roadside village of Villa Cerro Castillo at the finish of the walk. Most trekkers will find it simpler to come directly from Coyhaique or Puerto Ibáñez.

The nearest store is in Villa Cerro Castillo at the end of the walk. For the best range and price, Coyhaique is the place to buy supplies.

Access

The walk begins at Las Horquetas Grandes, 85 km south of Coyhaique. Las Horquetas Grandes is little more than a bend in the Senda Río Ibáñez (the name given to this section of the Carretera Austral) where two minor streams flow together. The Dirección de Vialidad has a small road works depot here on the west side of the road.

From Coyhaique you can take buses going

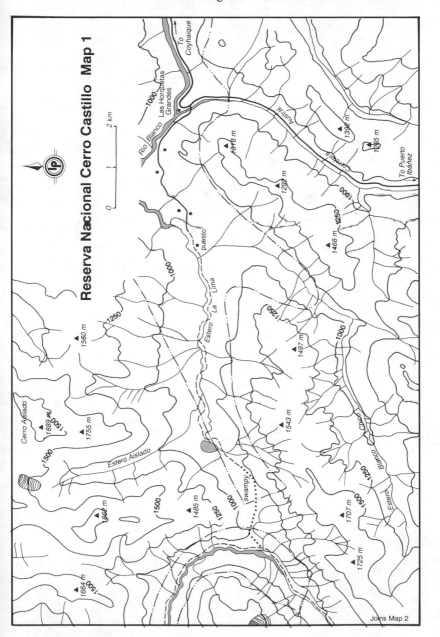

Reserva Nacional Cerro Castillo Map 1

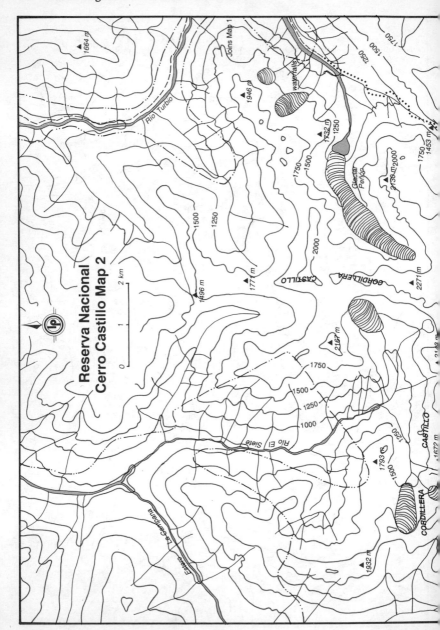

Reserva Nacional Cerro Castillo Map 2

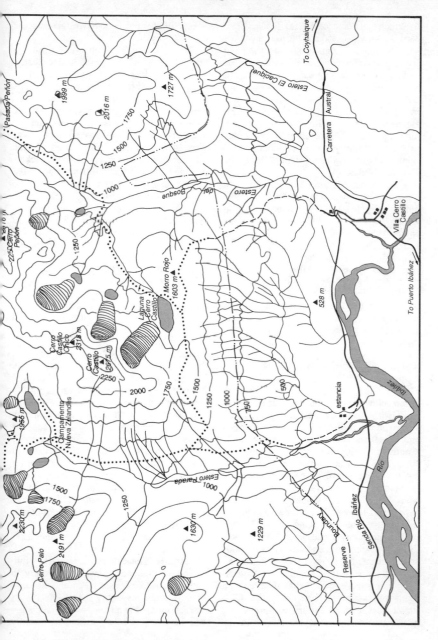

to either Cochrane or Puerto Ibáñez. The road is relatively good and the journey takes a bit less than two hours. In summer there are five Cochrane buses per week in either direction, usually departing early. Buses to and from Puerto Ibáñez leave daily. Sometimes colectivos also run this stretch. Buses leave rather less regularly to Puerto Ibáñez from Balmaceda, where the Region's sole national airport is located. If travelling from Cochrane in the south, you must continue for 20 minutes after Villa Cerro Castillo to cross the Paso Las Mulas.

The trek ends at Villa Cerro Castillo. In view of the majestic mountain itself, this small village lies 12 km down the road from the turnoff on the newly-opened Cochrane route. Although it is possible to flag down buses to Coyhaique from here, the chances of getting a ride are much better once you are back on the busier Puerto Ibáñez-Coyhaique road. If you are going on to Puerto Ibáñez, head south once you reach this intersection.

In this region of the country hitchhiking is exceptionally good. Both public and private transport are expected to increase as road conditions are steadily improved.

Stage 1: Las Horquetas Grandes to Upper Río Turbio

(16 km, 7 to 9½ hours)
From below the road maintenance station at Las Horquetas Grandes easily ford the Estero Paso Las Mulas above where it enters the Río Blanco to find a vehicular track. Continue 15 minutes along the left bank past a gate and a corral, then move up the slope to the left to arrive at a farmlet after 40 minutes. Follow the farmyard fence until you come upon the road once more. The way now heads through lenga forest which has been thinned out by logging.

This lumber road leads away from the Río Blanco into the Valle La Lima, and descends to the stream after 1½ hours. Scattered along the river are a few more small farms. Continuing along the eastern bank of Estero La Lima for 20 minutes, cross Estero Blanco, a small sidestream. A further 20 minutes on you reach the last occupied puesto in the valley. Interesting bare red ridges top the adjacent slopes.

The increasingly overgrown 4WD track gradually narrows to a well-trodden cattle trail. Keep close to the stream, which is forded two or three times. Passing the ruins of a farmhouse, after one to two hours the route leads out to a glade on the north bank. Here you should see the remains of an old wooden cattleyard, and there is the first clear view of the 'Pasada Peñón', a gap in the range to the south-west. A tiny brook trickles into the Estero La Lima, its source being the small glacier visible up a side valley to the north on Cerro Aislado.

Cross the clearing and pick up the path again. It takes you back over the stream a final time, leading through a difficult area of fallen trees. An extended belt of waterlogged mallín begins. When you reach a shallow lagoon, start moving left to the forest edge at the bottom of the slope.

The valley of the Estero La Lima does not terminate in a definite pass, but connects smoothly with the Río Turbio across an attractive moorland plain. You will hear the stream's surging waters before it actually comes into sight. Now 2½ to 3½ hours from the old cattleyard at Estero Aislado, walk down to the river bank to join a trail coming up the valley from Fundo El Encuentro on the shores of Lago La Paloma.

Staying close to the bank, make your way upstream. The path soon fords a channel of the river, but at no time attempt a crossing of the dangerous Río Turbio itself. The gradient is gentle and progress is rapid. Continue for one hour through small grassy pampas bordered by stands of deciduous beech. In the moister places there are patches of the native Magallanes strawberry. On the adjacent side of the river, numerous cascades spring from hanging glaciers and tumble off the sheer vertical cliffs.

Towards its head, the valley separates into two short branches. Ahead, or slightly to your left, is the 'Pasada Peñón', the only obvious route possibility. A little clearwater brook coming down from the gap enters the Río Turbio, just below a field of recently

Top: Glaciar Moreno, Parque Nacional Los Glaciares
Bottom: Laguna Torre from Base Camp, Parque Nacional Los Glaciares

Top: Altocumulus clouds, Parque Nacional Torres del Paine
Bottom: Parque Nacional Torres del Paine

deposited boulder-moraine. Directly west, the 'Glaciar Peñón' descends from the heart of the Cordillera Castillo.

The sidetrip to 'Glaciar Peñón' is recommended and can be done in one or two hours return. From above the junction of the two waterways, cross the left stream. Moving towards the ice mass, follow the south bank of the Río Turbio across newly colonised areas of grass and chaura bushes. There is no track, but despite loose rock the going is relatively easy. At the snout of the 'Glaciar Peñón' is a murky meltwater pool. For better views, you can climb the longitudinal moraine mounds on the glacier, but walking on the ice itself is very risky.

Camp Sites Except for the initial section, there is virtually unlimited camping along the whole way, and it is easy to break this stage up into two shorter days. The upper Río Turbio is, however, most recommended. Here many excellent camp sites can be found.

Stage 2: Upper Río Turbio to Estero del Bosque Junction
(6½ km, 5 to 6½ hours)
On the true right bank of the clearwater stream, pick up a prominent animal trail. This leads up through low forest for 1½ to two hours, until petering out at a sodden grassy slope near the tree line. Head on for another one to 1½ hours over unstable scree slopes to arrive at the 'Pasada Peñón', which at 1453 metres is the highest point of the trek. Unlike a classic pass, the gap is choked with frost-shattered rock debris. It is not possible to see both valleys at once. The high turquoise lake visible from the southern side of the pasada (at 50° true north) indicates the route ahead.

Keeping to the left, traverse the loose scree and drop down on to even more unstable slopes of glacial moraine. Where it is steeper, larger parties should take special care to dislodge as little rubble as possible. A spectacular sight opens out on the right, where a multitude of waterfalls drop from icefalls around Cerro Peñón. A rocky, gently

sloping silt-wash follows, formed by the course of the glaciers' meltwater.

Continue downward on the true left bank. The tree line begins a short way below. Here, pick up random trails down through the woods, or walk on cattle pads beside this narrow cascading stream. Only 1½ hours from the pass, this eastern branch of the Estero del Bosque intersects with the somewhat larger western arm. Make a ford 200 metres above the river junction.

Camp Sites After crossing the river, there is reasonable camping in the moist forest a short distance upstream. Some rather better camp sites, used occasionally by cattle musterers, are situated 500 metres below on the estero's true right bank. To get to these don't cross until you reach a wider section of the river, well down from the confluence. No other camping spots can be recommended.

Stage 3: Estero del Bosque Junction to 'Laguna Cerro Castillo'
(3 km, 3 to 4 hours)
Downstream from the junction the Estero del Bosque leads into an increasingly steep and difficult canyon. Hikers must not be tempted to use this route as a presumed faster exit, but should take the route described below.

Now inside the 'Y' formed by the two branches of the Estero del Bosque, make your way upstream. Several very small sidestreams are passed, and after 20 to 30 minutes a quite sizable tributary flows rapidly into the river at a sharp angle. Carefully select a crossing place some way above the stream intersection. Fallen logs may provide a convenient bridge.

Immediately ascend a very low ridge that divides the main stream from the small torrent just crossed. Pick up a faint track which now continues along the true left (ie north-western) bank. In places landslides and natural erosion have made it necessary to detour above the steep sides. Two to three hours on, a partially cut track through the weather-beaten vegetation emerges. Head up over sparse alpine pastures for a further 30 to 40 minutes to arrive at 'Laguna Cerro

Castillo'. A stunning sight, the lake lies at 1275 metres above sea level in a deep glacial basin which is directly under the imposing Cerro Castillo. Hanging glaciers periodically drop ice blocks onto the rock cliffs below, which shatter and occasionally hit the water.

Camp Sites The open stony ground around 'Laguna Cerro Castillo' offers scenic but extremely exposed camping. There are poor semi-sheltered camp sites 15 minutes (or one km) downstream from the lake in the scrub on the true right bank. This not far above where the meltwaters of an impressive icefall enter the stream. At this altitude firewood is a bit scarce.

Stage 4A: 'Laguna Cerro Castillo' to Villa Cerro Castillo (Via Estero del Bosque)
(9 km, 4 to 5½ hours)
This is the fastest and most direct way of walking out. However, trekkers should take care on the exposed first section of the route.

Cross the lake's outlet stream and start moving left up the stabilising moraine slope until you reach a terrace. Follow this natural walkway until you are about two thirds of the way along the length of the lake. Then head more or less straight uphill to a tiny tarn on the flat and barren saddle, 30 to 45 minutes from the camp. This spot offers a fine view to Cerro Castillo directly opposite (you will need a 28 mm lens to get it all in). The rocky crest on the left may also be climbed to reach the flat summit of 'Morro Rojo', from where there are views down the Valle Ibáñez as far as Lago General Carrera.

Contour around into a roughly easterly direction and traverse the sparsely vegetated south-facing slopes behind 'Morro Rojo' on animal trails for about 1500 metres. As you near the brushline, swing around south onto a steep indistinct ridge. If descending from the top of 'Morro Rojo' itself drop down at roughly 150° true north, taking care to avoid steep gullies on the east side of the hill.

Keeping well to the right of where the land drops away sharply into the Estero del Bosque, follow the ridge down through regenerating forest for 15 to 20 minutes until you arrive at an area that has been burn-cleared for grazing. From here on you will begin to find more definite cattle paths.

Continue for another 45 minutes until you begin to hear the river more clearly. Gradually ease over towards the stream to pick up a good trail. This now descends south-west through fire-damaged beech forest, passing by a corral and through a gate. Below some low cliffs, go left along the line of a badly eroding drain to meet a broad cut vehicular track. This road leads on past a farmhouse and crosses the Estero del Bosque on a bridge. Here the landscape changes abruptly into Patagonian steppes. Depending on the winds, the walk to Villa Cerro Castillo takes about 15 minutes.

Camp Sites No suitable camping is available until near the end of the trek. On the ridge down from 'Morro Rojo' water may be hard to find close to level ground. Once you get to the road, a few reasonable sites can be found just up from the bridge crossing the Estero del Bosque. If you ask permission you might be able to camp at Villa Cerro Castillo.

Stage 4B: 'Laguna Cerro Castillo' to 'Campamento Nueva Zelandés'
(8 km, 4 to 6 hours)
For stronger parties with sufficient time, this optional sidetrip to the mountaineers' base camp at the head of the Valle Parada is well recommended. The only difficulty involves traversing exposed land above 'Laguna Cerro Castillo' and dropping 600 vertical metres through steep trackless terrain until a trail on forested slopes above the river is met.

From the saddle below 'Morro Rojo' (see Stage 4A) head two km due east up the barren ridge until it levels out. The edge of this small flat area overlooks the valley, and you can best view the route possibilities below from here. The forest ends immediately upstream from where a deep gully curves left to join the Estero Parada.

Just south of this sidestream an obvious ridge also swings around to the left, but rather more sharply.

Descend one km down the steep spur at 240° true north then move slightly over to the right to pick up a small ridge. Follow this for 15 minutes as it takes you down a coarse gravel-wash. Look for the track near where sidestream, forest and the small ridge all come together.

The trail edges higher as it makes its way up the valley, maintaining a fairly constant course 500 metres from the Estero Parada. In a number of places bands of rock debris washed from the slopes above jut down through the forest belt and across the path, allowing impressive views towards Cerros Palo and Puntudo on the adjacent range.

The path meets the river after 1½ to two hours. Continue on the east bank for a further 45 minutes to one hour through attractive moist clearings and thinning lenga forest. The valley opens out considerably as you near its head. Some fireplaces and a mound of rocks on the true left bank of the stream a short way below the tree line indicate 'Campamento Nueva Zelandés', the site of the original base camp used by a 1971 climbing party from New Zealand. The expedition made a number of first ascents of peaks in this area, in particular Cerro Castillo.

The wild upper Valle Parada is enclosed on three sides by jagged summits of the Cordillera Castillo, and half a day or so might be spent exploring this area. A small lake set in bare surroundings under Cerro Castillo Chico can be visited from 'Campamento Nueva Zelandés' by heading up beside the narrow eastern branch of the Estero Parada. After the path peters out, continue over mossy slopes and glacial debris to the lake (one to two hours return). On the west side of the valley two more lakelets formed by end moraines are best reached by crossing the east stream and heading around underneath the cliff face (one hour return).

Camp Sites Although the campamento itself is hard to beat, there are numerous other spots in sheltered clearings above the junction of the two main branches of the stream. The land further down the valley is generally too steep for tents.

Stage 4C: Across the Pass to Valle El Siete

(To the Pass: 2½ km, 3 to 4½ hours)
From 'Campamento Nueva Zelandés', it is possible to climb up through the seemingly impassable cliff wall to reach the Valle El Siete on the other side. This trip is exclusively for more experienced trekkers however, and parties should only attempt the climb in fine conditions. Once over the 1672-metre-high pass watch the weather carefully to avoid becoming stranded by sudden loss of visibility due to low cloud or rain. A rope may be useful for packhauling.

There is no precise route, but try to pick out a way up from well back. Start on the granite slabs above the tiny aqua-blue lake near the cliff base, and then work your way up through continuous chutes and ledges. Watch out for rotten or loose rock and be prepared to downclimb and try again if you get stuck. The pass offers superb views down the valley.

The next valley can now be reached by heading left and walking along the cliffline for 15 minutes, before dropping down to the right past a small glacier. Crossing the violently flowing Río El Siete is hazardous and unnecessary. From here it is possible to trek a poor route down the river to Lago Azul and Lago El Desierto.

Stage 4D: 'Campamento Nueva Zelandés' to Villa Cerro Castillo

(13 km, 7 to 10 hours)
Backtrack down the valley to where you first hit the trail at the start of the fire-cleared area. Remaining high above the river, various tracks continue across fields of wild strawberries for one or two hours. Where the country starts to open out into the Valle Ibáñez, move slightly west of due south for one km down a spur to near the shore of the Estero Parada.

As the gradient moderates, trails follow the course of the river for a further one to two hours into increasingly typical Patagonian steppes of windswept calafate bushes and ñirre woodland. Pass an extensive homestead belonging to the Hueitra family to your the left. A wide and unmistakable track is reached shortly thereafter. This is a *senda de penetración* providing farms along the north bank of the Río Ibáñez with basic access.

Walking vaguely east, cross rich river flats and follow the track to where it meets the river underneath some low rock outcrops. The way becomes noticeably more transited, and rises and dips slightly to continue for one to two hours through lenga forest near the riverside. After it comes out at a sandy plain, the road heads in a straight line to meet a larger gravel road. Turning left, proceed for 20 minutes across the Estero del Bosque bridge and on to Villa Cerro Castillo.

Other Treks in Central Patagonia

UP THE RÍO PUELO – CHILE
(At least 6 days)
This long trek goes via the valley of the lightly settled Río Puelo just south of the Lake District. The Río Puelo rises in Argentina but flows west via Lago Puelo into the Pacific.

From the coastal village of Puelo (100 km south-east of Puerto Montt on Seno Reloncaví) take a chartered boat to the east shore of Lago Tagua Tagua. Here, follow a trail up the eastern bank of the river to its junction with the Río Manso, which must also be crossed by a locally-hired boat. The route continues to the Carabineros station at Llanada Grande and on past Lagos Azul, Blanco, Totoral, Las Rocas and Inferior to the Argentine frontier. Although locals often cross here, trekkers are generally not permitted entry in either direction and may be sent back by customs personnel.

Maps
Four Chilean IGM 1:50,000 maps cover the Río Puelo area: *Puelo* (Section H, No 62), *Lago Taguatagua* (Section H, No 63), *Río Traidor* (Section H, No 73) and *Llanada Grande* (Section H, No 74). See also the following section on Lago Puelo – Argentina.

PARQUE NACIONAL LAGO PUELO – ARGENTINA
(1 to 3 days)
This park is situated south-west by road from El Bolsón. From the north-east end of Lago Puelo there is a track leading west along the lake shore across the border into Chile where there are isolated settlements on the Río Puelo. Although locals often cross here, trekkers are generally not permitted entry in either direction and will probably be sent back by customs personnel.

Maps
Two Argentine IGM 1:100,000 sheets, *Cordón del Pico Alto* (Chubut, No 4372-3) and *Lago Puelo* (Chubut, No 4372-4), cover all of the park. See also the preceding section Up The Río Puelo – Chile.

PARQUE NACIONAL LOS ALERCES – ARGENTINA (LAGO MENÉNDEZ)
(2 to 3 days)
Los Alerces is a very large national park in the Cordillera to the west of Esquel in the north of Chubut Province. The park's northern sector offers some excellent hiking but the southern area of Los Alerces is dominated by Lago Situación, a huge hydroelectric dam. From Mermoud (55 km south by road from Cholila) an easy track can be followed along the south-east shore of Lago Menéndez before heading north to Laguna Hito and Lago Rivadavia. Access is by tour bus from Esquel.

Maps
Two sheets 1:100,000 produced by the Argentine IGM, *Lago Rivadavia* (Chubut, No 4372-10) and *Villa Futulafquén* (Chubut, No 2372-16) cover the trekking route.

PARQUE NACIONAL LOS ALERCES – ARGENTINA (LAGO FUTULAFQUÉN TO LAGO CHICO)
(4 to 6 days)

From Punta Limonao at the south-eastern end of Lago Futulafquén a track leads around the lake's southern side to Lago Krüger, where it is necessary to cross by boat in order to pick up a trail along the lake shore to Lago Chico. Access is from Esquel.

Maps

As for the previous Parque Nacional Los Alerces – Argentina (Lago Menéndez).

PARQUE NACIONAL QUEULAT – CHILE
(Approximately 2 days)

Queulat is a newly established national park on the Carretera Austral near Puyuguapi. A large part of the park is glaciated or covered by icefields, and the lower country is vegetated by dense coastal rainforest. The area's lack of trails and intensely wet climate make it a very challenging place to explore. From the guardería (two km off the Carretera) which looks out toward the spectacular Ventisquero Colgante a track is planned up the Río Ventisqueros (not to be confused with the nearby Río Ventisquero) into the wild country around the Nevado Queulat.

Maps

The Chilean IGM 1:50,000 sheet *Puyuguapi* (Section I, No 61) covers the central part of the park around Ventisquero Colgante.

Southern Patagonia

Southern Patagonia stretches south from the Península de Taitao and Lago Carrera/Buenos Aires south to the Straits of Magellan. Dominated by the two vast continental icecaps, the Hielo Norte and the Hielo Sur, this region is the most intensely glaciated part of the South American continent.

Unquestionably one of the world's most ruggedly, beautiful places, Southern Patagonia takes in the internationally renowned Los Glaciares and Torres del Paine national parks. Their towering granite peaks attract thousands of trekkers every year. There are also many other lesser known and less frequently visited areas. Wherever else you plan to go in the Patagonian Andes, be sure to include a trip to one of the superb parks of this region.

Reserva Nacional Tamango

The small Reserva Nacional Tamango is situated immediately north of the tiny township of Cochrane, south of Lago General Carrera on Chile's Carretera Austral. The reserve occupies the very western end of the Cordón Chacabuco, a range of low mountains that overlook Lago Cochrane (pronounced locally as 'cock-ran-ay').

Tamango is a gently forested plateau that undulates at about 1000 metres. Reaching 1722 metres, the highest peak in the reserve is Cerro Tamango. This rounded mountain rises abruptly from the nearby Río Baker, the most voluminous river in Chile, and the Carretera Austral. In the centre of the reserve are two attractive lakes, and numerous small alpine tarns lie hidden in the forest.

To the west, the Campo de Hielo Norte, the smaller and more northerly of Patagonia's two vast icesheets, greatly shelters the area around Cochrane from the savage weather typical of the coastal highlands. In fact, the reserve occupies a zone of climatic transition, with vegetation changing noticeably as precipitation levels drop away as you move eastwards.

The western parts are covered by light forest of predominantly deciduous lenga (*Nothofagus pumilio*). The ground cover often consists only of low herbs and mosses giving the forest a very open appearance. In many places the tree branches are covered with growths of stringy lichen called *barba del viejo*, or 'old man's beard'. Towards the east, the forest gives way to a drier landscape of tussock grasses and prickly cushion plants more typical of the Patagonian steppes. Birdlife is especially abundant here, and there are many species of ducks, swans and other water fowl around the isolated lakes and marshes.

Like other reserves in Chile's XI Region, Tamango is a sanctuary for the endangered huemul (*Hippocamelus bisulcus*), or Andean deer. The wildlife also includes guanaco, ñandú, native foxes and the Patagonian hare. Immediately north of Tamango lies the Valle Chacabuco, run as a vast (75,000 hectare) estancia which occupies the entire valley. A number of small farms are also situated around the reserve, and cattle and sheep often wander across its boundary.

Patagonian hares

166

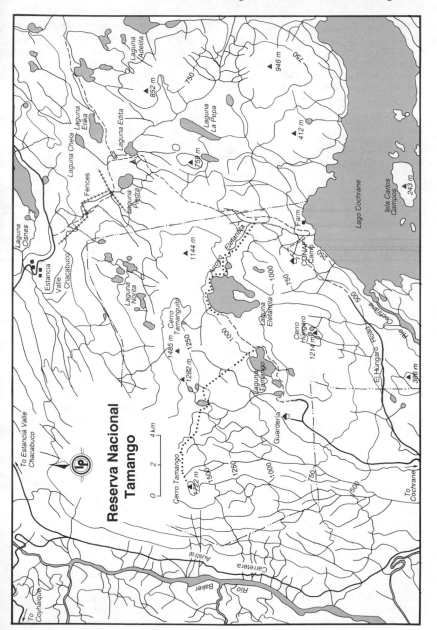

Reserva Nacional Tamango

TAMANGO CIRCUITS

Maps

Reserva Nacional Tamango is covered by one Chilean IGM 1:50,000 sheet, *Valle Chacabuco* (Section J, No 57). The map does not indicate the reserve or the walking route, but is otherwise quite accurate.

Days Required

There are two alternative circuit routes through the reserve. The longer version goes north through the Valle Chacabuco road and is best done in three leisurely days. The other option is via the El Húngaro road and can be done in two short days. A fairly long return day walk to Lago Tamango and Lago Elefantita is also possible from Cochrane.

Standard

The trek follows tracks and small roads for most of its distance, but the central three km section around Lago Elefantita is rather scrubby in parts. Stray livestock still graze in and around the reserve, and their trails confuse the route in places. There is usually little underbrush, however, and off-track walking is easy except where previous fires have destroyed the forest, as this causes vigorous regrowth. The route is largely unmarked, but with some care navigation should not be a major problem.

It is well worth paying a visit to the local CONAF office in Cochrane. This is located at Calle Teniente Merino on the Plaza de Armas. Either version of the trek is easiest to follow in the direction given below, and this is the recommended way to do the trek. The walk is rated easy to moderate. The Valle Chacabuco circuit total's 36 km. The length of the shorter version is 29 km.

Accommodation & Supplies

There are no huts specifically for trekkers in the reserve, but CONAF have established a semi-permanent camp on the slopes above Lago Cochrane and there is a newly-completed guardería in Tamango where it may be possible to stay a night. Nonetheless, all walkers should carry a tent.

Cochrane has at least two casas de familia, but there is nothing more up-market in town. Cochrane has several general stores with most necessary provisions. Prices reflect the town's relative remoteness so, if possible, do your shopping in Coyhaique or Puerto Aisén.

Access

The trek begins directly from Cochrane, 340 km by road south of Coyhaique. Together Aerobus and Buses Pudú run five minibuses per week from Coyhaique to Cochrane. Buses usually leave around 8 am and take around eight hours to complete the journey. At US$15 to US$18 one-way, bus fares are relatively expensive.

In summer, Don Carlos has three flights from Coyhaique to Cochrane each week. The cost of the single airfare is around US$35. Make sure that you sit on the right side of the plane for tremendous views of the northern continental icecap, if fine weather allows.

Due to the low volume of traffic, hitchhiking on the Carretera Austral south of Lago Carrera can be very slow. Both public and private transport are expected to increase as road conditions are gradually improved.

In August 1991 the eruption of Volcán Hudson, situated 110 km south-west of Coyhaique caused considerable damage to the local environment. The blast lasted two weeks and deposited ash and other volcanic debris over wide areas of southern-central Patagonia. This made a 25 km section of the Carretera Austral near the Río Ibáñez impassable, and access to Cochrane from Coyhaique was cut. Reconstruction of the road will begin almost immediately once the eruptions have subsided, but it may be some time before the Carretera Austral is reopened (check at the CONAF office in Coyhaique).

Stage 1: Cochrane to Laguna Elefantita
(10 km, 4 to 5 hours)

From the Plaza de Armas in Cochrane walk north one street block past the Liceo Municipal (school). Cross the small Estero Tamango stream on a bridge and follow a dirt road around to the left. The road leads up past a pine plantation to reach an intersection after 30 to 45 minutes. The slopes of low ñirre scrub overlook the township.

Take the left road branch and begin climbing more steeply beside the stream into light lenga forest. The road continues through the reserve entrance gate to reach a second fork after one to 1½ hours. The left branch goes 500 metres to a newly established CONAF guardería. Head one km along the right track around two mallínes to where it terminates.

Pick up a well-marked path and follow this gradually around to the right. The path leads past two attractive ponds in the lichen-covered lenga forest to reach Laguna Tamango after 30 to 45 minutes. Make your way around the lake's south-eastern shore for a further 15 to 20 minutes through a continuous band of clearings where guanaco sometimes graze. From the north-eastern outlet of Lago Tamango follow the stream's open soggy banks gently down for 1½ km until you come to the considerably larger Laguna Elefantita.

Camp Sites The two large ponds first passed by the track offer pleasant and sheltered camping. Good camp sites can be found at the eastern end of Laguna Tamango amongst the scrub. At Laguna Elefantita there are scenic but exposed sites near the inlet stream.

Stage 2A: Laguna Tamango to Cerro Tamango
(10 km return, 5 to 7 hours return)
This relatively straightforward sidetrip is recommended for moderately experienced trekkers.

From the outlet stream of Lago Tamango, head roughly 330° (ie north-west) up into the forest. Make your way over a low ridge to a small stream. Cross and continue one to two hours in the same direction until you come to an attractive wide saddle between Cerros Tamango and Tamanguito.

Move 500 metres west past some alpine tarns and begin ascending the open eastern slopes of Cerro Tamango via irregular ridges. As you get higher ease over right and follow a slightly more pronounced spur to reach the summit after a further 1½ to 2½

hours. In fine weather there are excellent views west towards the northern continental icecap. The great snow-capped massif some 60 km to the south-west is Monte San Lorenzo, the second highest mountain in southern Patagonia.

The western slopes of Cerro Tamango are dangerously steep. Do not try descending to the Carretera Austral from the summit, but return via the ascent route.

Stage 2B: Laguna Elefantita to Cochrane via El Húngaro road
(19 km, 5½ to 9 hours)
This is the shorter and easier route back to Cochrane.

Head around the northern side of Laguna Elefantita. Depending on the water level, either follow the narrow rocky shore line or make your way through the sometimes scrubby forest. The going is slow but mostly not difficult. As some clearings appear near the lake's east end, pick up a faint trail leading south-east to reach the small outlet stream after 45 minutes to 1¼ hours.

Continue 400 metres via stream-side clearings to pass left (north) around a swampy lakelet. Cross at the outlet and begin dropping down along the southern side of the cascading Arroyo Elefantita through occasional thickets. At the edge of an area of forest destroyed by fire, drop down steeply to the bottom of the slope. Here the Arroyo Elefantita is joined by another stream and swings around south. Cross the stream and head uphill until you intersect with a broad and well-trodden horse trail.

Turn right (south) and gradually descend towards Lago Cochrane. There are excellent views across the lake's turquoise waters to Isla Carlos Campos and other tiny islands. After two km the trail passes by a small farm on a level peninsula of Lago Cochrane. Wade the shallow Estero Elefantita 200 metres from the shore and begin climbing very steeply to the left of a deep gully. This leads up to a CONAF camp on the fire-charred slopes high above the lake. The camp consists of a large wooden building with a stable at the back.

From the CONAF camp the path contours south-west for three km and then becomes a road. Follow this road for two to three hours until you get to the junction passed in Stage 1, then proceed downhill to Cochrane.

Camp Sites There is camping near the Laguna Elefantita outlet on damp moss lawns. After this there are no recommended camp sites until you reach the CONAF camp. Here water can be collected at a small stream 100 metres on from the camp and it should be boiled.

Stage 2C: Laguna Elefantita to Laguna Edita
(9 km, 4 to 6 hours)
This is the longer route alternative back to Cochrane via the Valle Chacabuco.

As described above, make your way around the northern side of Laguna Elefantita before following the outlet stream (Arroyo Elefantita) down to meet the broad trail coming up from Lago Cochrane.

Turn left and head northwards, soon crossing the (unmarked) boundary of the reserve. The path gradually edges north-eastwards and leads through a pleasant area of moist meadows. Diverging animal trails confuse the route in some places. After passing through remaining pockets of low beech forest, the land drops away to give a sudden view of the Laguna Piedra (to your left), Laguna Erika (behind) and Laguna Edita below.

Drop down one km north-east towards Laguna Edita, sidling a few hundred metres right as you descend through rough tracks in the thick ñirre scrub. On the southern side of Laguna Edita is a strip of green pasture that contrasts sharply with the largely barren hills surrounding the lake. Here you come onto a horse trail leading down the valley from a puesto.

Camp Sites There is a nice grassy camp site at Laguna Edita by a cluster of ñirre trees on the lake's south-western corner. Camping is also possible in the area of open meadows beside the path. Laguna Erika is another possibility (see Stage 3 which follows). All water should be boiled.

Stage 3: Laguna Edita to Carretera Austral
(17 km, 5 to 7 hours)
Follow the trail 15 to 20 minutes north past the lake outlet to where another track leads eastwards across a footbridge in the direction of Laguna Erika. Continue around to the left (west) for one km through a wire fence gate. The trail now descends north-west across open undulating slopes, passing through a second gate to reach the Valle Chacabuco road two to three hours after leaving Laguna Edita.

Turn left and walk west along the road, reaching the administration centre of Estancia Valle Chacabuco after 2½ km. This consists of a dozen or so scattered buildings. Continue west through the dry eroded landscape of tussock grasses and calafate bushes. The road rises and dips to cross a number of small (mainly dry) streams and arrives at the Carretera Austral after three to 4½ hours.

From here it is a further 17 km (four to six hours walking) back to Cochrane. Sporadic local traffic is almost certain to stop for hitchhikers, and the infrequent minibus service from Coyhaique also passes here every now and then.

Camp Sites Due to the dry nature of the country on this section, good camp sites are limited. However, the Estero Tulín, crossed about halfway between the Estancia Valle Chacabuco administration and the Carretera Austral, has permanent water and is a reasonable camping option. It may also be possible to camp by the Río Baker, but the only access to the river is at the ferry crossing one km off the Carretera Austral (8½ km on from where it passes the Valle Chacabuco road).

Parque Nacional Los Glaciares

The vast Parque Nacional Los Glaciares stretches some 200 km north to south along the eastern edge of the southern continental icesheet in the south of Argentina's Santa Cruz Province. The park is accessible from the the rapidly growing tourist town of Calafate.

Bordered by the southern continental icesheet, or Hielo Sur, to the west, and largely separated from the Patagonian steppes by great glacial lakes or the enormous glaciers themselves, Los Glaciares is well protected by natural barriers. The park is probably the greatest single tract of true wilderness left in Argentina. Access to large parts of the park is only possible by boat, and entry is tightly controlled. Apart from supervised tourist launch excursions across Lago Argentino, venturing into the heart of the Los Glaciares is not encouraged. Park authorities seek to protect the delicate environment of Los Glaciares as much a possible.

As its name suggests, the Los Glaciares landscape is totally dominated by ice age glaciation, and continues to exhibit a variety of glacial phenomena. One of Argentina's most famous natural landmarks, the spectacular Glaciar Moreno lies in the southern sector of the park, and is easily visited by tour bus. The glacier periodically dams up a major branch of Lago Argentino until the immense pressure of the backwaters eventually breaks the ice wall in a marvellous show of natural forces.

Since large parts of Los Glaciares receive heavy winter snowfalls, the recommended time to visit the park is during the summer season from November to April. Despite this, winter conditions are not as severe as you might think, because the harsh Patagonian winds that constantly blow throughout the summer months drop away from around May to the beginning of September .

The SNPN has offices in Calafate at San Martín & 1 De Mayo, on the road leading west towards the mountains.

At the far north end of Los Glaciares lies one of the most magnificent and famous mountain areas in the Andes. Here the legendary diorite peaks of Cerro Torre and Cerro Fitz Roy rise abruptly from the flat Patagonian steppes, attracting climbing expeditions from all over the world. Short

lateral valleys lead into the ranges to below many of these peaks, giving trekkers relatively straightforward access to the finest scenery.

A number of different walks can be done in the northern sector of the park, here called the Fitz Roy area. Four of the these are described below in the recommended order. Permits to camp in Parque Nacional Los Glaciares are issued as you sign in at the Guardería Chaltén. You must give your intended route and the expected date of the party's return. Be sure to sign out before leaving the area.

Other treks, in the southern sector of the park, are described at the end of this chapter.

Maps

The best map covering the entire Fitz Roy area is a well-prepared sketch map scaled at roughly 1:75,000. The duplicated sheet shows all walking routes and places of significance to trekkers, but is not always drawn to scale. The map is produced in Calafate, and sold cheaply by 'CROC', at Avenida del Libertador 1474. Two newly printed Argentine IGM 1:100,000 sheets, *Estancia Kaiken Aike* (No 4972-26, Santa Cruz) and *Laguna del Desierto* (No 4972-20, Santa Cruz), cover the eastern Fitz Roy area, but exclude the crucial interior of the park. Although these maps are reasonably accurate topographically, they do not show hiking trails. Two other still unprinted sheets, *Glaciar Viedma* (Nos 4972-25 & 4975-30) and *Monte Fitzroy* (No 4972-19), would take in the spectacular mountainous area a little further to the west, and are sorely missed.

Accommodation & Supplies

The only accommodation in the Fitz Roy area specifically for visitors is the Hostería Chaltén. This is situated opposite the Guardería Chaltén. The hostería offers medium-range accommodation (US$15 per night) and also serves meals (US$8). There are two free campgrounds, two km apart, at each end of Chaltén. Firewood is often scarce. Calafate is the logical place from which to base your visit to Los Glaciares.

The town has many good to medium hotels and residenciales, and even a youth hostel.

Supplies still cannot be bought at Chaltén (or anywhere else within the park), so it is important to bring all you need with you from Calafate, where there are at least two small supermarkets and a bakery.

Access
The treks all leave from around the newly built administration village of Chaltén, some 240 km north of Calafate. From December to around Easter (check for exact dates), the Interlagos tour company runs a daily bus from Calafate to Chaltén. The round trip costs about US$13. The bus leaves Calafate at 7 am, and returns from Chaltén around 3 pm. The trip takes five hours each way. There is no problem breaking the journey, even if you want to stay a few weeks in the area.

Visiting Fitz Roy out of season usually requires organising your own transport. With enough people, a minibus or taxi will cost roughly US$25 per person each way. National parks and other service vehicles make regular trips up to Chaltén, and you may be able to arrange a ride in Calafate. Hitchhiking outside the busy summer months is lonely and very unpredictable.

CERRO TORRE
This recommended short walk takes you to an exhilarating camp site looking out on Cerro Torre. The polished, vertical rock walls of this classic granite needle were for decades considered impossible to climb. The eventual conquest of Cerro Torre in 1970 by Cesare Maestri provoked the most bitter controversy in climbing history, when it became known that the Italian alpinist and his party had used a portable compressor drill to fix a line of bolts to reach the summit.

Days Required
The trek is often done as a long return day trip. A more leisurely two days is recommended, however, with a night at the camp site above Laguna Torre. By taking a shortcut described in Stage 1B (which follows), the walk can easily be combined with the trek to Cerro Fitz Roy. This avoids a return to Guardería Chaltén, and increases the walks duration by several days.

Standard
The path to Laguna Torre is well marked and easy to follow. The shortcut track to the Fitz Roy Base Camp (Stage 1B) is well trodden at either end, but gets a bit vague in the central section. At the camp site above Laguna Torre is a tiny but sturdy refugio capable of sleeping about four people. There are two or three other very makeshift shelters nearby.

The 10 km return trek to Laguna Torre is rated easy. The shortcut is rated moderate.

Stage 1A: Guardería Chaltén to Cerro Torre Base Camp
(10 km, 4 to 5 hours)
After signing in at the ranger station, cross the Río Fitz Roy bridge and proceed past the neatly laid out village of Chaltén. Pick up the path some 200 metres south of a stockyard off the main road. The path leads west across the flat grassland, climbing steeply to overlook the valley of the Río de las Vueltas. Continue roughly south-west across undulating terrain of sporadic lenga woodland for one to 1½ hours until you come to a rise looking out over the beautiful upper Valle Fitz Roy towards Cerro Torre.

Traversing steep-sided embankments the path moves down towards the Río Fitz Roy, passing the signposted turnoff leading north to the Fitz Roy Base Camp (see Stage 1B which follows). Follow the riverbank for a further 45 minutes to one hour, before heading up past large boulders to reach the top of the moraine wall enclosing Laguna Torre.

Make your way along the narrow crest towards the towering figure of Cerro Torre with the ice-filled lake on your left. At the far end of the moraine ridge a track leads off to the right. This zig-zags steeply for 10 to 15 minutes to reach a terrace in the trees, long used as a base camp by mountaineers. There is a tiny A-frame refugio built by the military, with maximum sleeping capacity for four people. Other more makeshift shelters can also be found. Fetch water from the little stream a few minutes down the path to the right.

Camp Sites The scenic and well sheltered upper camp site at Laguna Torre is by far the best spot. Less spectacular camping exists along much of the upper Río Fitz Roy, particularly by the lake outlet and in the forest below the moraine wall.

Stage 1B: Shortcut Track to Fitz Roy Base Camp
(11 km, 3 to 4½ hours)
Backtrack 30 to 40 minutes to where the signposted track departs to your left. The track is initially well marked and follows ridges north-east onto a plateau at about 750 metres. Heading slightly east of due north, pass to the left of a swampy area to reach Laguna El Perro after 1½ to two hours. Make your way around the eastern side of Laguna El Perro, and continue on to a larger second lake (shown as Lago Capri on the IGM map). Move along the east shore of the lake to the outlet stream, and descend along the right side. The shortcut track intersects with the main path from Chaltén.

If coming from the other direction, look for the start of the track on the east side of the sidestream where it enters the Chorrillo del Salto.

Camp Sites There is good camping in the central part of the route, particularly between the two biggest lakes.

CERRO FITZ ROY
The local Tehuelche tribes venerated Cerro Fitz Roy, whose prominent form must have been a key landmark during their annual migrations from the Atlantic to the Cordillera. Believing Fitz Roy to be a volcano, the Tehuelche called the mountain 'Chaltén'. Francisco Perito Moreno gave the peak its present (Celtic) name after Captain Fitzroy of the Beagle, who in 1834 accompanied Charles Darwin up the Río Santa Cruz to within 50 km of the Cordillera. Fitzroy (the

original spelling of his name) and Darwin were presumably the first Europeans to view Fitz Roy's classic 3441-metre summit of smooth frost-polished granite. Cerro Fitz Roy is easily the highest peak in the area, and can be seen from many locations along the hiking trails. The closest viewing point to this extraordinary mountain is from a col in the upper Río Eléctrico.

Days Required
This is a return trek best done in four days.

Standard
The route to Piedra del Fraile is reasonably well marked and easy to follow, except for a short section leading out of the Río Blanco into the Valle Eléctrico. The track leads along riverbanks and through valleys the whole way.

The trek is graded easy to moderate.

Stage 1: Guardería Chaltén to Fitz Roy Base Camp
(9 km, 3 to 4½ hours)
Follow the road for two km by the village, passing a house immediately before you go through a campground in the low ñirre forest. Continue for 10 to 15 minutes to where an unsignposted path departs to the left.

Head north-west along this well-worn path up over low ridges, passing a lakelet on your right to reach the Chorrillo del Salto after one to 1½ hours. With the first spectacular views of the Fitz Roy Massif ahead, follow the ridge above the stream. Ten to fifteen minutes on, a trail heads off left up to the picturesque Laguna Capri. This is a worthwhile sidetrip of 30 to 45 minutes return.

Continue up the valley, passing another path leading off to the left. This is the shortcut track to Laguna Torre (see Stage 1A of the trek to Cerro Torre Base Camp). After crossing a very low watershed, the path leads across a lovely open and flat area at the head of the new valley. Make your way north-west for 30 to 40 minutes to reach the Río Blanco. Follow the track down a short distance to an improvised shelter at the edge of a clearing

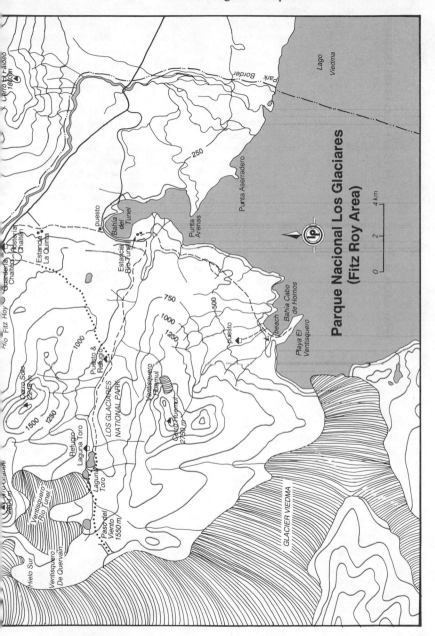

Parque Nacional Los Glaciares
(Fitz Roy Area)

looking out onto the spires of Fitz Roy, or cross the stream on stepping stones and head up into the lenga forest to where you will find two other crude huts. Built by mountaineers, these refugios are a rather messy and inhabited by voracious mice.

Camp Sites The best camping is in the upper valley of the Río Blanco around the scattered Fitz Roy Base Camp. There are also good camp sites by the tiny lake on the path above the Chorrillo del Salto.

Sidetrip: Fitz Roy Base Camp to Laguna Sucia From the camp on the west bank of the Río Blanco, pick up a trail heading southwest through the forest. The trail is poorly marked with tree blazings, and leads up the moraine ridge right of the river. After passing the tree line the route becomes fainter, but continue on through boulders and loose debris to a viewing point about 150 metres above Laguna Sucia. The lake is set in a glacial cirque of very spectacular proportions. The granite peaks of Fitz Roy can be seen behind a dramatic icefall above Laguna Sucia.

This sidetrip is 6 km return and takes two to three hours return.

Stage 2: Fitz Roy Base Camp to Piedra del Fraile
(9½ km, 4½ to 6½ hours)
Head downstream along the west side of the Río Blanco (the 1:50,000 map incorrectly shows the track on the east side). The route initially follows the immediate riverbank, where a minor rise in the water level would submerge sections of the track. The going is slower, and in places it is necessary to climb away from the stream to avoid getting your feet wet.

After 45 minutes to one hour the track meets a torrent descending through a mass of loose rock debris. From here a short and highly recommended sidetrip to Laguna Piedras Blancas can be made. Without crossing the stream, follow a vague path up the moraine ridge. A glacier winds around from in front of Cerro Fitz Roy in a series of icefalls to calve into the small lake.

Cross the Chorrillo Las Piedras Blancas a way above where it enters the Río Blanco, and continue downstream along the left shore. At first the going is tiresome due to the eroding banks, but further down the valley the track becomes more pronounced. Occasional cairns mark the best way through the boulders and other alluvial rubble of the river bed. As the valley gradually widens, carefully look out for more cairns and coloured streamers on trees, one to 1½ hours from Las Piedras Blancas. These markings indicate where the trail into the Valle Eléctrico leaves the Río Blanco and heads off left.

Follow the path into the forest, and make your way through an a series of attractive meadows. From here there are a number of route variations. The best option is to head slightly north of west, climbing a little until you come onto a well-transited horse track. The track contours gradually around to a north-west course and meets the milky Río Eléctrico after 45 minutes to one hour. Various other trails head more directly towards the river, following the banks upstream through thick scrub.

Continue up the valley through beautiful riverflats of beech forest for one to 1½ hours, until you get to a wide grassy field. The Refugio Piedra del Fraile is located at the near end of the great erratic block of granite by the river. The refugio belongs to the Gendarmería Nacional, who keep it locked between patrols. A few makeshift shelters exist nearby. It is worthwhile spending a day doing the two sidetrips described below. Return to the Guardería Chaltén via the same route.

Camp Sites The best camping is on the lawns around Refugio Piedra del Fraile itself, but firewood is very scarce. There are also good potential camp sites beside the Río Eléctrico and the lower Río Blanco.

Sidetrip: Lago Eléctrico (4 km return, 1 to 1½ hours return). From Refugio Piedra del Fraile, pick up a path leading up the valley between the Piedra del Fraile itself and the river. The path first skirts the stream before

Top: Lago Grey, Parque Nacional Torres del Paine
Bottom: Los Torres, Parque Nacional Torres del Paine

Top, Middle & Bottom: Laguna de las Tres Marías, Parque Nacional Tierra del Fuego

crossing an area of swampy ground. The final stage goes over an interesting series of wave-like moraine ridges to reach the dramatically bleak Lago Eléctrico. Winds from the nearby Hielo Sur are fierce and incessant.

Sidetrip: Cerro Fitz Roy Lookout ($2\frac{1}{2}$ km, 2 to 3 hours return). Follow an indistinct route up the southern side of the valley between two obvious streams tumbling down the steep slopes. Continue along a low ridge towards the great granite spires ahead to a rocky col. From here you have a spectacular panorama of the north face of Fitz Roy and various other peaks.

LAGO TORO

Lago Toro (not to be confused with the Laguna Torre) lies at the head of the Río Tunel, south of Guardería Chaltén. The entrance to the small valley is cut by a deep ravine, preventing easy access and the area is less often visited than other parts of the Fitz Roy region. Lago Toro is a small turgid meltwater pool at the snout of the Ventisquero Río Tunel. Although perhaps less picturesque than other lakes in the park, Lago Tunel's raw glacial setting makes an interesting contrast to the very attractive upper Valle Tunel. The central area of Valle Toro is open and surrounded by high ridges on either side. Towering over the valley along the edge of the Hielo Sur stand the glaciated 2400-metre peaks known as the Agujas del Río Tunel. Pleasant lenga forests and meadows fringe the roaring milky-coloured stream. The Valle Tunel is also an access route to the Paso del Viento, a difficult pass that leads out towards the huge southern continental icesheet, the Hielo Sur.

Days Required

The return trek to Lago Toro can be done in two longish days. It is worth spending an additional day exploring the upper Valle Tunel and area around the lake. If also doing the return trek up to the Paso del Viento allow a long day. Combining the walk with Glaciar Viedma extends the number of trekking days to around four.

Standard

This trek is less popular with walkers and follows a generally poorly marked route. In most places there is more or less a discernible track, but on the central section of Stage 1A the route goes over trackless ridges where some basic routefinding will be required. In the middle section of the trek it is necessary to wade the Río Tunel. While this ford is easier than anywhere further downstream, extended periods of sunny weather may cause the stream to rise considerably.

There are two small refugios in the valley, on the central Río Tunel and just below Lago Toro. Although the walk is possible without taking a tent, it is recommended that parties carry one.

It is possible to make a return trip up to the Paso del Viento (Stage 3). Here a short section of the lower Glaciar Tunel is crossed. Although there are no real crevasses on this part of the glacier, meltwater streams and sinkholes in the ice call for caution. The approach up to the pass is very loose and rocky, and there is no track. There is also a refugio on a rock ridge within the Hielo Sur near the Paso del Viento, but it can be hard to find in bad weather.

The trek to Lago Toro is rated moderate, and the total return distance is 34 km. The 14 km return sidetrip to Paso del Viento is rated difficult.

Stage 1A: Guardería Chaltén to Puesto Río Tunel

(9 km, 3 to $4\frac{1}{2}$ hours)
Pick up the track from behind the guardería, and head over to the left through a fence gate. The path moves around into a southerly direction to cross a tiny stream on a footbridge after 20 to 30 minutes. Follow sporadic route markings of blue ribbon up the slopes, passing clumps of calafate bushes and isolated stands of forest. The path moves away from the stream, gradually becoming harder to follow. Make your way south-west through a series of clearings onto a small plateau, where an attractive shallow lake lies in a slight depression. Continue up to the open slopes looking out over the Valle Tunel

towards the prominent north wall of Cerro Huemul on the adjacent side. This point is two to three hours from Guardería Chaltén.

Sidle one km west across the wind-eroded ridge towards the distant glacier at the head of the valley. Begin descending south-west, picking up the route beside an old wire fence leading down the fire-cleared slopes to just above the Puesto Río Tunel. The simple shack is in a green meadow a short way from the river, 500 metres upstream from where the glacial stream descending from Ventisquero Huemul flows in. Puesto Río Tunel is still used by cattle musterers from nearby estancias, but is never locked. There is one bed and space for a few more sleepers on the dirt floor.

Camp Sites There is excellent camping by the river near the puesto. Suitable camp sites can also be found in the vicinity of the small lake on the broad ridge before you descend into the Valle Tunel.

Stage 2: Puesto Río Tunel to Refugio Lago Toro

(8 km, 2½ to 3½ hours)
Wade the icy Río Tunel below the shelter. If the water level is high, walk a short way upstream to where you can cross via a number of smaller channels. Head up the valley along the south bank on easy trails through mainly open country. Progress is good, and after 1½ to 2½ hours the route passes an old climbers' camp hidden in the forest. Continue a further 30 to 45 minutes to Lago Toro, crossing the Río Tunel a way before you reach the lake. The Refugio Lago Toro is situated on north bank about 300 metres from the river on the downstream (east) side of the obvious rock ridge. The small orange A-frame hut (identical to the one at Laguna Torre) sleeps a maximum of four people.

Camp Sites There is virtually unlimited camping along either bank of the Río Tunel. The north shore of Lago Toro is too exposed for safe camping.

Stage 3: Paso del Viento

(14 km return, 8 to 11 hours return)
The heavily glaciated area behind Lago Toro is interesting to explore, but ice and loose rock make this difficult and potentially dangerous terrain. The very close proximity of the continental icesheet makes weather extremely unpredictable, and this sidetrip is recommended only to very experienced parties.

Make your way around the difficult rocky southern side of Lago Toro. The lake's north shore seems an easier route, but accumulated glacial sediment makes the inlet stream hazardous to wade. Climb through the steep broken rock and head high up the slopes to the right of the Ventisquero Río Tunel. This wild isolated area is one of the few places

Huemul

around Fitz Roy where there are huemul, or Andean deer. Continue up the valley around a tiny lake at the snout of a second glacier and ascend difficult scree slopes south-west to reach the Paso del Viento after four to $5\frac{1}{2}$ hours. The pass looks out over the continental icesheet. A refugio has been constructed for scientific research some four km south of Paso del Viento on a rock peninsula in the ice.

GLACIAR VIEDMA

This is another infrequently visited part of the Fitz Roy area. Glaciar Viedma is the largest glacier in South America. After carving its way east down through the ranges surrounding the vast southern Patagonian icesheet, the Hielo Continental Sur, the Viedma Glacier's five km wide snout calves directly into Lago Viedma. The 50-metre high wall of ice drops enormous chunks into the lake. A peninsula jutting out into the lake in front of the great wall of ice provides a natural viewing point, and frequently strands icebergs as they float by.

Days Required

The return trek can be done in two relatively long days from Guardería Chaltén. A route variation allows you to combine this trek with that to Lago Toro, lengthening the walk by at least two days.

Standard

The path follows a relatively straightforward route around the northern side of Lago Viedma. The only serious part of the trek is in the middle section, where it is necessary to wade the Río Tunel. The Río Tunel is a small but fast fast-flowing stream of turgid meltwater with many channels. During periods of warm sunny weather its glacier-fed waters can rise considerably.

The area around the lake shore in the vicinity of Glaciar Viedma is extremely exposed, with relatively little shelter from vegetation. In summer, freezing winds blow almost continually off the glacier across Lago Viedma, and sudden storms often

sweep down from the Hielo Sur virtually without warning.

There is a rustic puesto on the slopes above the lake, but it is difficult to find.

The trek is graded easy to moderate.

Stage 1A: Guardería Chaltén to Península El Ventisquero

(21 km, 7 to 11 hours)

From the guardería walk one km south-east along the main road past cliffs on your right and pick up a clear track leading off south across the flat pampa. The track is easily followed for 20 to 30 minutes to the Estancia La Quinta, where a hostel for tourists has recently been opened. Cross the farmyard and continue south for 30 to 45 minutes. Passing to the right of a neat red shack, descend a short way to the road around Bahía Tunel. Follow the road three km south around the bay to Estancia Río Tunel.

Pick up a track at the end of a paddock behind the row of poplars and follow this to the river. The Río Tunel is high and fast-flowing in summer, and best waded a short way downstream where the river is broken up into numerous smaller channels. Head around the southern banks to find the trail near a fence gate and climb the steep slopes. The path contours south high above Lago Viedma with a nice view across the lake towards two sandy peninsulas on the adjacent shore line.

After 45 minutes to one hour gradually move around into a south-westerly direction and continue through open ridges where the vegetation has largely been destroyed by fires. Make your way through lush depressions (where horses graze) towards the broad front of Glaciar Viedma, and drop down onto the pebble beach of Bahía Cabo de Hornos. Follow the shore around to Península El Ventisquero, from where the massive glacier is best viewed. Great blocks of ice frequently lie stranded around the peninsula's southern shore.

Camp Sites There is an old puesto three km from Bahía Cabo de Hornos on the north side of the large stream which flows into the bay.

Good camp sites can be found in the woods around Bahía Cabo de Hornos. Península El Ventisquero is very exposed to winds and is not suitable for camping.

Stage 1B: Estancia Río Tunel to Puesto Río Tunel

(9½ km, 3 to 4 hours)
From the estancia take the road towards the Río Tunel, turning right at a fork, to where the road peters out. Pick up a track along a ramshackle fence running straight up the hillside. Head into the obvious gap at the right, where a steep loose-rock ascent leads out into a dry gully after 30 to 45 minutes. Another fence-line is followed through lenga forest far above the deep ravine of the Río Tunel until the fence turns sharply away to the right after 30 to 45 minutes.

Continue up the valley through a long series of mallines and clearings interspersed with woodland. Infinite cattle trails criss-cross the path and confuse routefinding. Stay well above the river until the valley begins to open out. Descend a way down from where the large sidestream enters the river and follow the bank for 30 to 45 minutes to the Puesto Río Tunel (see the description for Lago Toro).

Other Treks in Parque Nacional Los Glaciares

FITZ ROY AREA – LAGUNA DEL DESIERTO

(4 to 7 days)
This is a return trek of moderate standard. From the park administration a road can be followed north across the Río de las Vueltas to the Gendarmería Nacional outpost. From here various good routes continue upstream to Laguna del Desierto and beyond to the disputed border area around Lago O'Higgins/San Martín.

Maps
Two new Argentine IGM 1:100,000 sheets

cover this route. These are *Península MacKenna* (Santa Cruz, No 4972-14) and *Laguna del Desierto* (Santa Cruz, No 4972-20).

LAGO ARGENTINO – BRAZO SUR & LAGUNA FRÍAS

(4 to 7 days)
The Brazo Sur is one of two southern arms of the Lago Argentino which are periodically blocked off and dammed by the Glaciar Moreno flooding the surrounding lake shore up to 30 metres above the normal water level.

From Calafate there is a road 53 km south-west to Estancia La Jerónima from where a rough vehicle track leads south to the Río Frías. From here it is possible to wade the fast-flowing glacial stream and proceed north around the western side of the Brazo Sur. The true right (ie southern) bank of the Río Frías can also be followed upstream to Laguna Frías and Glaciar Frías. This is a difficult trek suitable for experienced parties only. A permit must be obtained from the Parque Nacional Los Glaciares administration office in Calafate before departing.

Maps
The only map of any real use is the recent Argentine IGM 1:250,000 *El Calafate* (Santa Cruz, Nos 5172-I & 5175-II).

Access
Transport to the start of the trek must be specially arranged in Calafate.

Parque Nacional Torres del Paine

Possibly South America's most famous national park, the Torres del Paine area lies some 100 km to the north of Puerto Natales, in far southern Chile. The uniqueness of the 2422-sq-km park was recognised in 1978 when Torres del Paine was given UNESCO world heritage status.

Standing quite apart from the lower ranges

that surround it, the craggy mountains of the park make a breathtaking sight when first viewed from the eastern approach road. The roughly quadrilateral-shaped Macizo Paine forms the heart of the park and displays many of the area's most unique and spectacular features. Rising out of a largely flat and barren plain at barely 100 metres, the massif's highest summits reach heights in excess of 3000 metres.

The park gets its name from three magnificent frost-polished columns of pink granite, the Torres del Paine, which jut out of directly from above an icefall that spills into a small alpine lake. The Cuernos del Paine are interesting jagged turrets of a resistant layer of sedimentary black shale covering the granite base, and rise up imposingly from immediately north of Lago Nordenskjöld. Situated on the western flank on the Paine Massif, Cerro Paine Grande is the highest peak in Torres del Paine. Cerro Paine Grande is capped by so-called *hongos de hielo* (ice mushrooms), a phenomenon almost peculiar to the loftier summits of the far southern Andes.

Parque Nacional Torres del Paine is sandwiched between the vast windswept steppes of Patagonia and the massive southern continental icesheet, from which three major glaciers descend into the park. The area occupies a zone of climatic transition, with highly localised weather conditions. There is a corresponding diversity in flora and fauna. Guanaco and ñandú are frequently sighted in the eastern sector which is characterised by sparse steppes and grassland typical for much of Patagonia. As you move further to the west there are dense forests of lenga and coigüe. Condors are often sighted soaring around precipitous peaks.

The origins of the park's name are in some doubt. Although the word *paine* (pronounced 'pie-nee') means 'pale blue' in the Mapuche language and could, therefore, be a reference to the colour of the area's half dozen or so large glacial lakes, southern and most of central Patagonia belonged to Tehuelche tribes and the Paine area is well outside the territory originally inhabited by the Mapuche. Another theory is that 'Paine' was the name of an early climber of Welsh origin.

Up until the declaration of the national park in 1959, most of the Torres area was leased out to several local estancias. In the grassy steppes of the park's periphery, signs of the area's former use as grazing land are still visible in old fences and outstation huts, and cattle and horses roam wild in the more remote western sectors. The graziers' use of fire to clear forest has greatly modified the landscape, particularly in the eastern sector of the park. Regeneration is occurring only slowly, a reminder of the destructive effect of fire in these parts. The administration headquarters at Lago del Toro is the former Estancia Paine building and was donated by

Nandú

the previous owners to the newly established national park.

In recent years tourism has boomed in Torres del Paine, and development is now beginning to accelerate. New roads and tracks are planned which will increase the accessibility of remoter parts of the park. Modern hotels are to be constructed close to the park boundaries.

The best time to visit the park is from November to April, as much of the central area is covered by snow in winter. From around May to the beginning of September, however, the otherwise severe and incessant Patagonian winds more or less completely cease. This means that winter trips are much less extreme than might be expected.

Maps

There is no IGM sheet which covers the area that has a useful scale. A sketch map of the Torres del Paine has been produced by CONAF for walkers, and is issued free upon entry to the park. Scaled at roughly 1:150,000, this map shows topographic detail very vaguely, and incorrectly indicates certain track routes and the location of refugios.

Accommodation & Supplies

There are currently seven refugios within the park and the construction (or replacement) of others is planned. Many of the refugios are former puestos dating from the days when the area was given over to sheep and cattle grazing. With the exception of the newly renovated refugio at the administration village, there is presently no charge for their use.

In recent years, however, the idea of privatising the management and maintenance of the huts has been adopted by the park authorities, and it is likely that in future any new or renovated huts will be staffed by a fee-collecting warden. Despite the relatively large number of refugios, the route possibilities for parties who don't carry a tent are still fairly limited. For this reason all serious trekkers are strongly advised to bring a tent with them.

There are two hotel-type alternatives at Torres del Paine. These are the Posada Río Serrano at the administration village at Lago del Toro (US$15 per night) and the more up-market Hostería Pehoé (from about US$40) on Lago Pehoé. There is a newly renovated refugio at the administration village with bunk-style accommodation and hot showers (US$6). There are also two organised campgrounds at Lago Pehoé and on the Río Serrano with hot showers (both US$6 per site).

The Posada Río Serrano is the only place at Torres del Paine where you can buy supplies. Prices are exorbitantly high and the range of items is very limited, so try to bring all you need with you. You can leave well-packaged food for later treks at the administration centre.

Access

The town of Puerto Natales is the gateway to Parque Nacional Torres del Paine. Many travellers arrive in Puerto Natales on the ferry *Tierra del Fuego* from Puerto Montt. There are a number of daily buses from the provincial capital of Punta Arenas, some six hours south by road.

During the summer season, Buses Fernández run one bus every day except Sunday from Puerto Natales to the administration centre at Lago Pehoé. The return fare costs around US$10, and there is generally no problem staying in the park for several weeks before using the return ticket. There are a growing number of smaller operators running minibuses or taxis. These are a bit more expensive, but allow a more flexible itinerary. They can also drop you off at more remote parts of the park where the regular bus service does not go. Drivers often arrange to pick up trekkers at specified times and places.

A minibus service operates between Puerto Natales and Calafate in Argentina three times per week between November and March. On the way the minibus passes the turnoff to Torres del Paine, some 50 km from the park administration centre. From the turnoff it may be possible to hitch a ride or flag down the bus coming from Puerto Natales. Don't try it out of season.

A new road is currently being constructed via a much shorter southern route via Lago del Toro and the Río Serrano. When completed, the park will become far more easily accessible.

A nominal fee is charged for entry into the park.

TORRES DEL PAINE CIRCUIT

The Torres del Paine circuit is the longest and one of the most popular treks in the park. The walk circumnavigates the Paine Massif, offering constantly changing views of this extraordinary range. The vast 17 km-long Glaciar Grey is the central feature of the north-west corner of the park. Glaciar Grey disgorges into Lago Grey, sending numerous icebergs to gradually drift south across the lake's turquoise waters. Where the Glaciar Grey and Lago Grey meet there are interesting ice caves created by the action of meltwater.

Days Required

The full circuit is normally done in seven days. Sidetrips and rest days might stretch the walk out to 10 days or more. Do not underestimate your walking times, and be sure to carry enough supplies for a safe, comfortable trek.

If you are unable to do the entire Torres circuit, a shorter return trek to Ventisquero Grey (basically Stage 5 to Stage 7 in reverse) requiring three days is a recommended alternative. The day walk to Campamento Británico would take an additional day.

Standard

The path is marked with orange stakes and paint, and is so well trodden that serious navigational difficulties should not arise. Little track maintenance is carried out, however, and especially in the forested central section of the circuit fallen logs often make the going slow and strenuous. In a few places landslides and avalanche debris bury the path. Several small but fast-flowing glacial streams must also be forded.

There are three official refugios along the route. These are at Lago Pehoé, Lago Dickson and Lago Paine. A disused outstation building on the Río Paine, about halfway between Guardería Laguna Amarga and Lago Paine, is not intended for use by trekkers, but could serve as emergency shelter. Refugios also exist at the beginning and end of the trek. The standard CONAF map shows a refugio at Lago Grey, even though this burnt down many years ago. This makes the trekking distance between huts impossibly long, and it is essential to carry a tent. In any case, all refugios are prone to overcrowding and are generally run down and rodent-ridden.

The trek is best done in an anticlockwise direction. This saves the hardest sections until later, and means that you finish at the administration centre (where modern amenities exist) rather than at Laguna Amarga or the more remote portería at the park entrance.

The Torres del Paine circuit is rated moderate. The total distance is 86 km, but optional long sidetrips to the Torres del Paine (32 km return) and Campamento Francés (20 km return) would considerably lengthen the walk.

Stage 1: Portería Lago Sarmiento to Guardería/Refugio Laguna Amarga

(5½ km, 2 to 3 hours)
After signing in at the park entrance, pick up an unsignposted track leading north along the left side of a fence forming the park boundary. Rising gently through grassy greens where guanaco graze, you begin heading in a more north-easterly direction to pass a lake on the right after one hour. Now move steadily downhill until the milky waters of the Río Paine come into view. The track descends through a shorter steeper section to meet the road. Follow this left to reach the Guardería Laguna Amarga a few minutes on. The Refugio Laguna Amarga is located just down from the ranger station. Officially, the refugio has space for six people. In high season many more than that may be staying there.

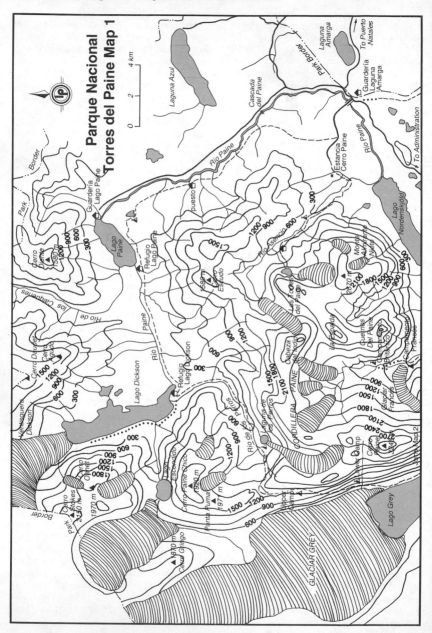

Parque Nacional Torres del Paine Map 1

Camp Sites There is little good camping along this very short section. Parties should aim to reach the Guardería Laguna Amarga before nightfall.

Stage 2: Guardería/Refugio Laguna Amarga to Refugio Lago Paine (or Coirón)
(24 km, 7 to 10 hours)
This very long section can be broken up into two easier days. The highly recommended sidetrip to the Torres del Paine lookout (see the later description of it as a separate walk) can easily be combined with Stage 2.

Below the guardería two suspension bridges allow a crossing of the Río Paine via a tiny island. In mid-summer, when glacial meltwater raises the level of the river, it may be necessary to wade the shallow waters. Immediately after reaching the opposite bank, you come to a signposted track junction. Take the right-hand path that leads across bare and rather dull country once given over to grazing. The track continues near to the river for one to 1½ hours passing the Cascada del Paine, where the cloudy waters of the Río Paine drop four metres.

Continue following the gentle if somewhat monotonous western bank of the Río Paine. The path stays fairly close to the river, and leads through a long series of wide riverflats. As you move up the valley, the vegetation gradually becomes lusher.

After three to four hours an abandoned puesto is reached. Although in sound structural condition, the building is apparently not intended for use by trekkers and is kept locked.

Pick up the trail below some old animal pens. After 45 minutes to one hour you leave the river and climb left over barren ridges to reach a small and picturesque horseshoe-shaped lake (not marked on maps). Pass around the tiny beaches on southern shore, and follow orange stakes west in steep switchback curves up the slopes leading directly through a small pass. From here you have a wonderful panorama of Lago Paine below, with a variety of peaks along the Chile-Argentina frontier behind Lago Dickson at the head of the valley.

Traverse the steep slopes above Lago Paine, as the track gradually descends to near lake level. The Refugio Lago Paine (or Coirón) is reached after 1½ to two hours. The primitive open-sided tin shack has space for a maximum of eight trekkers on the dirt floor.

Camp Sites There is good camping on the banks of the Río Paine for most of its lower course. Most recommended is the small lake passed on the track after leaving the Río Paine. Although recent fires have spoilt the place a bit, there is excellent camping by the beachy shores. Only very poor camp sites exist on the steep slopes on the southern side of Lago Paine. Good spots can be found at the western end of Lago Paine or upstream from where the Río Paine enters the lake.

Stage 2: Refugio Lago Paine to Refugio Lago Dickson
(8½ km, 3 to 4 hours)
Follow the track roughly south-west some distance from the Río Paine across open grassland. The track enters a boggy section and passes the burnt-down ruins of a small puesto. Rising gently you come to a prominent ridge of old glacial moraine, from where the refugio and Lago Dickson appear. A former homestead, Refugio Lago Dickson has a stove and toilet, with sleeping space for around 30 people. Set on an attractive broad pampa with the impressive backdrop of Ventisquero Dickson, an appendage of the southern continental icecap, the area is a good place to put in a rest day.

From Refugio Lago Dickson various sidetrips are possible for more experienced parties. Ventisquero Dickson can be reached via the west shore of Lago Dickson (cross the Río de los Perros at the point where it enters the lake. Lago Escondido and Cerro Ohnet are more challenging possibilities.

Camp Sites The best camp sites are by Lago Dickson at the end of a short path from the refugio, or further along the track by the Río de los Perros.

Stage 3: Refugio Lago Dickson to Campamento 'Laguna de los Perros'
($8\frac{1}{2}$ km, $4\frac{1}{2}$ to $6\frac{1}{2}$ hours)
Follow the trail on for 15 to 20 minutes to meet the Río de los Perros, and begin heading south-east up the steepening slopes beside the river. Fire-damaged slopes soon give way to virgin beech forest as you enter the wildest and least accessible section of the trek. After climbing for one to $1\frac{1}{2}$ hours the track comes onto a clearing beside a beautiful moor, from where there are good views in most directions.

The main tributary of the Río de los Perros, a torrent coming down from the Cabeza del Indio, is crossed on a log bridge upstream from the junction of the two streams. The path heads off right, but soon returns to the riverside to meet a small thunderous ravine.

Continue upstream through rich beech forests, with few views until the valley widens some one to $1\frac{1}{2}$ hours on. Shortly after crossing two very small streams of obvious glacial origin, the track comes to several log bridges spanning the the main channel of the river. None of these is particularly satisfactory, and crossing requires concentration.

Make your way up through a gravel wash with many smaller channels, and continue to some high mounds of glacial end-moraine forming the natural dam wall of the lovely 'Laguna de los Perros'.

A tiny glacier calves directly into the lake, noisily dropping small icebergs which can be seen floating in its frigid waters or lying stranded around the shores. The campamento is situated in the forest on the upper valley side of the lake.

Camp Sites Reasonable camp sites can be found on the upper Río de los Perros, but the only recommended camping is at the official campamento above the lake.

Stage 4: Campamento 'Laguna de los Perros' to Ventisquero Grey (Upper Camp)
($5\frac{1}{2}$ km, $3\frac{1}{2}$ to 5 hours)
Pick up the path from behind the camping area and make your way along the south side of the Río de los Perros. Now much smaller, the river is easily waded 10 to 15 minutes on. Continue over often very soggy ground for one to $1\frac{1}{2}$ hours until you reach the tree line near the head of the valley. Here, below a tiny chasm, recross the stream.

An unmistakable line of orange-painted rocks and cairn markings leads left up the increasingly bare slopes. A small glacier coming down from the south side of Cerro Paine Chico comes into full view as you get higher. The pass is gained $2\frac{1}{2}$ to $3\frac{1}{2}$ hours from the Campamento 'Laguna de los Perros'. At around 1300 metres above sea level, the pass is the highest point on the circuit. There is an awe-inspiring view of the enormous Ventisquero Grey, a fractured mass of ice choking the valley.

Following route markings, head a way diagonally left and drop down in zig-zags to the tree line. A steep and in places very slippery track descends into light beech forest for one to $1\frac{1}{2}$ hours to arrive at the official campamento above Ventisquero Grey.

Camp Sites The only recommended camp site is the Upper Camp. Collect water from a brook a short distance downhill.

Stage 5: Ventisquero Grey (Upper Camp) to Ventisquero Grey (Lower Camp)
(5 km, 3 to 4 hours)
Continue roughly south along the forested slopes at the edge of Ventisquero Grey. The track is not maintained, and fallen logs and occasional landslides hinder progress. In places the track rises sharply to avoid cliffs formed by the glacier. The pleasant Lower Camp is situated by the track where a waterfall plummets down through a quebrada from the Paine Massif.

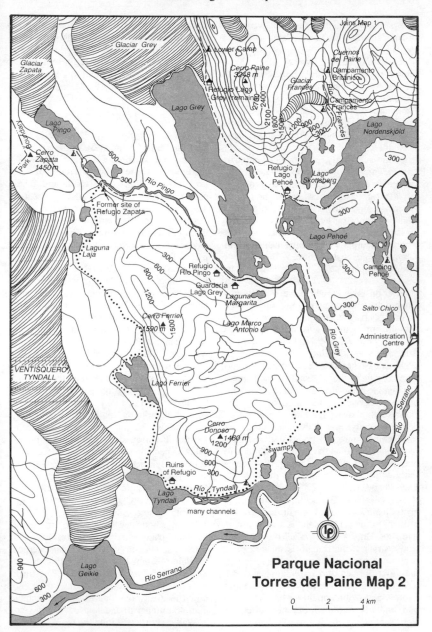

Parque Nacional
Torres del Paine Map 2

Camp Sites No good sites exist between the Upper Camp and the Lower Camp.

Stage 6: Ventisquero Grey (Lower Camp) to Refugio Lago Pehoé
(12 km, 5 to 7 hours)
Cross the stream 20 metres below the Lower Camp and climb the difficult eroding banks. Continue down alongside Ventisquero Grey for 40 to 50 minutes until you come to a fork in the track.

A short and highly recommended sidetrip to some interesting ice caves on the rim of the Ventisquero Grey can be made by following the right path to where a meltwater torrent runs around the side of the glacier. Here look for cairns leading left over the low grassy ridge to the ice caves. These wonders of natural sculpture are formed in spring and summer by meltwater action. With sufficient care and discretion it is usually possible to enter the caves.

Head on towards where the Ventisquero Grey calves into Lago Grey. Impressive views of Cerro Paine Grande are seen as you pass the burnt-out remains of Refugio Lago Grey (this refugio is still shown on the standard park map). Continue through clearings of calafate bushes on the eastern side of Lago Grey. Driven by the incessant winds, numerous giant icebergs drift away from the snout of the glacier across the waters of the lake. Head south above Lago Grey for four km, before moving away to the south-east. The track climbs onto flat ridges and passes a scenic small lake on the right, 45 minutes to one hour before descending through a shallow dry valley to arrive at the Refugio Lago Pehoé.

Refugio Lago Pehoé is situated on a grassy plain looking out onto the picturesque brilliant turquoise lake, and is a very attractive spot. Only a day's walk from the park administration, the refugio is in very poor condition due to overuse. There is space on the floor for about 15 trekkers, and the refugio has a wood stove (very smoky) and a toilet. Sanitation conditions here are very bad and all water should be boiled or sterilised.

Camp Sites There are few especially good spots to camp by Lago Grey. The small lake passed by the track a short way before you reach the refugio offers scenic semi-sheltered sites. Near Refugio Lago Pehoé there is sheltered camping by the lake shore, five minutes away along the path to Campamento Francés.

Stage 7A: Refugio Lago Pehoé to Campamento Francés, Campamento Británico & Cuernos del Paine
(20 km return, 7 to 11 hours return)
Pick up the signposted track and head eastwards above the shore of Lago Pehoé. The track soon swings around into a more northerly direction and makes its way through undulating terrain of mixed grassland and light forest, passing two small lakes. Traverse below the lightly forested south-east slopes of Cerro Paine to meet the Río Francés after 1½ to 2½ hours.

Move around left to enter the deep and narrow valley. Following the river's western bank upstream, the path crosses two areas of boulder moraine to reach some camp sites (Campamento Francés) in the scrub a short way below Glaciar Francés. Wade the swift-flowing waters of the Río Francés below the snout of the glacier and head up the obvious loose moraine ridge on the adjacent side. Continue for 1½ to 2½ hours to reach a small hut built by some British climbing expeditions. This awesome and magnificent location is surrounded by high peaks on all sides. Especially spectacular are the Cuernos del Paine lying directly to the east.

Stage 7B: Refugio Lago Pehoé to Administration Centre
(17 km, 4½ to 6½ hours)
Take the signposted track to the far side of the small pampa, and sidle the grassy ridges above Lago Pehoé. The spectacular Cuernos del Paine become increasingly visible as you make your way around the lake. The track rises well above the lakeside before dropping down to a tiny bay opposite some islands after 45 minutes to one hour.

Walk a short way along the flat shore line,

before heading south-east away from the lake. The track leads across open fields to meet the cloudy-green Río Grey, a major stream draining Lago Grey. Follow downstream above the the river's often steep banks for 1½ to 2½ hours. The path gradually turns around eastwards and crosses a wide expanse of windy steppes. Small groups of ñandú can often be observed here. After one to 1½ hours the path comes out at a road. Turn left and continue for one km to the administration centre.

Camp Sites Excellent camp sites can be found along the initial stretch after leaving Refugio Lago Pehoé, especially at the small bay of islands. The banks of the Río Grey are generally not much good for camping because sites tend to be either too steep or unsheltered. Camping too close to the administration centre is discouraged, and it is recommended that you stay at the newly renovated refugio.

TORRES DEL PAINE LOOKOUT
This short trek is the most spectacular in the park and should not be missed. The Torres del Paine stand just north of the Cuernos peaks within a deep valley of the Paine Massif. The 'torres' themselves are three distinctive pinnacles of hard Andean batholith rock, and are all that remains of a great cirque that has been sheared away by the relentless forces of glacial ice. The summit of the tallest tower stands some 2900 metres above sea level and and imposingly overlooks the intensely glaciated and barren surroundings 250 metres below.

Refer to the Parque Nacional Torres del Paine Map No 1 in this chapter.

Days Required
The trip can be done as a long day walk from Guardería/Refugio Laguna Amarga. If you arrive by bus at the main portería and then walk to Guardería Laguna Amarga, however, there will not be enough time to return the same day. For this reason many parties stretch the trek out to two days by either returning to Laguna Amarga the same day or making a camp somewhere along the Río Asencio. A further one day could also be spent exploring the the upper Río Asencio. The trek is easily combined with the Torres del Paine circuit.

Standard
This return trek follows a reasonably well marked and tracked route all the way. The walk makes a long day, and slower parties might consider making a camp somewhere along the way. There is a tiny shelter with space for two people in the upper Río Asencio, and good camp sites in a number of other places along the track.

The trek up to the Torres del Paine lookout is rated moderate.

Access
See the Access section for the Torres del Paine circuit. This trek begins and ends (unless you continue via the Torres del Paine circuit to the administration centre) at the Guardería Laguna Amarga, a more northerly alternative entry point to the park. Fernández company buses usually don't pass through here, but many other tour bus operators visit the Laguna Amarga area. It is possible to walk to Guardería Laguna Amarga from the main portería, or hitchhike from the turnoff on the main road.

Stage 1: Guardería/Refugio Laguna Amarga to Torres del Paine Lookout
(32 km return, 7 to 11 hours return)
Cross the Río Paine on the suspension bridges, and turn left at the track intersection on the other side of the river. Head around north-west along an old vehicle track for one to 1½ hours to arrive at Estancia Cerro Paine, now the only freehold property left within the park. On the down-slope side of the estancia, follow marker-tape around the outside of a wire fence past a corral and continue around the fenceline before dropping down left to the Río Asencio. Although not wide, the river is swift-flowing and should be forded with caution.

Cross the wash plain and make your way up the adjacent gravel ridge. The trail ascends beside an interesting gorge through layered black rock, before entering the more enclosed upper valley of the Río Asencio through a narrow windy section. Continue two km and drop down the steep loose hillside to reach some nice camp sites in a calafate clearing on the river bank.

Head upstream along the western bank of the Río Asencio. The track ascends the slopes to traverse a distance above the river, passing a number of cascades on the range opposite. The raw glaciated crags on the western side of Monte Almirante Nieto can be seen by virtue of a severe forest fire, which has largely destroyed the tree cover along this part of the route. Moving back into the forest, the track dips and rises constantly to reach a small glacial stream flowing down from the left. Directly ahead, an attractive stand of dwarf lenga shelters a tiny two-person hut built by a mountaineering expedition.

Begin climbing to the left of the small glacial stream through the increasingly bare boulder-moraine. No single track seems to exist, but with some rock-hopping the route eventually climbs over a rock mound to arrive at the spectacular lookout immediately below the granite Torres del Paine. A turgid grey-green lakelet in the foreground adds to the scenic harmony.

The return to Guardería Laguna Amarga is made via the same route. Remember that the level of the glacier-fed Río Asencio is likely to be higher in the afternoon, and recrossing this fast-flowing stream should be undertaken with care.

For hiking parties intending to walk the Torres del Paine circuit, a shortcut route avoids backtracking the whole way to the Río Paine, saving at least one hour. At a left fork in the road, 500 metres after passing a large boulder marked 'Cerro Paine' (or 15 to 20 minutes on from Estancia Cerro Paine), head north across lush pampas. Follow occasional tape markings along endless diverging cattle tracks which meander through ñirre thickets. These eventually lead out onto the open plains of the Río Paine by way of a long green meadow.

Camp Sites If asked, the owners of Estancia Cerro Paine will let you camp close to the homestead. Further up, there are a number of good camp sites along the banks of the Río Asencio. Excellent sheltered camp sites near the very small climbers' shelter in the lenga forest below the Torres del Paine lookout are the most recommended.

LAGO PINGO

The wild area of the park's more inaccessible interior behind Lago Grey is worth visiting. Lago Pingo is on the south side of Lago Grey in this remote eastern sector of the park. The source of both the lake and its outlet, the Río Pingo, is Glaciar Zapata. This relatively small but spectacular glacier spills down from the Hielo Sur, or continental icesheet, to calve in the freezing waters of Lago Pingo. The Pingo Valley is forested with attractive stands of largely open lenga forest. Along the undulating riverbanks are continuous thickets of calafate bushes which in February and March produce abundant berries. Pumas are attracted by the area's relative isolation and are probably seen most often in this sector of the park.

Refer to the Parque Nacional Torres del Paine Map No 2 in this chapter.

Days Required

The Lago Pingo trek takes one full day in either direction. An additional day spent exploring this lovely area is highly recommended. The walk can easily be done as part of a circuit via Lagos Ferrier and Tyndall (see the description which follows), extending the walking time by three or four days. The trek is rated as easy.

Standard

The simple return trek to Lago Pingo follows a marked and very well trodden path up the Río Pingo (also called the Río Avutardas), and presents little routefinding difficulty. The gradient rises very gently along the course of the river, and there are no really strenuous sections.

The Pingo area is close to the edge of the southern continental icecap. As in other parts of the park, this makes local weather very unstable. It is not uncommon to experience heavy downpours close to the mountains while sunshine is visible on the steppes just a few km to the east. The chilling effect of the freezing winds that in summer blow incessantly off the great glaciers should not be underestimated.

Unfortunately a fire some years ago destroyed the only refugio on the upper Río Pingo, so it is now no longer possible to do the trek without carrying a tent. There is a small tin refugio located just a short way from the start of the track, but while welcome, this hut can't really serve as a base for a return day's walk to Lago Pingo.

Access
The trek begins from the carpark of Guardería Lago Grey. From the administration centre follow the road south across the Río Grey bridge and continue right (east) along the road on the river's southern side. The total distance is 18 km. In summer it is usually possible to arrange with drivers of tour buses, taxis or minibuses to take you from the administration centre to Lago Grey. You can walk out to Guardería Lago Grey in four to six hours.

Stage 1: Guardería Lago Grey to Lago Pingo
(15 km, 6 to 8 hours)
Before setting out, it is worthwhile making the short sidetrip (one to $1\frac{1}{2}$ hours) to Lago Grey. Cross the Río Pingo on the suspension bridge opposite the guardería, and head a short way upstream to where a senda de interpretación introduces various geological and biological features of the park. It is possible to walk out along a spit of fine glacial sand jutting into Lago Grey, from where you get a view of the distant Ventisquero Dickson and icebergs in the lake.

From above the guardería, follow the path up the west side of the river to reach Refugio Río Pingo after 20 to 30 minutes. The well-constructed tin cottage has a good wood stove and two bunks, with space on the floor for about four more.

Continue up the valley for through a long series of clearings and riverside meadows, from where you get occasional views of Cerro Paine to the north-east. In March the many calafate bushes along this pleasant valley are laden with berries. After $3\frac{1}{2}$ to five hours the track steers around right into a grassy open riverflat. This was the site of the Refugio Zapata (or Pochongo) which burned down in 1989.

Pick up the track from above the clearing and continue up the valley. The track crosses a bare gravel plain to meet a narrow but deep and swiftly flowing stream of glacial origin after 15 to 20 minutes. Cross via the make-shift wire bridge. Follow the path through endless calafate thickets, only meeting the river every now and then to reach Lago Pingo $1\frac{1}{2}$ to $2\frac{1}{2}$ hours from the former site of Refugio Zapata. The spectacular Glaciar Zapata slides down from the continental icesheet to calve into the lake. Icebergs are driven south by the incessant winds and beach on the sandy southern shore.

Camp Sites There is almost unlimited camping along the Río Pingo, but perhaps the nicest spot is the Upper Camp site itself. Camping is also possible in the scrub close to Lago Pingo behind glacial dunes on the southern shore, but these sites are very exposed to the frigid winds blowing down the lake and are thus less recommended.

PINGO-TYNDALL CIRCUIT
An extension of the walk to Lago Pingo, this trek takes you through the wildest and most remote part of Parque Nacional Torres del Paine. The trek follows a course immediately to the east Ventisquero Tyndall (also known as Ventisquero Geikie). Until relatively recently this very large glacier spilled over into a number of lakes along the route. Signs of glaciation are a predominant feature of the landscape.

Days Required
The full circuit takes about five days, including the initial walk to Lago Pingo. Parties may be delayed by poor weather and

route finding errors, and at least one extra day should be allowed.

Standard

There are supposedly plans to cut a foot track along this route at some time in the future, but until then this trek is exclusively for experienced and fit parties with very good navigational skills. After leaving the Lago Pingo track, the trek traverses relatively high country crossing an indistinct watershed at around 600 metres. The route is fairly straightforward but has almost no route markings. Until you reach Lago Tyndall there is no real track.

The close proximity of the continental icesheet and Ventisquero Tyndall means the weather is even less predictable than in other parts of the park. The area is very exposed to strong icy winds from the west. The final stage from Lago Tyndall back to the road follows a mostly overgrown track.

The Pingo-Tyndall circuit is probably best done in an anticlockwise direction. This leaves the rougher sections until last, but makes routefinding more simple. Apart from an almost useless makeshift shelter by the Río Tyndall, there are no refugios along the route and it is essential to carry a good tent.

The trek is graded difficult. When the first section from the guardería up the Río Pingo is included, the total trekking distance is 63 km.

Access

As an extension of the Lago Pingo route this trek begins from the path on the Río Pingo (see the previous details of Access under the Lago Pingo track notes).

Stage 1: Upper Río Pingo to 'Laguna Laja'

(6 km, 3 to 5 hours)
From the former site of Refugio Zapata, walk up the valley along the path for 10 to 15 minutes. When you reach an open windy section, head off left to the edge of some cliffs and climb up through smoothed rock slabs still showing glacial scratch marks. As you get higher there is a good view towards

Lago Pingo to the north-west. Make your way southwards to meet a cloudy-water lake after one to $1\frac{1}{2}$ hours.

Move around to the inlet and follow it upstream along the banks. The river makes a wide curve to reach a small lake above a series of waterfalls, 45 minutes to one hour further on. Head a short way up to another much larger lake, 'Laguna Laja', set in impressive barren rocky surroundings. Continue around the lake on slanted terraces of rock strata. Numerous erratic boulders and smaller rocks indicate recent glacial recession. Progress is surprisingly good, and the sandy shore near where the main inlet stream cascades into the southern end of 'Laguna Laja' is reached after a further one to $1\frac{1}{2}$ hours.

Camp Sites Due to the lack of natural shelter, camping tends to be rather exposed. Reasonable camp sites can be found at the inlet and outlet streams of 'Laguna Laja', or in the scrub by the stream below 'Laguna Laja'.

Stage 2: 'Laguna Laja' to Lago Ferrier

($8\frac{1}{2}$ km, 4 to $5\frac{1}{2}$ hours)
Follow the eastern side of the outlet stream, where moraine terraces provide a convenient walkway. These lead up beside tumbling cascades and tiny gorges past where a major sidestream descends from the bare slab rock of the adjacent slopes. Continue south-east and higher into the valley, where the sparse vegetation allows good views down the slope as far as Glaciar Zapata.

Find your way up through ñirre thickets, crossing the stream wherever necessary. In many places an old stock track can still be followed. As you near a raw cirque on the left, the valley opens out and the ground becomes boggy, with numerous small stagnant ponds. Make your way gradually up the valley to cross the indistinct watershed $2\frac{1}{2}$ to four hours after leaving 'Laguna Laja'. The turquoise waters of Lago Ferrier are visible ahead for most of the time as you descend beside a small stream. The going is fairly straightforward and the lake is reached after a further one to 1½ hours.

Camp Sites It is possible to camp near the stream for much of the way, though the ground is often soggy. Good camp sites can be found at Lago Ferrier on the lake's western side.

Stage 3: Lago Ferrier to Lago Tyndall
(10 km, 4 to 7 hours)
Cross the small inlet stream, and head around towards the western side of Lago Ferrier. Although it seems like a more direct route, the eastern side of the lake is covered by dense scrub and the shoreline is fringed by low cliffs. The ground is often sodden, but the going is relatively easy. Clear areas within the light forest can be followed for most of the way.

It is possible to do a short sidetrip to view Ventisquero Tyndall, otherwise barely seen on the trek. Make your way up the open slopes on your right. At the top of the ridge head west to where the great glacier spills down from the Hielo Sur.

Continue south-east along the shore to reach the outlet stream two to three hours from the northern end of Lago Ferrier. Begin heading down the right bank through continual clearings. The gradient steepens dramatically as you move into moist beech forest after 30 to 45 minutes. Move well to the right of the stream and descend rapidly through the forest which is relatively free of underbrush. This leads out onto a wide expanse of forest destroyed by fire in the 1940s, one to 1½ hours on. The icy waters of Lago Tyndall are visible immediately below.

Make your way down slab terraces just to the right of the tumbling stream onto the charred slopes above the lake. Fallen logs and occasional thickets of calafate bushes may slow you down, but you should reach the shore after a further one to 1½ hours. The stream is best forded on the flat plain near where it enters Lago Tyndall. The lake is fed by stray chunks of ice and a meltwater

cascade spilling over from Ventisquero Tyndall. To get a closer look take a vague track off to your right up the bare rocky lakeside.

Camp Sites There is little suitable camping until you reach Lago Tyndall. Here excellent camp sites exist on clover flats 300 metres from where the Río Tyndall flows out of the lake.

Stage 4: Lago Tyndall to the Administration Centre
(23 km, 7½ to 11 hours)
Follow the track down the valley along the very exposed shore line of Lago Tyndall, passing the ruins of an old puesto. The faint path leads down the left side of the Río Tyndall, the lake outlet. Avoid the steep river bank by climbing up left onto the grassy slopes, from where there is an interesting view south-west across a broad floodplain towards Lago Geikie.

After contouring one km across small ridges and rock ledges, descend to the river and make your way downstream. Where there is no track, you can walk on the pebbly sandbanks between little channels in the river. The route continues across minor tributaries to reach a riverflat just upstream from where the Río Tyndall flows into the mighty Río Serrano, 1½ to 2½ hours from Lago Tyndall. A crude wind shelter of stacked tree trunks and brush can be found here near a brook at the edge of the open lenga forest.

Pick up the track some 300 metres downstream where cliffs fringe the water's edge. The path now gradually heads away from the Río Serrano, generally following a course just above where the flat swampy ground meets the higher forested slopes. In places the track is very badly overgrown, and progress is slow and tiresome. It is often necessary to move right to cross waterlogged sections of the river plain. After three to 4½ hours you come to a line of low fire-cleared ridges.

From here on it becomes difficult to follow the track, as the way is confused by numerous crisscrossing animal trails. The best route to take probably goes a way eastwards below the slopes, before heading north-east across the hills through ñirre and calafate scrub. After descending onto the windy steppes, wade a large glacial stream and continue 700 metres to reach the Lago Paine road after 1½ to 2½ hours.

If walking in the opposite direction, head south-west across a triangular clearing by the road one km after crossing the Río Paine bridge. The six km stretch back to the administration centre can be walked in 1½ to two hours.

Camp Sites The best camp site on the Río Tyndall is in the forest near the log shelter, a short distance above the river's confluence with the Río Serrano. Unfortunately, the area is infested with biting gnats. Other camping possibilities exist by small sidestreams along the route. It is prohibited to camp close to the road. Avoid further damage to forests by exercising extreme care with campfires.

Other Treks in Torres del Paine

LAGUNA VERDE
(2 to 3 days)
An easy trek across pampa steppes to some small lakes where birdlife and guanacos can be observed. A foot track leads north-east from the administration centre to Laguna Verde. The return trek can be made via two other paths that connect with the park's main access road.

LAGUNA AZUL & LAGO PAINE
(2 to 5 days)
A good signposted trail leaves the road north of Laguna Amarga and heads north-west to the western side of Laguna Azul. From here continue north-west to the northern shore of Lago Paine, where there is a refugio.

Other Treks in Southern Patagonia

RESERVA NACIONAL JEINEMENI – CHILE
(2 to 4 days)
Lago Jeinemeni (pronounced 'hey-ni-may-ni') lies in the heart of this large reserve. It is situated 60 km by road south of Chile Chico, a town on the southern shore of Lago General Carrera.

From Lago Jeinemeni a short walk can be made west to Lago Verde, a spectacular lake enclosed by high glaciated cliffs. From Jeinemeni's eastern shore another much longer track leads south up the Estero San Antonio to an attractive pass, then continues down the Estero La Leona to eventually reach the Valle Chacabuco. At present the road ends at Lago Jeinemeni, but in time it will be extended along the route of the present foot track so that it connects with the Cochrane/Paso Rodolfo Roballos road.

Maps
The Chilean IGM 1:50,000 sheet *Lago Verde* (Section J, No 49) covers the central part of the reserve around Lago Jeinemeni.

Access
Irregular minibus tours during summer to the Cueva de los Manos (prehistoric Indian cave paintings) are the only public transport out to the reserve.

RÍO PINTURAS – ARGENTINA
(2 to 5 days)
The Río Pinturas is 185 km by road south-east the town of Perito Moreno in northern Santa Cruz Province. The river is best known for its ancient rock paintings found at the small Cuevas de las Manos reserve, but 150-metre high canyons and gorges within the area also provide a backdrop for interesting walking. The surrounding country is largely grazing land set amongst semi-arid steppes and rugged *mesetas* (small tablelands), and is best suited to more experienced trekkers.

Maps
Four 1:100,000 Argentine IGM sheets cover the Río Pinturas area. These are *Arroyo Telken* (Santa Cruz, No 4772-18), *Cerro Negro* (Santa Cruz, No 4769-13) *Río Pinturas* (Santa Cruz, No 4772-24) and *Cañadon Charcamac* (Santa Cruz, No 4769-19).

Access
There is a local bus from Perito Moreno township to the reserve several times a week during the summer months.

COCHRANE TO VILLA O'HIGGINS – CHILE
(10 to 14 days)
This very long (approximately 170 km one-way) trek follows sendas de penetración (graded horse tracks) through the remote backcountry along the Chile-Argentine frontier. From Cochrane on Chile's Carretera Austral, the track leads south, passing Lago Esmeralda and Monte San Lorenzo (3706 metres), and follows the Río Salto to cross a pass. The route then continues down the Río Bravo before heading off south-east past Lagos Alegre, Guitarra, Cristie and Riñon to the Río Mayer and on to Villa O'Higgins. Occasional farms are passed but most of the country is uninhabited. Unfortunately, forest fires in the 1940s have destroyed large stands of forest in places. This trip is for experienced backcountry trekkers only and might be better done on horseback.

Maps
The Chilean IGM 1:250,000 two has new colour sheets, *Cochrane* (No SL-18-12) and *Lago O'Higgins* (No SM-18-3), in its Carta Terrestre series which indicate the track fairly accurately. The Chilean IGM also has most or all of the necessary sheets scaled at 1:50,000. Two recent Argentine IGM 1:250,000 colour sheets, *Lago Belgrano* (No 4772-III) and *Monte Tetris* (No 4972-I) also cover the area but do not show the route.

Access
Villa O'Higgins will eventually be the final termination of the Carretera Austral but at present the tiny village can be reached only by an irregular air service from Coyhaique (around US$50 single fare). It is, therefore, recommended that parties fly in to Villa O'Higgins (with plenty of supplies) and do the trek south-to-north.

PARQUE NACIONAL PERITO MORENO – ARGENTINA
(At least 7 days)
Parque Nacional Perito Moreno is a superb wilderness area that lies roughly 250 km directly south-west of the provincial town of Perito Moreno in Argentina's Santa Cruz Province. Just north of the park is the mighty San Lorenzo Massif, whose major summit, Monte San Lorenzo (or Cochrane to the Chileans) is the second highest point in southern Patagonia. Unfortunately, the Argentinian authorities simply lack the funds necessary to provide a basic infrastructure at this very remote park, and the administration centre near Estancia Lago Belgrano was never opened after its construction in 1981.

The area is enclosed by some eight major lakes which reach out into the Patagonian steppes from the park's mountainous interior. Dirt roads and rough musterers' tracks give access to the eastern sectors, but the interior is a complete wilderness and offers some wonderful scenery. A circuit route leads along the southern side of Lago Belgrano to Lago Azara then south to Lago Nansen before returning via the northern shore of Lago Burmeister. Another rough route leads around the northern margin of Lago Volcán to the Chilean border but requires wading a section of Lago Península and crossing the fast-flowing rivers Lácteo (shown on maps as 'Río Late'), Penitentes and San Lorenzo.

These are difficult treks suited only to experienced and well equipped parties. All food and supplies must be brought in.

Maps
Two relatively recent Argentine IGM 1:100,000 sheets, *Lago Belgrano* (Santa

Cruz, Nos 4772-33 & 4772-32) and *Monte Tetris* (Santa Cruz, No 4972-3), cover all of the park. An adjoining northern sheet, *Cerro Pico Agudo* (Santa Cruz, No 4772-27), includes the nearby Monte San Lorenzo and may also be useful to trekkers (and climbers) in this area.

Access
Visitors without their own transport will find access very difficult. Transport to Estancia Lago Belgrano must be arranged from either Perito Moreno or Gobernador Gregores.

RESERVAS NACIONALES MAGALLANES & LAGUNA PARRILLAR – CHILE
(1 to 2 days)
These two small reserves are situated on the Brunswick Península west and south-west respectively from Punta Arenas. Both lie in pleasant but generally unexciting country of rolling hills covered in low lenga forest. At Reserva Nacional Magallanes there are modest skiing facilities. At Reserva Nacional Laguna Parrillar you can camp by the lake, from where walks can be made into the surrounding area.

Maps
The CONAF office in Punta Arenas has the only maps of the reserves that are of any real use. They may allow you to borrow these for photocopying.

Access
Reserva Nacional Magallanes can be reached on foot or by chartered taxi from Punta Arenas. Reserva Nacional Laguna Parrillar is difficult to reach without private transport.

Tierra del Fuego

The mountains of southern and western Tierra del Fuego present one of the most exciting wilderness areas in the southern Andes. The extreme climate and inaccessibility of most of this area (partly due to the border that arbitrarily divides the island between Chile and Argentina) means that only the eastern parts of the Fuegian mountains can be easily visited by trekkers.

Parque Nacional Tierra del Fuego

Argentina's Parque Nacional Tierra del Fuego forms a narrow strip of 630 sq km in rugged mountainous country running along the Chilean frontier north from the Beagle Channel to include a large area on the north side of Lago Kami. The national park begins just 10 km west of the rapidly expanding tourist city of Ushuaia, and is surrounded by other more expansive areas of largely undisturbed and equally spectacular country.

Rather than following the general north-south line of the main Cordillera, the Fuegian Andes run in an east to west direction. This gives the mountains somewhat greater shelter from westerly winds, though it also makes them a bit more exposed to southerly storms that can sweep in from the large expanse of open ocean below the great island.

Sphagnum bogs are a major feature of subalpine Tierra del Fuego. Sphagnum bogs thrive anywhere drainage is poor and are known locally as *mallínes* or *turbales*. Mallínes cover extensive areas of the lower valleys, where they are gradually colonised by encroaching forests. The bogs form beautiful spongy peat mounds of red and gold colours that are often dry enough to walk on. Due to the southerly latitude, the forests tend

to be less dense than further north, with only light underbrush. The southern beech species lenga (*Nothofagus pumilio*) dominates the highland areas. Lower down coigüe de magallanes (*Nothofagus betuloides*) is also common.

Regrettably, North American beavers (*Castor canadensis*) now inhabit most forested streams all over Tierra del Fuego. The gnawed tree stumps and the animals' often surprisingly high dams are a constant hindrance and eyesore. Reindeer have also been introduced to the park area. Fortunately their numbers have stayed low enough (reportedly around forty head) to make them still something of a novelty, and their discarded antlers are occasionally found. Native guanaco are common throughout the park area and their trails often provide excellent natural walkways.

Compared to the mighty Darwin Range a short distance to the west in Chile, the mountains of Argentine Tierra del Fuego are of a more modest height. Yet although none of the summits exceed 1500 metres, the heavily glaciated ranges are still very impressive. Small but deeply carved glacial valleys are enclosed by jagged peaks dotted with tiny glaciers. The upper limit of alpine vegetation is around 550 metres and the permanent snowline is just a few hundred metres above this. This gives the mountain ranges a 'miniaturised' feel that makes it easy to forget the relatively low altitudes. The eastern Fuegian Andes are a fascinating area to explore.

Maps
The Argentinian IGM has still not published maps of the area that are of any use to trekkers. The only topographical map currently available that covers the entire area of the walks described below is a Chilean IGM sheet of the 1:250,000 Carta Preliminar series: *Canal Beagle* (No 5468). Due to its

basic form and large scale, this map shows all detail very poorly. A local tourist brochure of Parque Nacional Tierra del Fuego has a sketch map showing the first stage of the trek as far as Lago Kami. Although worth having, the brochure shows parts of the walking route incorrectly and is otherwise misleading. The locally available map of Tierra de Fuego by Rae Natalie Prosser de Goodall is of no use to trekkers.

Caminante, a commercial guiding company based in Ushuaia, plans to produce a map of the Fuegian mountains featuring tracks and routes. When published this will probably be the best available trekking map of the area.

LAGO KAMI CIRCUIT

This challenging walk passes through some of the finest country in the southern Andes, traversing the wild mountains from the Beagle Channel to isolated lagoons and inlets on the southern shores of Lago Kami. The lake is still more commonly known by its European name, Lago Fagnano. The trek's first section follows the route of a long-disused railway, built to carry lumber from the rich forests of the Río Pipo Valley.

Lago Kami is incomparably the largest lake on Tierra del Fuego. It more or less divides the largely flat and much drier northern part of the island from the more rugged southern strip that leads west into the long peninsula formed by the Darwin Range. The lake's 105-km-long form was gouged out by Pleistocene glaciers and has roughly similar dimensions to the nearby Beagle Channel. The Lago Kami basin also drains west and extends across the Chilean border into the more mountainous and heavily glaciated country to Seno Admirantazgo on the Fuegian west coast.

Days Required

No less than six days should be considered for the circuit, and slower parties might need an additional two or three days walking time. The area also has many interesting off-route features that are worth spending more time to explore. Some parties may decide to return

from Lago Kami via the same route, which would shorten the walk to a minimum of four days.

Standard

The trek follows a poor route through rugged and challenging country, and is suitable only for very fit and self-reliant trekkers. The recommended time to do the trek is from December to April. Trips made outside of this time are still possible, but there is an increased possibility of bad weather. Even in summer the weather is highly erratic, with frequent storms and snow falls in the mountains. Less confident parties are advised to opt for the shorter mini-circuit described below.

A track of poor-to-reasonable standard goes as far as Bahía Grande on Lago Kami. Thereafter, only a poorly marked cross-country route exists, and very good navigational skills are necessary. Fortunately there is much open walking through clearings, mallín country or above the tree line, and a little 'bush bashing' is necessary. The circuit crosses two exposed passes above the tree line at around 500 metres, which may be snow-covered early or late in the season. The ground is often waterlogged due to the work of introduced North American beavers as well as the naturally peaty soil, and trekkers may prefer to wear rubber boots.

Routefinding will generally be easier if the circuit is done in an anticlockwise direction, starting in Parque Nacional Tierra del Fuego. This trek is not for the inexperienced, and all sections are rated difficult. The total walking distance for the full circuit is 83 km.

Accommodation & Supplies

In Parque Nacional Tierra del Fuego there is camping with facilities at Lapataia. There are no huts or any other reliable shelter along the route of the trek, and it is essential to carry a good tent.

Ushuaia is the only logical base for all trips into the park. The city has quite a number of middle range hotels, but more economical accommodation is sometimes

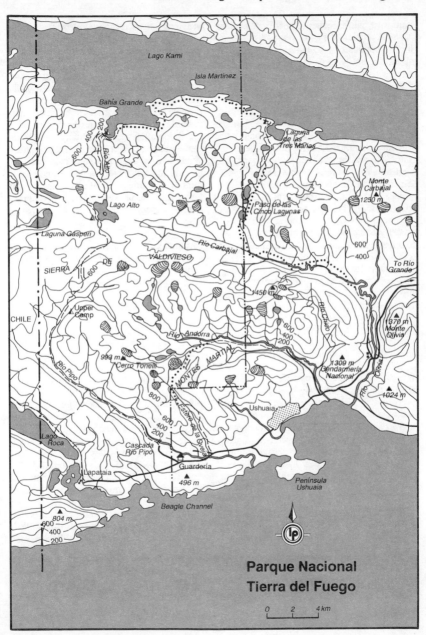

Parque Nacional
Tierra del Fuego

0   2   4 km

harder to find. Cheaper range hiking equipment is available in Ushuaia and all other basic supplies can be bought in a modern supermarket.

Access

The circuit begins at the termination of the Río Pipo road, 21 km from Ushuaia within the national park. Throughout the warmer months a local outdoor tourist company operates a minibus service out to the park. These leave three times a day from the Caminante office in Ushuaia at Deloqui 368. The one-way fare is around US$6.

The walk out to the trailhead from Ushuaia takes three to four hours (watch out for the quarry trucks on the first stretch of road). If arriving on foot or by private vehicle, turn right at the signposted road 1½ km after passing the park portería. A nominal entry fee is payable here.

The trek ends at the Gendarmería Nacional post, some 11 km from Ushuaia on the main road north (Ruta 3) from where you will have to organise your own transport back to town. Colectivos often pass by here and traffic is generally busy enough to make hitchhiking a reasonable possibility.

Stage 1: Río Pipo Carpark to Upper Río Pipo Camp

(16 km, 7 to 10 hours)
Follow the Río Pipo road through moorland and pretty river flats to where it ends at a small carpark. From here a short trail goes along the riverbank to the low and uninteresting 'cascada'. Instead take the wide but unsignposted old logging route leading up left into the forest.

Begin the long trek north-west up the valley, rising very gradually through pleasant beech forest. The track is often very wet and muddy, with continual boggy areas and fallen tree trunks along the path to slow you down. Where possible, stay on the higher ground well away from the river, as an endless series of beaver dams have flooded lower areas. There are occasional tree blazings and other route markings.

Stay within the Valle Pipo (disregarding the route shown on some tourist maps going via a tiny side valley). After four to six hours the valley widens out considerably into a long strip of saturated turbal. Trace the old road above the forested western side to reach a large sidestream coming down from the left, one to 1½ hours on. Ignore an overgrown logging route branching off here towards the Chilean border, and continue up the main valley which gradually turns northeastwards. The path crosses the now small Río Pipo after a further one to 1½ hours, and then follows the east bank for another 45 minutes to one hour through noticeably lower forest to arrive at the Upper Camp. A crude tee-pee shelter has been constructed here.

Camp Sites Excellent camp sites can be found along the river bank for most of the way, and completing this long section in single day is unnecessary.

Stage 2: Upper Río Pipo Camp to Lago Alto

(9 km, 3½ to 5 hours)
Wade the stream from the camp site and pick up the track. Head up the steepening western bank to a clear stream with strikingly white rocks and move up to your right away from the river. As the alpine scrub becomes patchy, find your way across mushy ground and climb north to gain a pass after two to three hours. From here you get a nice view of the upper Valle Pipo. On the other side is a lovely highland valley where there is a good chance of seeing hoofed wildlife.

Descend to the tiny stream and continue down the valley through open waterlogged country. The valley soon curves left (ie north) to reach a beaver dam above a waterfall, where Lago Alto comes in to view. Wade just below the dam wall and follow marker poles leading down to where the stream enters the lake. Lago Alto is a beautiful alpine lake surrounded on all sides by impressive glaciated peaks.

Camp Sites Reasonable semi-sheltered camp sites can be found near the inlet stream to Lago Alto, or about midway around the lake, 30 to 40 minutes on. Camping higher up is either too exposed, steep or boggy.

Stage 3: Lago Alto to Bahía Grande (Lago Kami)

(9 km, 4 to 6 hours)

Cross the inlet stream and begin heading around the western side of Lago Alto. The route leaves the immediate shoreline to avoid small peninsulas. Where vegetation is thick a trail has been cut, but on more open sections marker poles show the way. At the north-west corner of the lake, follow the track a short way up from the lake into a tiny side valley, before descending to the small sidestream. Cross and make your way around the wet grassy northern shore to reach the Río Alto, the outlet of Lago Alto, one to 1½ hours after crossing the southern inlet stream.

Most maps incorrectly show Lago Alto's outlet as the stream flowing eastwards into the Valle Carbajal).

Drop down 500 metres beside the cascading outlet stream and wade to the east bank. The track goes down through a succession of swampy clearings and beaver dams until steep rock sides force another crossing. The route now climbs away left to follow more sporadic marker poles across flattened rock ridges well above the stream for 45 minutes to one hour.

Shortly after passing through a pretty area of mallínes Lago Kami becomes visible. Here watch carefully for cairns or other route markings that lead off to the right. Move down the slope a short way and contour 300 metres to pick up a cut trail. This heads steeply down a broad ridge toward the junction of the Río Alto and an obvious side valley coming down from the south-west. The track descends quickly into the rich tall coigüe and lenga forest, still untouched due to the area's inaccessibility.

Follow the well-blazed trail along the gently dropping west side of the Río Alto for 1½ km to where the river falls sharply in a series of cascades. Climb left through an area of fallen trees onto where a natural lookout

gives an excellent view of Bahía Grande ahead. Make your way carefully down the steep rocky ridge back to the streamside, and continue for 30 to 45 minutes, passing a major waterfall shortly before you reach a sheltered inlet of Bahía Grande, itself part of the great Lago Kami. This lovely semi-enclosed bay makes a nice spot to spend a rest day.

Camp Sites There is fair camping along the river where the ground is not too steep or damp. Excellent camp sites can be found in the forest on the east bank of the river at Bahía Grande.

Stage 4: Bahía Grande to Laguna de las Tres Marías

(21 km, 10 to 14 hours)

The marked track finishes at Bahía Grande. From here on the going becomes rather more rugged, though routefinding is fairly straightforward. Most parties will need at least two days to do this long section.

Heading eastwards, pick up a faint livestock trail. Follow this around through an area of burnt forest to pass a tiny peninsula at the mouth of the inlet after 45 minutes to one hour. Cross a small stream flowing into a pebbly cove, and continue east along the lakeside for a further one to 1½ hours. Turn north and make your way via a mostly good track and stretches of beach until you come to a low but prominent peninsula at the entrance of Bahía Grande, four to five hours from the Río Alto camp sites.

Walk along the coast of Lago Kami, generally staying as close to the lakeside as possible. Head east to reach a larger beach after 1½ to two hours, and continue on past the adjacent Isla Martinez, some two km offshore. In places the track peters out and it is necessary to find your own way through the largely open lenga forest until the route reappears.

As you leave the island behind, progress becomes slower and more strenuous. For the next five km the coastline is interrupted by high rock cliffs and small promontories alternating with isolated sandy bays. Ruins of fences and an old cattleyard indicate previous livestock grazing from the Chilean side of the border. Follow animal trails roughly south-west to cross a small stream flowing out of a marshy lagoon, and continue for another one to 1½ hours until you arrive at Laguna de las Tres Marías.

This beautiful little inlet has a narrow opening sheltered by tiny islands. A cut track leads around the shore past the remains of a burnt-down fishing lodge (the Hostería de los Renos, which at some time may be rebuilt).

Camp Sites Except for a long section adjacent to Isla Martinez, where cliffs cut off access to the water, camps can be made in frequent spots along the way. Winds off the lake can be very strong, so choose a sheltered site. At Laguna de las Tres Marías excellent camp sites can be found around the western shore.

Stage 5: Laguna de las Tres Marías to Upper Río Carbajal via 'Paso de las Cinco Lagunas'
(11 km, 6 to 8 hours)
Take the track around the shore line until you get to a small stream flowing into the inlet after 30 to 40 minutes. Head up the west bank for 500 metres before crossing, and continue up the valley close to the stream, recrossing where necessary. The first lake is reached 45 minutes to one hour from Laguna de las Tres Marías.

Pick up notched tree blazings leading around the east shore through an area of sodden moorland on the lake's south-eastern side. Cross again and follow the stream for 1½ km, then climb left to avoid difficult terrain. Smooth rock ridges and wet grassy slopes can be followed through occasional sections of steep scrub.

When you come to the smaller second lake, descend to the shore and follow it around the east side. As before, make your way high above the stream, and continue ascending through small clearings to reach the third lake after 30 to 45 minutes. At the far end of the third lake is a spectacular

waterfall spilling down directly into its waters.

From the southern side of the third lake, climb ahead over an obvious crest. Drop down immediately to the shore of the fourth lake, and once more begin moving around the eastern side. This is the largest of these lakes, with a peninsula jutting out into the water about halfway. Cut off the peninsula by following markings that lead up left over a low ridge to a small mossy bay. First make your way around the beavered shore line, then head up left through some clearings to the inlet stream.

Follow the course of the stream through increasingly sparse alpine vegetation. Picking up good animal trails, continue up past two very small lakes to arrive at the 'Paso de las Cinco Lagunas' after 45 minutes to one hour. There are superb views back down the valley towards Lago Kami.

Drop down the bare slopes to a final lake just below the pass, and follow around its east shore. On your right, a tiny glacier comes down from an impressive peak. From the outlet, continue 500 metres down the left bank of the stream, then cross and make a rapid descent through a continuous series of soggy clearings which lead out into the Valle Carbajal after 45 minutes to one hour.

If coming from the other direction, turn north up into the first side valley on your right 1½ km after an obvious division of the main Valle Carbajal.

Camp Sites Some excellent camp sites can be found by the lower four lakes passed on the way up, but the terrain higher up is mostly exposed and waterlogged, and less suitable for camping. Faster parties are advised to continue over the pass into the Valle Carbajal, where numerous good camp sites exist in the trees along the riverflats.

Stage 6: Upper Río Carbajal to Río Grande-Ushuaia Road (Ruta 3)
(17 km, 7 to 10 hours)
Head downstream, following wild cattle trails along the banks of the milky Río Carbajal. The trails lead to numerous fords of the

small meandering stream, and in many places beaver dams blocking the route must be avoided. After initially passing through areas of light forest, you come to an extended belt of moorland.

Make your own way east to south-east across the red bogs for two to three hours, keeping to the northern side of the river. Although sometimes tiring to walk on, the spongy peat provides a direct and scenic route. Where you come to an obvious forested lateral moraine pick up a good animal trail along the low ridge for 1½ km. The moraine ridge peters out near a large beaver dam.

Head across to the opposite side of the valley, again fording the Río Carbajal to meet an ancient overgrown logging road. Follow the track as it gradually improves and swings around to the south. The route skirts the moorland, leading through occasional clearings in the rich lenga forest to pass an aviation beacon three to four hours on. From here follow the vehicle track past a modern peat cutting operation (watch out for the dogs), and continue across the Río Olivia to reach the main Ushuaia-Río Grande road after another one to 1½ hours. A major post of the Argentinian Gendarmería Nacional is situated here, with radio contact to Ushuaia.

There is no local public transport this far out of town, though taxis often run this route. Traffic on this road is generally busy. The walk back to Ushuaia is about 11 km and takes two to three hours.

Camp Sites Despite beaver activity and extensive areas of moorland, good camp sites can be found in many places along this section.

TIERRA DEL FUEGO MINI-CIRCUIT

The Montes Martial rise up abruptly from behind Ushuaia. In winter, there are small skifields on the treeless upper slopes of the range that looks out south across the Beagle Channel. A popular tourist walk goes directly up from Ushuaia via a chairlift to the snout of the Glaciar Martial.

Despite is closeness to Ushuaia, the country behind the Martials is almost completely wild and undisturbed, and mostly belongs to the Parque Nacional Tierra del Fuego. Although only the higher peaks of the range reach more than 1000 metres, several glaciers cling to its upper slopes. Like glaciers all over the world, these have been receding during the last few generations and are now quite small.

This very accessible mini-circuit completely circumnavigates the Montes Martial range. The route leads up an idyllic valley that drains south into the Beagle Channel and over a watershed where it enters the national park. In the secluded Valle Andorra the vegetation is mainly attractive light beech forest and areas of Fuegian turbal.

Days Required
The trek can be done in two long days, but the ideal walking time is three days.

Standard
The trek is shorter and much less demanding than the full circuit described previously, and follows a rough yet straightforward route that crosses a low pass situated at roughly 600 metres above sea level. A track of sorts can be followed over most of the walk, but in certain places it may be necessary to find your own way.

The circuit route is more easily followed if walked in a clockwise direction, as there are various diverging roads to confuse those coming the other way. The trek is graded moderate and has a walking distance of 22 km (or 34 km if walking from and back to Ushuaia).

Access
The trek starts from a road bridge passed on the way to the national park, 8 km west of Ushuaia. A local guiding firm, Caminante, runs three daily minibuses out to Lapataia during the extended tourist season. These leave from outside the Caminante office in Ushuaia. The one-way fare is around US$6. From Ushuaia the walk out to the start of the trek takes two to three hours. This trek ends

at the Río Grande-Ushuaia road (Ruta 3), just four km from the centre of town.

Stage 1: Puente Estero de la Oveja to Upper Cañadón de la Oveja

(5 km, 3 to 4 hours)

If starting out from Ushuaia, follow the Lapataia road (watch out for trucks) a short way past the local rubbish tip to the Puente Estero de la Oveja. At about eight km west from the centre of town, this unsignposted bridge is the first one you will come to.

Walk 20 to 30 minutes up the grassy eastern side of the stream past a racing speedway on your right to where the forest begins at the start of a tiny valley. Head uphill on scrubby cattle pads and pick up a cut track leading into the narrow forested valley.

The path can be followed for 700 metres before petering out. From here find your own way through the largely open woodland along the banks of the Estero de la Oveja. The route then continues another two to three hours over grassy meadows bordered by thickets of scrub to reach a small area of avalanche rubble that descends right down to the west side of the stream.

Camp Sites Although it is possible to camp in the damp forest lower down the valley, the small grassy clearings found on both sides of the upper Cañadón de la Oveja are the most attractive.

Stage 2: Upper Cañadón de la Oveja to Upper Río Andorra

(6 km, 3 to 6 hours)

Continue up the valley through the thinning vegetation, crossing the small stream where necessary. Pick up guanaco trails that lead towards the head of the valley around to the right (north-east). These provide a quick ascent over grassy green slopes before you reach the stony open pass marked with a rock cairn after one to two hours. From here on there are some good views north towards the mountains of the Sierra de Valdivieso.

Following this natural path, drop down rapidly to the tree line. Here the route again disappears. Make your way down, either directly through the wet forest beside the cascading stream or via faint animal trails on the slopes to your right. A rough horse track on a small eastwards-flowing stream is reached, 45 minutes to one hour from the pass.

Turn right along the steep south side of the sidestream. The track rises and dips many times, and in places diverging cattle pads lead off-route. After two km the stream leads out into the much broader Valle Andorra where the path becomes less distinct.

Camp Sites After leaving the upper part of the cañadón the camping is poor until the valley opens out after reaching the Río Andorra.

Stage 3: Upper Río Andorra to Río Grande-Ushuaia Road (Ruta 3)

(11 km, 5 to 9 hours)

Head roughly east along the southern side of the Río Andorra, mostly some distance from the river. The path leads through attractive beech forests repeatedly interrupted by expanses of moorland and open flowery meadows. The valley is enclosed by glaciated ranges and there are some fine views of surrounding peaks. Look out for occasional route markings, as often no definite route exists until the track re-enters the forest.

Continue until the route merges into an old and partly overgrown logging track. Follow this for two to three hours as it gradually widens and comes out at a graded road. The road winds its way five km past a peat cutting operation, isolated farms and holiday houses to connect with the Ushuaia road. From here you can walk back to town in one to 1½ hours.

If coming from the other way, watch for a cement works situated on the left, immediately where the turnoff leaves the Ushuaia-Río Grande road.

Camp Sites On the first part of this section excellent camp sites can be found anywhere the land is dry enough and close enough to water. Camping further down the valley is not recommended.

Other Treks in Parque Nacional Tierra del Fuego

BAHÍA ENSENADA TO LAPATAIA
(2 to 3 days)
From Bahía Ensenada a rough route leads west around the coastline to the park administration headquarters at Lapataia. Other shorter day-walks are possible from here.

Maps
A recent Chilean IGM 1:50,000 sheet, *Puerto Navarino* (Section L, No 188) covers this area well.

Access
Transport is by daily Caminante minibus from Ushuaia.

LAGO ROCA
(1 to 2 days)
From Lapataia follow the road north to pick up a trail leading north-west around the eastern shore of Lago Roca. The trail continues over the border into Chile. The frontier area is regularly patrolled (usually by boat) and should not be crossed without written permission from the Chilean Consulate (at Maipu & Kuanip) in Ushuaia.

Maps
As for the preceding walk, Bahía Ensenada to Lapataia.

Isla Navarino

Isla Navarino lies on the Beagle Channel just to the south of the Fuegian 'mainland'. The island is large, measuring roughly 100 km by 40 km and has a stark subantarctic climate. The only real settlement on Navarino is the Chilean naval base of Puerto Williams, which is now considered the most southerly town in the world.

Physical isolation and severe climatic conditions on Navarino have effected the island's wildlife. There is less diversity of tree species compared to areas further the north, with deciduous lenga and ñirre species predominating in the mountains. Where exposure to the elements becomes extreme, vegetation is reduced to beautiful stunted forms. Waterlogged peat bogs and attractive mossy lawns compete with the forest at all elevations.

There are no land-dwelling predators on Navarino. As a consequence, the flightless steamer duck (*Tycheres pteneres*) is relatively common on the island. Small flocks of this large bird can sometimes be encountered roaming through the brush or foraging around streams, well away from the protection of any sizable body of water. Isla Navarino also has a large population of guanacos. Without the threat from pumas, the animals are much less shy than their cousins on the mainland, and can often be observed in their wild state from close range.

Unfortunately, introduced North American beavers have caused major damage to the forests and river systems of Navarino Island. Beavers gnaw down trees alongside the streams, building often enormous dams to create their favoured habitat. These industrious rodents will block even the smallest watercourse right up to the tree line, inundating large parts of the valleys. As on Tierra del Fuego, from where the beavers migrated in the early 1950s, the absence of foxes and pumas means there is no biological control of the beavers, and their numbers are still increasing.

DIENTES CIRCUIT
In the little-visited interior of Navarino is a superb wilderness of many hundreds of lakes and craggy mountain ranges. A spectacular range of jagged pinnacles known as Los Dientes de Navarino are the highest peaks on the island. In fine weather the Dientes can be seen directly from Puerto Williams and are a key landmark for boats on the Beagle Channel.

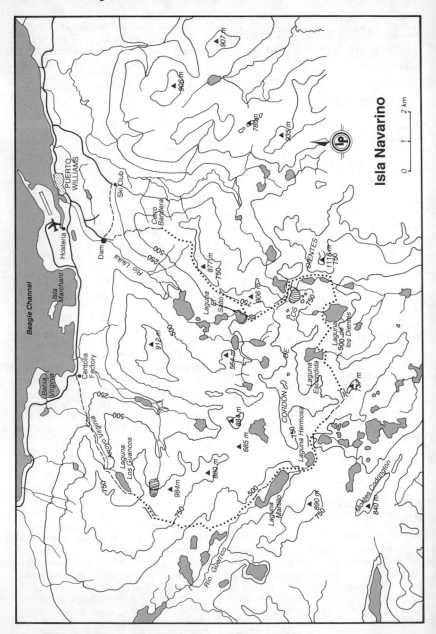

Isla Navarino

Maps

The central ranges of Navarino Island are covered by two Chilean IGM sheets scaled at 1:50,000: *Puerto Williams* (Section L, No 190) and *Lago Windhound* (Section L, No 203). Although very new, these maps fail to show many lakes and have other major topographic inaccuracies (such as incorrect vegetation). They do not indicate the circuit route. These attractive sheets are, nevertheless, of considerable use to walkers.

Days Required

The Navarino circuit is probably best done in five relatively short days. The walking stages given below are suggestions only. As good camp sites can be found along much of the route, parties can move at their own pace. The ranges of the island's interior are easily accessible and invite further exploration. The numerous possible off-route sidetrips would lengthen the trek by many days.

Standard

The interior of Navarino is wild country, and this trek should not be taken lightly. Although somewhat protected by the mountains which lie further to the west, the island often experiences savage weather, with strong winds and snowfalls even in summer. The trek is best done from early December to the end of March, though more experienced and well prepared parties can go at least a month earlier or later.

The circuit follows a rough route only. Most of the hiking route goes through relatively exposed terrain above the tree line, and in the central area of the Dientes there is no vegetation whatsoever. The advantage of this is that there is open walking for much of the way. In many places excellent guanaco trails indicate the best route and can be easily followed. Beavers, however, have flooded large parts of the forested valleys with their (usually shallow) dams, making the going harder. On some sections peaty bogs must be crossed and in these areas the ground is quite waterlogged. The route is variously marked with tree blazings, cairns, coloured tape and paint splotches. Nevertheless, careful routefinding is required.

Isla Navarino is a military zone under the jurisdiction of a naval commander. Officially you are required to get permission to trek and camp from the commander's office in Puerto Williams. The nearest CONAF office is in Punta Arenas, but staff at the town's excellent museum or the small tourist office may be able to provide limited information on conditions.

The walk has been rated as moderate to difficult. The total distance is 55 km.

Accommodation & Supplies

There are no walker's refugios (nor any other buildings) along the route and it essential that parties carry a good tent. The Hostería Wala is two km west of Puerto Williams and offers more up-market accommodation (around US$30 per night). There are three or four other cheaper casas de familia in town.

All necessary supplies can be bought at the general store in Puerto Williams. Considering the town's isolation, prices are not unreasonable. There is also a small bakery.

Access

Navarino is only accessible by plane or boat.

From Punta Arenas, Aerovías DAP have one regular weekly flight (usually Tuesday) to Puerto Williams. A one-way airfare is around US$50. DAP and the Chilean airforce (FACh) also have many irregular flights between Punta Arenas and Puerto Williams. Airforce flights are generally on an at-short-notice basis and are, therefore, not able to be reserved.

During the summer season there is a weekly tourist boat from Ushuaia, in Argentinian Tierra del Fuego, to Puerto Williams. The boat usually leaves early on Saturday and returns in the afternoon. In past years disagreements between Argentine and Chilean maritime authorities have interrupted the service, so check on the current situation. The return fare is around US$15. Naval ships run irregularly between Punta Arenas and Puerto Williams, and there is a supply ship about once a month. The trip takes two days and follows the spectacular fjord-pocked coast of southern Tierra del Fuego. Fares are usually very reasonable.

Many private yachts on their way to and from Cape Horn or Antarctica pass through Punta Arenas, Ushuaia or Puerto Williams. During the summer months it is often possible to hitch a ride on one of these boats.

Stage 1: Puerto Williams to 'Laguna El Salto'
(11 km, 6 to 8 hours)
The first section of the walk takes a cleared track up to Cerro Bandera. This is a popular day walk for locals. With light daypacks, the return trip to Cerro Bandera can be done in four to five hours.

One km west of Puerto Williams there is a statue of the Virgin Mary at a road intersection that marks a turnoff heading inland. Follow this road for 40 to 50 minutes, turning right at a fork. The road leads up beside the Río Ukika to a small dam (the water supply for the township). From above the small carpark by the dam two marked paths depart. The left path has tree blazings dabbed with red paint and eventually leads back to town.

Take the right track, at first following the east bank of the stream. The track soon turns left, and after 15 minutes continues steeply uphill in a series of switchbacks through the lenga forest. One to two hours on, the tree line suddenly gives way to wind-battered beech brush. A short hop straight up the grassy slope leads to the now fallen sheet-metal Chilean flag. When standing, the flag is clearly visible from the Hostería Wala, and was originally erected here in the early 1980s during the tense period of military confrontation with Argentina. Magnificent views from Cerro Bandera stretch out along the Beagle Channel to Ushuaia and beyond.

Cerro Bandera is actually a spur, and not a peak in itself. A stony and extremely exposed plateau extends out to the south. In very fine weather it is possible to follow the ridge-line. Head gradually right, following cairns some way above the irregular line of weathered shrubbery. Pick up a good guanaco trail that skirts the tree line. In

places loose scree is difficult to cross. There are nice views of numerous lakes in the forested valley with the Dientes behind. Continue until a course-rock talus slope comes down across the trail, and then descend to the shore of 'Laguna El Salto'.

Sidetrips An interesting area of lakes, set in a barren landscape north-east of 'Laguna El Salto' and below the Dientes Range, is easily accessible. The area can be explored from 'Laguna El Salto' by following the route to the tiny shallow lake (see the following description) and heading over the lateral ridges. In places there are guanaco trails which indicate the easiest routes.

It is also possible to climb the steep lichen-covered ridges to (near) the summits of some of the Dientes peaks. The rock is mostly rotten and heavily fractured. A marked route leads up a rubble-filled couloir from a cairn on the first col. Other ascent possibilities exist in the range.

Camp Sites It is possible to camp at the Hostería Wala near Puerto Williams (but ask permission first). There is good camping in the picnic area by the Ukika dam. At 'Laguna El Salto' there are pleasant camp sites on moist cushion-plant lawns around the lakeside. Below 'Laguna El Salto' many other possibilities exist. Higher up the terrain is very exposed and there is no firewood.

Stage 2: 'Laguna El Salto' to 'Laguna de los Dientes'
(11 km, 4 to 5 hours)
Continue around the shore of 'Laguna El Salto' to the inlet cascade. Head up the side of the steep stabilised rubble chute on the right. The route follows the small stream, soon crossing the vegetation line. Only sparse lichen grows up here, so it is all open walking.

Approaching the Cordón de los Dientes you pass a tiny shallow tarn and the stream soon disappears. Swing around left (eastwards) towards the ridge to reach a large rock cairn, one to 1½ hours from 'Laguna El Salto'. A lake set in barren surroundings comes

Top: Ushuaia, Tierra del Fuego
Bottom: Lago Kami Circuit, Parque Nacional Tierra del Fuego

Top: Navarino Circuit, Isla Navarino
Bottom: Paso Bevan, Parque Nacional Tierra del Fuego

into view. To the right, another slightly lower pass can be seen across the lake.

Do not descend the whole way to the shore, but traverse around towards the pass, remaining about 35 metres above the lake on rock ledges. Some scrambling might be necessary, but the pass is gained easily.

Head down into the tiny attractive valley, passing a small glacier at the right. Take the east bank of an elongated lake and descend to another smaller lake. Pass this via its western side. The valley opens out just below the lake's outlet stream. The south coast becomes visible behind a multitude of lakes on the low-lying waterlogged land in the south of the island. Immediately before this, look out for route markings leading off to the right. Guanaco trails head east over a low ridge through stunted vegetation to the sizable 'Laguna de los Dientes'.

Camp Sites The elevated route section above 'Laguna El Salto' is very exposed and unsuitable for camping. The tree line is not again reached until 'Laguna de los Dientes'. The more thinly wooded slopes above the lake are preferable for the pitching of tents.

Stage 3: 'Laguna de los Dientes' to 'Laguna Martillo'
(8 km, 4 to 6 hours)
From the upper side of 'Laguna de Los Dientes' head north-west up a gentle but distinct side valley. An interesting ridge of rock needles running off the Cordón de los Dientes should be on your right. Another big lake, Laguna Escondida, appears after 40 to 50 minutes. Set in stark surroundings, the lake is enclosed on three sides by steep craggy peaks.

Sidle left around the beaver-cleared lakeside to cross the outlet stream. Move immediately onto the rise of low beech thickets and continue across a short section of rock rubble. From here the route to be taken is clear. An obvious pass, some 2½ km distant, lies to the south-west at roughly 240°.

Make a bee-line for the head of the attractive, tiny valley. Pick up excellent guanaco trails that lead up to the crest of the pass, which is marked by a high rock cairn. A whole new panorama of lakes, forest and jagged peaks comes into view. Do not head directly down the slope from the pass, but follow trails that contour to the right along the ridge. Some 300 metres on, the route ahead becomes more clearly visible. To the north-west at about 310° is yet another low, easy pass.

Gradually descend the broken rock slopes to the tree line. Circle around on the higher ground to your right to avoid the more difficult terrain of boggy beaver dams and beech thickets. Follow occasional cairns and other route markings leading up the slope to the pass. 'Laguna Hermosa', as its name suggests is a lovely liver-shaped lake with a tiny island on its left side. It is reached just after crossing the pass. The lake is the source of the Río Guerrico, which drains into the Beagle Channel.

Pick up trails that go well above the impenetrable scrub growing around the lake's southern shore. Where the vegetation thins out ahead, move down to cross the cascading outlet stream to continue down the true right bank. 'Laguna Martillo', a long and in places very narrow lake begins. Make your way around the north-eastern side of the lake. The route first stays close to the shore, but moves up at about half way to cut off the broad peninsula near the southern end of 'Laguna Martillo'.

Camp Sites There are many potential camp sites along the route, though low vegetation generally provides poor shelter. The ground is often soggy, so choose your site carefully. Most recommended camp sites are above 'Laguna Hermosa' and on the north-eastern shore of 'Laguna Martillo'.

Stage 4: 'Laguna Martillo' to 'Laguna Los Guanacos'
(8 km, 4 to 5½ hours)
Proceed down the valley on the northern side of the Río Guerrico, avoiding the waterlogged ground close to the river. A range of spectacular spiked peaks rises abruptly on

the left. To the right, a lower and more gently contoured range can be seen. At about 345° on the lower end of this range is a slight depression. This is the fifth and final pass crossing.

Two km from 'Laguna Martillo', follow tape markings up from the river through the narrow clearing along a small stream. Move diagonally upwards to above the tree line until you come to a sloping terrace. Well-trodden trails up a tiny ridge covered with green cushion plants lead the way onto the range. There are superb views over the stony slopes to Ushuaia, the western Cordillera Darwin and other peaks. Interesting peaks on the neighbouring Isla Hoste also stand out.

Head across the barren plateau towards mountains on the adjacent Tierra del Fuego, passing two icy tarns. After 20 minutes you come to the edge of the flat area. The land falls away abruptly into a magnificent classic glacial lake, 'Laguna Los Guanacos'. Large snowdrifts and loose scree cover the precipitous slopes enclosing the lake. Follow markings and cairns a short way around to the right, where scree slides allow a rapid 200-metre descent to Laguna Los Guanacos. Avoid occasional snowdrifts which are dangerously icy.

Guanaco

Camp Sites There is good camping by the Río Guerrico downstream of 'Laguna Martillo', but to find dry, flat ground you may have to look hard. The scenic 'Laguna Los Guanacos' lies partially sheltered in a deep glacial trough, and there is plenty of beavered driftwood around the shores of the lake. Less exposed sites exist just below the outlet stream.

Stage 5: 'Laguna Los Guanacos' to Puerto Williams
(17 km, 5½ to 8 hours)
A guanaco trail, so good in places that it seems it was deliberatley constructed by humans, traverses the rocky western side of 'Laguna Los Guanacos'. The trail continues past the outlet stream and down below the tree line. The Arroyo Virginia is crossed without difficulty a number of times. Lower down, beavers have left many areas inundated or swampy, and the route is harder to follow. There are occasional markings to guide you, but otherwise keep close to the river.

After descending for two to three hours, the valley of the Arroyo Virginia becomes narrower. Wait until a burnt-out area below some low cliffs fringes the river. Then make your way on cattle and horse pads across cleared slopes to arrive at the the Mac Lean centolla processing plant on the coast road. The 12 km stretch back to Puerto Williams can be walked in two or three hours. Occasional vehicles usually stop for hitchhikers.

Other Treks in Tierra del Fuego

ALTOS DE BOSQUERÓN
(1 to 2 days)
The Altos de Bosquerón are a low range of hills overlooking Bahía Inútil in Chilean Tierra del Fuego. Although scarcely wilderness, the area has historical Fuegian gold rush ruins dating from the around the turn of the century.

Maps

The area is covered by two Chilean IGM 1:50,000 sheets, *Porvenir* (Section L, No 103) and *Concordia* (Section L, No 104).

Access

The Altos de Bosquerón are easily accessible from Porvenir.

Index

MAPS

PLACE NAMES

Map references are in **bold** type

Keep in touch!

We love hearing from you and think you'd like to hear from us.

The Lonely Planet Newsletter covers the when, where, how and what of travel. (AND it's free!)

When...is the right time to see reindeer in Finland?
Where...can you hear the best palm-wine music in Ghana?
How...do you get from Asunción to Areguá by steam train?
What...should you leave behind to avoid hassles with customs in Iran?

To join our mailing list just contact us at any of our offices. (details below)

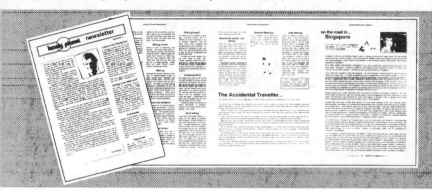

Every issue includes:

- *a letter from Lonely Planet founders Tony and Maureen Wheeler*
- *travel diary from a Lonely Planet author - find out what it's really like out on the road*
- *feature article on an important and topical travel issue*
- *a selection of recent letters from our readers*
- *the latest travel news from all over the world*
- *details on Lonely Planet's new and forthcoming releases*

Also available Lonely Planet T-shirts. 100% heavy weight cotton (S, M, L, XL)

LONELY PLANET PUBLICATIONS
Australia: PO Box 617, Hawthorn, 3122, Victoria (tel: 03-819 1877)
USA: Embarcadero West, 155 Filbert Street, Suite 251, Oakland, CA 94607 (tel: 510-893 8555)
UK: Devonshire House, 12 Barley Mow Passage, Chiswick, London W4 4PH (tel: 081-742 3161)

Guides to the Americas

Alaska – a travel survival kit
Jim DuFresne has travelled extensively through Alaska by foot, road, rail, barge and kayak. This guide has all the information you'll need to make the most of one of the world's great wilderness areas.

Argentina, Uruguay & Paraguay – a travel survival kit
This guide gives independent travellers all the essential information on three of South America's lesser known countries. Discover some of South America's most spectacular natural attractions in Argentina; friendly people and beautiful handicrafts in Paraguay; and Uruguay's wonderful beaches.

Bolivia – a travel survival kit
From lonely villages in the Andes to ancient ruined cities and the spectacular city of La Paz, Bolivia is a magnificent blend of everything that inspires travellers. Discover safe and intriguing travel options in this comprehensive guide.

Brazil – a travel survival kit
From the mad passion of Carnival to the Amazon – home of the richest and most diverse ecosystem on earth – Brazil is a country of mythical proportions. This guide has all the essential travel information.

Canada – a travel survival kit
This comprehensive guidebook has all the facts on the USA's huge neighbour – the Rocky Mountains, Niagara Falls, ultramodern Toronto, remote villages in Nova Scotia, and much more.

Central America on a shoestring
Practical information on travel in Belize, Guatemala, Costa Rica, Honduras, El Salvador, Nicaragua and Panama. A team of experienced Lonely Planet authors reveals the secrets of this culturally rich, geographically diverse and breathtakingly beautiful region.

Chile & Easter Island – a travel survival kit
Travel in Chile is easy and safe, with possibilities as varied as the countryside. This guide also gives detailed coverage of Chile's Pacific outpost, mysterious Easter Island.

Colombia – a travel survival kit
Colombia is a land of myths – from the ancient legends of El Dorado to the modern tales of Gabriel Garcia Marquez. The reality is beauty and violence, wealth and poverty, tradition and change. This guide shows how to travel independently and safely in this exotic country.

Colombia – a travel survival kit
Colombia is a land of myths – from the ancient legends of El Dorado to the modern tales of Gabriel Garcia Marquez. The reality is beauty and violence, wealth and poverty, tradition and change. This guide shows how to travel independently and safely in this exotic country.

Costa Rica – a travel survival kit
This practical guide gives the low down on exceptional opportunities for fishing and water sports, and the best ways to experience Costa Rica's vivid natural beauty.

Ecuador & the Galápagos Islands – a travel survival kit
Ecuador offers a wide variety of travel experiences, from the high cordilleras to the Amazon plains – and 600 miles west, the fascinating Galápagos Islands. Everything you need to know about travelling around this enchanting country.

Hawaii – a travel survival kit
Share in the delights of this island paradise – and avoid its high prices – both on and off the beaten track. Full details on Hawaii's best-known attractions, plus plenty of uncrowded sights and activities.

La Ruta Maya: Yucatán, Guatemala & Belize – a travel survival kit
Invaluable background information on the cultural and environmental riches of La Ruta Maya (The Mayan Route), plus practical advice on how best to minimise the impact of travellers on this sensitive region.

Mexico – a travel survival kit
A unique blend of Indian and Spanish culture, fascinating history, and hospitable people, make Mexico a travellers' paradise.

Peru – a travel survival kit
The lost city of Machu Picchu, the Andean altiplano and the magnificent Amazon rainforests are just some of Peru's many attractions. All the travel facts you'll need can be found in this comprehensive guide.

South America on a shoestring
This practical guide provides concise information for budget travellers and covers South America from the Darien Gap to Tierra del Fuego. The *New York Times* dubbed the author 'the patron saint of travellers in the third world'.

Also available:
Brazilian phrasebook, **Latin American Spanish** phrasebook and **Quechua** phrasebook.

Lonely Planet Guidebooks

Lonely Planet guidebooks cover every accessible part of Asia as well as Australia, the Pacific, South America, Africa, the Middle East, Europe and parts of North America. There are five series: *travel survival kits*, covering a country for a range of budgets; *shoestring guides* with compact information for low-budget travel in a major region; *walking guides*; *city guides* and *phrasebooks*.

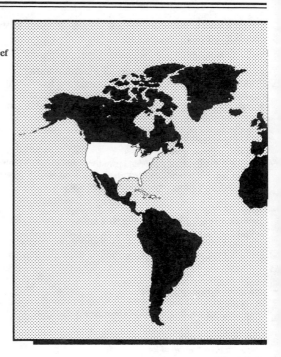

Australia & the Pacific
Australia
Bushwalking in Australia
Islands of Australia's Great Barrier Reef
Fiji
Melbourne city guide
Micronesia
New Caledonia
New Zealand
Tramping in New Zealand
Papua New Guinea
Bushwalking in Papua New Guinea
Papua New Guinea phrasebook
Rarotonga & the Cook Islands
Samoa
Solomon Islands
Sydney city guide
Tahiti & French Polynesia
Tonga
Vanuatu
Victoria

South-East Asia
Bali & Lombok
Bangkok city guide
Myanmar (Burma)
Burmese phrasebook
Cambodia
Indonesia
Indonesia phrasebook
Malaysia, Singapore & Brunei
Philippines
Pilipino phrasebook
Singapore city guide
South-East Asia on a shoestring
Thailand
Thai phrasebook
Vietnam, Laos & Cambodia
Vietnamese phrasebook

North-East Asia
China
Mandarin Chinese phrasebook
Hong Kong, Macau & Canton
Japan
Japanese phrasebook
Korea
Korean phrasebook
Mongolia
North-East Asia on a shoestring
Seoul city guide
Taiwan
Tibet
Tibet phrasebook
Tokyo city guide

West Asia
Trekking in Turkey
Turkey
Turkish phrasebook
West Asia on a shoestring

Middle East
Arab Gulf States
Egypt & the Sudan
Egyptian Arabic phrasebook
Iran
Israel
Jordan & Syria
Yemen

Indian Ocean
Madagascar & Comoros
Maldives & Islands of the East Indian Ocean
Mauritius, Réunion & Seychelles

Mail Order

Lonely Planet guidebooks are distributed worldwide. They are also available by mail order from Lonely Planet, so if you have difficulty finding a title please write to us. US and Canadian residents should write to Embarcadero West, 155 Filbert St, Suite 251, Oakland CA 94607, USA; European residents should write to Devonshire House, 12 Barley Mow Passage, Chiswick, London W4 4PH; and residents of other countries to PO Box 617, Hawthorn, Victoria 3122, Australia.

Indian Subcontinent
Bangladesh
India
Hindi/Urdu phrasebook
Trekking in the Indian Himalaya
Karakoram Highway
Kashmir, Ladakh & Zanskar
Nepal
Trekking in the Nepal Himalaya
Nepal phrasebook
Pakistan
Sri Lanka
Sri Lanka phrasebook

Africa
Africa on a shoestring
Central Africa
East Africa
Trekking in East Africa
Kenya
Swahili phrasebook
Morocco, Algeria & Tunisia
Moroccan Arabic phrasebook
South Africa, Lesotho & Swaziland
Zimbabwe, Botswana & Namibia
West Africa

Central America
Baja California
Central America on a shoestring
Costa Rica
La Ruta Maya
Mexico

North America
Alaska
Canada
Hawaii

Europe
Dublin city guide
Eastern Europe on a shoestring
Eastern Europe phrasebook
Finland
Iceland, Greenland & the Faroe Islands
Mediterranean Europe on a shoestring
Mediterranean Europe phrasebook
Poland
Scandinavian & Baltic Europe on a shoestring
Scandinavian Europe phrasebook
Trekking in Spain
Trekking in Greece
USSR
Russian phrasebook
Western Europe on a shoestring
Western Europe phrasebook

South America
Argentina, Uruguay & Paraguay
Bolivia
Brazil
Brazilian phrasebook
Chile & Easter Island
Colombia
Ecuador & the Galápagos Islands
Latin American Spanish phrasebook
Peru
Quechua phrasebook
South America on a shoestring
Trekking in the Patagonian Andes

The Lonely Planet Story

Lonely Planet published its first book in 1973 in response to the numerous 'How did you do it?' questions Maureen and Tony Wheeler were asked after driving, bussing, hitching, sailing and railing their way from England to Australia.

Written at a kitchen table and hand collated, trimmed and stapled, *Across Asia on the Cheap* became an instant local bestseller, inspiring thoughts of another book.

Eighteen months in South-East Asia resulted in their second guide, *South-East Asia on a shoestring*, which they put together in a backstreet Chinese hotel in Singapore in 1975. The 'yellow bible' as it quickly became known to backpackers around the world, soon became *the* guide to the region. It has sold well over half a million copies and is now in its 7th edition, still retaining its familiar yellow cover.

Today there are over 120 Lonely Planet titles in print – books that have that same adventurous approach to travel as those early guides; books that 'assume you know how to get your luggage off the carousel' as one reviewer put it.

Although Lonely Planet initially specialised in guides to Asia, they now cover most regions of the world, including the Pacific, South America, Africa, the Middle East and Europe. The list of *walking guides* and *phrasebooks* (for 'unusual' languages such as Quechua, Swahili, Nepalese and Egyptian Arabic) is also growing rapidly.

The emphasis continues to be on travel for independent travellers. Tony and Maureen still travel for several months of each year and play an active part in the writing, updating and quality control of Lonely Planet's guides.

They have been joined by over 50 authors, 54 staff – mainly editors, cartographers, & designers – at our office in Melbourne, Australia, 10 at our US office in Oakland, California and another three at our office in London to handle sales for Britain, Europe and Africa. In 1992 Lonely Planet opened an editorial office in Paris. Travellers themselves also make a valuable contribution to the guides through the feedback we receive in thousands of letters each year.

The people at Lonely Planet strongly believe that travellers can make a positive contribution to the countries they visit, both through their appreciation of the countries' culture, wildlife and natural features, and through the money they spend. In addition, the company makes a direct contribution to the countries and regions it covers. Since 1986 a percentage of the income from each book has been donated to ventures such as famine relief in Africa; aid projects in India; agricultural projects in Central America; Greenpeace's efforts to halt French nuclear testing in the Pacific and Amnesty International. In 1993 $100,000 was donated to such causes.

Lonely Planet's basic travel philosophy is summed up in Tony Wheeler's comment, 'Don't worry about whether your trip will work out. Just go!'